Andy Lavender

Hamlet in Pieces

Shakespeare Reworked:
Peter Brook, Robert Lepage, Robert Wilson

London

Nick Hern Books

www.nickhernbooks.co.uk

A Nick Hern Book

Hamlet in Pieces first published in Great Britain in 2001
as a paperback original by Nick Hern Books Limited,
14 Larden Road, London W3 7ST.

Hamlet in Pieces copyright © 2001 by Andy Lavender

Andy Lavender has asserted his moral right
to be identified as the author of this work

Cover design: Ned Hoste, 2H

Typeset by Country Setting, Kingsdown, Kent CT14 8ES
Printed and bound in Great Britain by Biddles, Guildford

British Library Cataloguing data for this book
is available from the British Library

ISBN 1 85459 61 87

Andy Lavender is a Senior Lecturer at Central School of Speech and Drama, and Course Leader of the School's MA in Advanced Theatre Practice. His work as a director includes productions of devised mixed-media shows, 'lost' classics and mime/physical pieces. He has written on theatre and the arts for a range of publications, among them the *Guardian*, *The Times* and the *New Statesman*. He is the author of a chapter on liveness in mixed-media performance in *Theatre in Crisis?: Performance Manifestos for a New Century* (Smith and Kraus, forthcoming) and a chapter on new and experimental theatre in *Theatre in a Cool Climate* (Amber Lane Press, 1999).

Contents

Sixteen illustrations from the three productions lie between pages 148 and 149

This book is dedicated to my parents, Rita and Eric Lavender

Acknowledgements

I was fancy-free and childless when I started this book. I finish it as the partner of a good woman and the father of two children. Such complete alteration might suggest that I've been tardy in the writing. On the other hand, it feels to me as though I've acquired a family at breakneck speed. One thing has become obvious, through the sleep-deprived fug. Being someone else's direct ancestor makes you a lot more mindful of your own forebears. In this frame of mind, I realise that this book is an attempt to come to terms with some cultural forefathers. It's a very selective reckoning. Three of the figures I'm interested in, whose influence pervades the modern theatre scene, are still working. The other is separated from them by around four hundred years.

I spent much of my time at university skirting around William Shakespeare. This was when arguments about the literary canon were in full sway, and who could be more canonical, more canonised, than Shakespeare? What's more, I was studying at a time when it was deeply unfashionable to concern yourself with stuff about the author's life and circumstances. What did it matter who Shakespeare was, if the text itself, in all its glorious (in)sufficiency, was what counted? It soon became clear that there was no escaping the Bard, at least for a student of English Literature in that department at that time. I decided to sideline my cautions, scruples, prejudices – call them what you will – and try to get to grips with Shakespeare. Did he really deserve such pre-eminence? I turned to *Hamlet* – what else? – Shakespeare's biggest, best, most evidently Shakespearean play. I wanted to know how it worked.

At about the same time, I realised that I wanted to make theatre as well as simply watch it and study it. That's what drew me to the work of Peter Brook, Robert Lepage and Robert Wilson. All were held up as exemplars of modern theatre-making. But why? Did *they* deserve it? And how did they do what they did? The first production by Robert Lepage which I saw was *The Dragon's Trilogy*. In common with many others, I found myself moved, delighted and hugely impressed by this six-hour-long piece of devised theatre. It featured a cast who doubled and trebled with ease, telling a story which had an epic reach, across generations and continents. *The Dragon's Trilogy* was full of bravado. It was also deft, conscious of its audience, consistently pleasurable. It flew in the face of orthodoxy (six hours long!), yet told a story and worked through theatrical transformations. It was very modern and oddly traditional.

I came to Peter Brook's work relatively late. I had read about it and seen some of it on video, but the first show I saw in the theatre was *The Man Who*. As with Shakespeare, Brook's near-deification seemed faintly offputting. I found his lauded book *The Empty Space* vaguely priestly, which didn't help. My attitude to Brook's work underwent a rapid transformation once I started to watch it at first hand. I was enraptured by the consummate craft of actors and director. Here was theatre which really knew what it was doing, where everything was meant and nothing was wasted.

Robert Wilson had for a while been something of an enigma to me. I was reading the most extravagant eulogies to his work. On the other hand, there were people around who didn't really know who he was, nor care very much. What was the fuss all about and why, in some parts, was there no fuss whatsoever? The first show of Wilson's which I saw was *Dr Faustus*

Lights the Lights in Edinburgh. I experienced what seems a common response in the face of Wilson's work: a mixture of incipient boredom, for things happened very slowly, and utter absorption in the control, precision and, yes, beauty of the staging. This sort of theatre was difficult, disciplined and more purely aesthetic than anything I had seen before.

I kept up with the work of these three luminaries. I didn't keep up quite as zealously with Shakespeare. I saw some fairly humdrum productions as a reviewer for the London magazine *City Limits*, which brought on a rising impatience and the view that Shakespeare ought to be given a rest. But then there were eye-opening productions by directors like Declan Donnellan, Peter Sellars and Yukio Ninagawa, and by accomplished companies from Eastern Europe. And one of the wittiest productions of *Hamlet* I saw was a solo version presented in a tiny room above Maison Bertaux, a coffee shop in Soho. Interesting things were being done to Shakespeare. All over the place.

These paths converged when the three directors presented their variations on Shakespeare's *Hamlet* in quick succession. I was lucky to see Lepage's *Elsinore* in Brussels. The National Theatre had arranged a recce to the production. A couple of the tickets weren't being used, and Nick Starr, assistant to the then-Director, Richard Eyre, asked if I'd like to go. Perhaps I could write something about the show when it came to London. Little did he know that I'd end up writing quite so much. My thanks to Nick for the invitation which set me off on an enjoyably long journey. I made trips to Paris to see Brook's *Qui Est Là* and Wilson's *Hamlet: a monologue*, covering them for an Arts page with its eye on this kind of work abroad. I'm grateful to Richard Morrison who, as Arts Editor of *The Times*, commissioned me to write about these shows and found space for pieces on the kinds of theatre which I found exciting.

I have been helped by a number of people in the writing of this book. I am grateful to the Research Committee at

Goldsmiths College, University of London, for granting me a sabbatical term, part of which was spent on this project. Thanks, too, to my current colleagues at Central School of Speech and Drama for giving me leeway as I neared completion. Jen Harvie read the chapter on *Elsinore* and made useful suggestions, and has been consistently supportive. Tricia Reid helped me see what I was trying to say in Chapter 5. Paul Allain read and commented aptly on my epilogue. I have spent many an hour in one of the reading rooms at the British Library. Free and friendly, the Library is a real benchmark of decency. My thanks to the anonymous hands who deliver all those books on request. My parents provided a dependable retreat from work and have been superb grandparents. Sarah and Paddy have also helped me by helping Tricia with the children. I'm grateful to Caroline Downing, my copy editor at Nick Hern Books, who has responded with alacrity, made only helpful comments and been a model of good humour. And thanks in particular to Nick Hern, who said Yes, showed great patience and offered the soundest advice. I couldn't have wished for a more understanding publisher.

I was treated generously by my three subjects. Peter Brook doesn't allow observers in his rehearsal room, and understandably made no exception in my case. But he did grant me his time, and his assistant, Nina Soufy, fielded all my enquiries in a friendly manner and put me in touch with Brook's collaborators. In researching Robert Wilson's work I spent some time at the Byrd Hoffman Foundation, which administers Wilson's activities. Geoffrey Wexler, the Foundation's archivist, was helpful before, during and after my visit, and his management of the archive is admirable. I am also grateful to the Archive for making available various unpublished writings by Wilson and by other commentators on his work. Thanks, too, to Robert Wilson himself for allowing me to watch one of his performances from backstage. I had most extensive access to

Robert Lepage's company and his rehearsal room. I spent three weeks in Quebec observing rehearsals, where Ex Machina's staff were kind and attentive, not least the company's receptionist, Nathalie Beaulieu, archivist Christine Borello and *Elsinore*'s technical director Richard Gravel. I'd like to thank Pierre Bernier for being so approachable, Peter Darling for accepting the presence of a chronicler with good grace, and in particular Robert Lepage, whose openness to observation strikes me as brave and generous. And I found his calm attentiveness inspiring. My thanks, too, to the various collaborators whom I interviewed over the course of writing this book, some of whom welcomed me into their homes to discuss their work. I am aware that this positions me rather strangely – part-critic, part-admirer. I've enjoyed attempting to walk that particular wire. If I lose my balance in places, I hope it's through overreaching rather than stepping back.

I mentioned my children. Of course there's a significant other. My thanks to Tricia, who has supported this project in all sorts of ways, many of which have involved sacrifices on her part. She is my anchor and my best friend, and she's changed everything.

I conducted a number of interviews with the three directors and their collaborators. Where I quote from these, I do so without giving a reference, to avoid cluttering the text with too many notes.

The Play without the Play

1

The Play without the Play

'. . . for look where my abridgement comes'

William Shakespeare, *Hamlet*, 2.2

Departures

Within the space of a year, between 1995 and '96, three extraordinary shows were produced by three celebrated figures in
world theatre: *Qui Est Là*, directed by Peter Brook, *Elsinore*,
directed by Robert Lepage and *Hamlet: a monologue*, directed
by Robert Wilson. Each was a version – at least in part – of
Shakespeare's *Hamlet*. None of them treated the play in anything like an orthodox manner. Lepage and Wilson both
'starred' in their own one-man shows (Lepage wasn't quite
solo, since he worked with a double). Wilson's monologue was
the more spare, relying on striking stage imagery and a
sophisticated sound design. Lepage's show was a feat of technical bravado, using revolving screens, slide and video projections and live computerised treatments of voice and image.
Brook's production was a glimpse of possible stagings of
Hamlet within an audacious framework: the performers discussed the play in the light of the theatrical approaches of five

eminent European directors (Stanislavsky, Meyerhold, Craig, Artaud and Brecht) and a thirteenth-century Noh master named Zeami. Five years later Brook followed through and staged a full production of the play. Each practitioner's show was eagerly awaited. Each created a buzz.

I live in London. I saw *Hamlet: a monologue* and *Qui Est Là* in Paris, and *Elsinore* in Brussels. I further encountered the shows and various personnel involved in their staging in London, Amsterdam, Paris and Quebec City. I mention this to highlight the cosmopolitan nature of the productions and the particular niche they occupy. I was a member of the audience for professional purposes, writing about each show for an Arts page which would occasionally report theatre events from abroad – those so eye-catching that reviews about them circulate even in countries which the productions are not scheduled to visit (*Qui Est Là* and *Hamlet: a monologue* have not been staged in Britain). Publicity departments (and to an extent newspapers) are happy to pay expenses to enable the coverage of theatre which is recognisably international. These are not large-scale shows in the sense of *Miss Saigon* or *Cats*, which enjoyed long runs in London's West End before being cloned and reproduced in theatre capitals around the world. The three *Hamlet*-variations are in their way no less global – but they give out a more exclusive allure. Each is a one-off, a unique approach to a classic text by an influential director. Each trades upon an identity as art – or rather, as 'artertainment': arthouse theatre which appears sexy rather than obscure.

This really is select work for an international clientele. I didn't see any of the shows 'at home' until *Elsinore* came to the National Theatre in London. I had to become a tourist. But then the theatre companies themselves were tourists, moving from one culture-capital to another. *Qui Est Là* played a longish run to its Parisian audience at Brook's base at the

Théâtre des Bouffes du Nord, and *Hamlet: a monologue* opened at the Alley Theater in Houston, Texas, under a co-production arrangement. That said, none of these shows would have been made (or made in the way they were) if they had not toured internationally. And here the identities of the three directors function like a marque. Their theatre is a near-global commodity, stamped with their respective names. We can of course say the same of Shakespeare.[1]

The frisson offered by each production lay in the apparent radicalism of their approaches to *Hamlet*. Here was an iconic text of world theatre seized upon – at around the same time, strangely – by three of the western world's most brilliant theatre-makers. You might agree with the view of W. B. Worthen that directors turn to Stratford's most famous son not to get at some authentic Bardic truth, but to 'authorize their own efforts by locating them under the sign of "Shakespeare".'[2] It is certainly a neon-bright sign. To be fair, neither Brook, Lepage nor Wilson claimed to be uncovering the heart of the original text, but Shakespeare's name was indeed displayed to suggest the weight and significance of their respective projects. As Peter Brook said, 'Our group of actors, which is an international group, coming together round the play that is perhaps the best-known play in the world, can't fail to find that this evokes all sorts of immediate questions of theatre.' Lepage and Wilson might have been inclined to say something similar. 'Immediate questions of theatre' are raised by all three productions.

Variations

In case you're not familiar with one or more of this trio of directors, here are some common observations.[3] Peter Brook perhaps needs the least introduction. Born in 1925 and based in Paris since 1970, he is widely thought of as 'the major

British director of our time'.[4] His recent work has attempted transcultural fusion (*Conference of the Birds*, 1979 and *The Mahabharata*, 1985), the figuring of neurological processes (*L'Homme Qui/The Man Who*, 1993/94 and *Je suis un phénomène*, 1998) and reappraisal of the qualities of 'classic' theatre pieces (Beckett's *Oh! Les Beaux Jours*, 1997, Chekhov's *The Cherry Orchard*, 1981, revisited in 1988, and Shakespeare's *The Tempest*, 1990). His theatre seeks to plunder a variety of sources in order to tap what is 'transcendent' or 'universal'. This is accompanied by a quest for purity where the stage features nothing extraneous. Brook's actors present themselves in play, and simultaneously in communion with what might be described as a graceful sense of human potentiality. This is spiritual in its implications, evoking as it does the registers of Zen-like masterliness through humility. Theatre, for Brook, is a means of drawing audiences into transcendent structures which are always mythic and metaphorical.

Born in 1957, Robert Lepage is a notorious internationalist, jetting from his native Quebec to cities in Japan, Sweden, England and Germany, although he has reoriented his work in Quebec of late. He is adept at using improvisation as a basis for creativity, whether in his one-man shows (*Vinci*, 1986, *Needles and Opium*, 1991, and *Elsinore*) or in the work which he has developed with other actors, notably *The Dragon's Trilogy* (1985-87), *Polygraph* (1988), *Tectonic Plates* (1988-91), *The Seven Streams of the River Ota* (1994-97) and *The Geometry of Miracles* (1998-99). The starting points for this work might be multiple and disconnected, but Lepage moulds them into a form of theatre which trades in thematic and visual connections and which exploits the stage in order to create striking transformational effects, often using the most ordinary objects and technologies. This, then, is a theatre of the imagination. Lepage is a pioneer of mixed-media performance, in particular involving video and slide projection in his shows, and he talks persuasively about the production of theatre for an audience weaned on television and cinema.

Robert Wilson, born in 1944, is a director-scenographer-lighting designer, unquestionably a *magus* of the visual. His achievement has been to concretise on stage a brand of spectacular neo-surrealism. On seeing Wilson's *Deafman Glance* in 1971, Louis Aragon famously wrote to the dead André Breton, 'He is what we, from whom Surrealism was born, dreamed would come after us and go beyond us.'[5] This has laid Wilson open to charges of emptiness and decadence, as if the work were nothing more than fancy images. In fact his radicalism lies in his formalist daring. He has staged shows longer than most (*KA MOUNTAIN AND GUARDenia TERRACE* presented at the Haft Tan Mountain in Shiraz, Iran in 1972, lasted for over 168 hours) and has resisted more than any other established theatre artist the claims of representation (shows which are clearly *about* something) in favour of those of pure presentation. Wilson is noted for his collaborations – with Sheryl Sutton, Lucinda Childs, Philip Glass, Jessye Norman, Heiner Müller, William S. Burroughs, Tom Waits – but he is also held in high regard as the definitive theatre auteur, painting with space, light and movement in order to manifest his own idiosyncratic vision. He sells his two-dimensional drawings and paintings, and works additonally as a sculptor and installation artist. For many his pre-linguistic understanding of shape and visual dynamics are unsurpassed in theatre.

All three have things in common. None is what we might describe as a 'jobbing' director, waged to produce other people's plays. Each has forged a career out of a very personal signature, making outcomes which are 'Brookian', or 'Lepagean', or 'Wilsonian'. Each is the subject of extensive coverage in the broadsheets and in scholarly publications. Each has established his own base for research and development. Each devotes more time than is usual to workshopping and rehearsal. So in the first instance this book is about the work of three distinguished and distinctive individuals.

Theatre directing, as we understand it, is a late-nineteenth-century and twentieth-century phenomenon. Directors didn't used to exist at all. Of course there would be someone calling the shots – a playwright or actor-manager, usually, often working for a patron. The role of the director as someone who marshals the work of specialised colleagues – a technocrat of the stage – has emerged relatively recently. The director is now functionally embedded in modern theatre, although the march of collaborative and devised theatre might once again reformulate the prevailing hierarchy of production. For all that they are treated as auteurs, Brook, Lepage and Wilson are expert facilitators of the work of a range of collaborators. That has always been part of the director's role, but the difference here is that these collaborators really are co-creators. This means that the composition of a piece of theatre does not reside quite as readily with the playwright-director duopoly. Changed responsibilities make for innovative theatre-making, because the very moulds and presses are different.

So this book is also about theatre direction at a time when directorial practices are in a state of transition. It is, more modestly, about three approaches to Shakespeare's *Hamlet*. The play has commonly been seen as the gateway through which an actor passes to a more exalted realm. In the latter part of this century, in England alone, Olivier, Burton, Pryce, Branagh, Rylance and Fiennes (to name but a few) have presented their interpretations of the role. *Hamlet* is now not just the actor's challenge *sine qua non*, but the auteur's.

The coincidence of the first three approaches to the play – the *Hamlet*-variations – seemed too good to miss. What made three of the leading directors in international theatre turn to the same play, with the same dismantling intent, at the same time? The productions found some of its topics – incest, madness, fratricide, contemplation and play-acting – especially modern. Taken together, they suggest a late-twentieth-century fascination with the existential and psychological strands of the play, and with the business of being theatrical. The contiguity of the three productions also allows us to say something about the processes by which they were made, and about emergent practices in theatre-making. Brook's full production of the play squares the circle and offers a nice point of comparison.

In writing this book, I set myself a simple initial objective: to find out how the variations on *Hamlet* were created. It is easy to mystify theatre-making, assuming that the writer and/or the director is a genius, or that actors have a gift which makes them more sensitive than the rest of us. I don't seek to deny the special talents of the individual directors nor the skills of fine actors. But theatre-making is a job of work, and like any work it involves management and organisation, sets of decisions, relationships between individuals and systematised processes of creativity and production. A shrewdly-handled creative process is more likely to produce an effective outcome, even in this mercurial business. I wanted to uncover the various steps of rehearsal of each production, cast light on the shaping input of a range of collaborators and discover who did what, when and to what effect.

Needless to say, I found that the traces of rehearsal work were already blurred. But I was able to get close enough to see the outlines of different sorts of theatre-making which had interesting overlaps. Each production, for instance, was developed through a collaborative, partly improvisatory rehearsal process. Each required extensive development time, much of it in the rehearsal room physicalising ideas or instincts. Each process prizes the operation of intuition. And the work of all three practitioners brings us especially close to a 'theatre theatrical' as opposed to a theatre which is a *medium* for play-

9

texts. Of course theatre usually involves configurations of body, space, voice and sound, in time, for a gathered audience – elements which are all quite other than literary. But in general over the last century the playtext has dominated as the authority for the things which are staged. Words come first, and actions (which do not necessarily speak louder) serve to underline them. With *Qui Est Là*, *Elsinore* and *Hamlet: a monologue* we are in the presence of something rather different.

The three shows were made within the workshop-space and on the stage. They were worked up with collaborators (actors, stage doubles, co-directors, designers, lighting and sound designers, musicians). They are stained with the sweat and grease of rehearsal – except that this is more than rehearsal, it is the making of something entirely new out of that old warhorse *Hamlet*. Let's be honest: none of the three productions really, centrally, stages the play. Instead they perform their own modernity. In so doing they subject Shakespeare to the (modern, selective, ruthless) creativity of accomplished theatre artists. Their drastic insistence upon theatricality first and last is all the more piquant if the starting point is that resonantly Eng. Lit. text, *Hamlet*.

Has Shakespeare therefore been 'betrayed'? Bardolators await round many a corner, eagle-eyed for anything which smacks of upstartish traducing of Shakespeare's foundational text. On the other hand, such is the saturation of Shakespeare-performance that companies and directors can only guarantee the currency of their work by offering a definitively new staging. The current economy of Shakespearean production makes auteurish innovation inevitable – and simultaneously marks out the genuinely innovative production for controversy. Each of the three directors paid scrupulous regard to their authorial source, although in ways which also appear to license them to take the most extreme liberties with his work. According to Wilson, Shakespeare is a 'rock'.

For Lepage, Shakespeare's text is so dextrously made that 'you could walk on it with golf shoes and it survives.' Peter Brook has built a career on radical stagings of Shakespeare, but he is tart in his estimation of the Bard: 'In rehearsal and privately one uses very severe words in relation to Shakespeare, who on one hand one admires more than any other author, and on the other hand one doesn't hesitate to say, "This is unbelievably boring, let's cut it".'

Hamlet went under the knife in all three productions. But to what end? I confess that my interest here is less in the object of textual surgery, and more in the techniques by which the surgeons carved it up, and in the new bodies which they produced. Of course, Brook, Lepage and Wilson were not the first to approach Shakespeare with a gleam in their scalpels. They follow a long line of text-slashers – some more cavalier than others, but a good number of them concerned with the same thing: the production of theatre which works for its audience. In this they are no different from the theatre workers of Shakespeare's time – no different from Shakespeare himself. There is a long history of *Hamlet* adaptation. It begins, near enough, with William Shakespeare.

Renaissance playhouse practice: the indeterminate *Hamlet*

Enough is known of Renaissance theatre practice for us to sketch a producing culture entirely different, in many respects, from our own. Authors were hired hands, producing work which would then belong to the company rather than the individual playwright. Stephen Orgel explains the system:

> The company commissioned the play, usually stipulated the subject, often provided the plot, often parcelled it out, scene by scene, to several playwrights. The text thus produced was a working model, which the company then

revised as seemed appropriate. The author had little or no say in these revisions: the text belonged to the company, and the authority represented by the text – I am talking now about the *performing* text – is that of the company, the owners, not that of the playwright, the author. . . . the very notion of 'the author's original manuscript' is in such cases a figment.[6]

This immediately situates playtexts as commodities which are useful only insofar as they are *usable* by performing artists. Any single play might involve more than one writer – up to five authors might collaborate on the plot, then work separately on individual segments – much like the writers of current American sitcoms.[7] The play would then be rehearsed very quickly and knocked about in whatever manner seemed most effective for its production. Actors would work from a running order of scenes. Some of the more elaborate set-pieces would be blocked and rehearsed. The actors would otherwise bring themselves on and off according to the appropriate cue points and perform with little reference to any scenic or production concept as we might expect of post-nineteenth-century theatre. The playwright might then revise parts of the play in response to feedback and requests from the company. Even the office of the Master of the Revels, who signed off the prompt-copy and thus licensed the play for performance, was not enough to ensure a stable script. This playhouse manuscript could be cut – and probably was, in different ways for different performances – but not added to. It is difficult to see how this edict could be policed, however, and the exigencies of Elizabethan performance mean that the prompt copy is likely to have been a full version of a possible production rather than a word-for-word transcript of an actual performance.[8]

Shakespeare himself, as an actor, might have performed in different plays on different days of the week. Gary Taylor paints an enjoyably hectic picture of Shakespeare the thespian: 'Many times he would rehearse one play in the morning and perform in another that afternoon. On most days he probably played more than one character; Elizabethan actors doubled, tripled, quadrupled roles, their versatility helping to hold down costs.'[9] With the energies left after this whirl of rehearsal and role-playing, Shakespeare would turn to the activity for which he is better known. He delivered his plays at a prodigious rate (Taylor lists five, including *Hamlet*, written in two years at the turn of the seventeenth century), and had them performed by his company who would rehearse and learn their new parts while appearing in other work. Richard Burbage, the first actor to play Hamlet, probably ad-libbed some of his lines – and no wonder.[10] For all we know, some of these ad-libs 'took', were repeated the next performance, and were worked into the texture of the script.

So Shakespeare was exceptional, an artist who rose above an artisan-like culture? Stephen Orgel differs, suggesting that 'he was simply in on more parts of the collaboration'.[11] His subsequent pronouncement that 'we know nothing about Shakespeare's original text' is rather brisk. Of course we know a good deal about work likely to have been by Shakespeare, produced under his nose and performed by his colleagues (sometimes acting alongside the writer himself) according to his guiding input. But it is true that a good deal is uncertain and that no single, definitive 'original' exists. The exasperating absence of scrupulous notating and documentary procedures 400 years ago is not the only reason for such uncertainty. The nature of the theatre industry of Shakespeare's time meant that the text was always subject to revision in the light of particular performing circumstances, the composition of the company, the time and place of performance and the happenstance of a theatre culture whose final authority is what goes down on the stage rather than the page. Performance rather than the playtext was the gold standard of Elizabethan theatre. The similarities with the shows which are the subject of this book hardly need underlining.

The words initially penned by the playwright were a starting-point, then, not the end-point. The 'final' text would be noted by the book-keeper (not the playwright), who would copy out each actor's part and keep a complete copy himself. But that complete copy would be subject to change since companies would amend their productions on each revival, perhaps involving the original playwright in any rewrites, or perhaps inviting other writers to do the work. Moreover the play may well have been developed through a degree of ad-libbing, and as scenes were added, cut or altered according to public reception of the work.

There are economic imperatives to this set of practices. Plays were fluid, not fixed. They could easily incorporate a range of contemporary references and be altered to suit the delicacies of the historical moment, the place of production or, in the case of command performances, the regal presence. Plays were made for audiences. That was the priority. The production itself – immediate, transformable, freshly wrought by the company – was central. The convention that we under-stand today of observing the primary authority of the *written* text simply did not exist in Shakespeare's time. Of course you could always say that Shakespeare was so brilliant that he trans-cended his working conditions to establish his own playtexts as more authoritative than anything anyone might subsequ-ently do to them. On the other hand you could say that, with-out the hothouse theatre-making culture in which he worked, he would not have come up with those scripts in the first place.

Shakespeare's *Hamlet* was based on another play of the same name, produced around ten years before Shakespeare's version. This source is known as the *Ur-Hamlet*, and its text is long lost. We cannot know how Shakespeare rendered his source material. He produced a revenge tragedy – but perhaps he was *parodying* a revenge tragedy (his revenger takes so long to get down to business, then botches the job). In any case, the greatest dramatic work by Shakespeare / of the Renaissance / in the western world / of all time (delete as you wish) is certainly not 'original'.

The three crucial texts of Shakespeare's *Hamlet*, the First Quarto (Q1), the Second Quarto (Q2) and the First Folio (F1), have intriguing histories. Q1, the first extant Shakespearean *Hamlet* document, was published in 1603 – two or three years, probably, after the play's first performances.[12] There is general acceptance among scholars that it was pirated (copied without the authorisation of Shakespeare's company), and it is known as the 'Bad Quarto'. Theatre companies would rush out their own publication to spoil the advantage that such a bootleg version might temporarily obtain. It is assumed that Q2, published in 1604 (although four of the seven extant copies are dated 1605), was prepared from a Shakespearean script which might, nonetheless, have been a draft.[13] Shakespeare died in 1616. His complete works were first published in 1623, seven years after his death, and this edition is known as The First Folio. Its version of *Hamlet* was largely modelled on that of Q2.

None of the Quartos of any of Shakespeare's plays show any markings of act or scene divisions, except for the 1622 Quarto of *Othello*, printed after Shakespeare's death.[14] Only in Nicholas Rowe's 1709 edition of Shakespeare's plays were act and scene divisions standardised. Rowe therefore provided the plays with structures which were not necessarily explicit in the sources from which he worked. Nearly a century after his death, Shakespeare's dramas were ordered into forms which we might recognise today. But the entire history of Shakespearean textual study is fraught with indeterminacy, and muddied by the hands of many scribes, text-looters, interpolators and editors.

It is rare in any case not to resort to a spot of editing when we stage Shakespeare. The prevailing custom in presenting *Hamlet* is to adopt the version published in F1 – which is notoriously long at a running time of around four hours. Only the messy-headed leave this sprawling monster uncut. As Clement Scott said (disapprovingly), 'There are not many audiences which will relinquish their beer for the sake of art.'[15] Enabling people to make last orders is a good enough reason to make cuts in the play, but there are others.

Any production of *Hamlet* is bound to involve interpretative decisions, perhaps more far-reaching than those of any other Shakespearean text. If you're interested in this particular challenge, Q1 is well worth reading.[16] It comes across vividly as a performance text. It is less than two-thirds the length of F1 (Q1 has 2221 lines, F1 3907), although it contains some material which is absent from Q2 and F1. Individual lines and even whole sections familiar to us from F1 appear in different parts of the play in Q1. Some characters are absent, with lines distributed to others. Key speeches are filleted in a way that continually gets to the nub of an exchange or a statement. Much interconnective, explanatory material in F1 is missing, with, I think, virtually no loss of clarity – the opposite, indeed. All of which makes for a text which has a striking freshness, familiar in the general run of the story but bracingly swift and decisive.

The 'To be, or not to be' soliloquy, for instance – which in Q1 begins, 'To be, or not to be, I there's the point,' is placed before the passage in which the King and Polonius (named Corambis in Q1) spy on Hamlet's encounter with Ophelia; before the entry of the Players; and before the King's meeting with Rosencrantz and Guildenstern (Rossencraft and Gilderstone in Q1), who report that they have not yet fathomed the cause of Hamlet's 'lunacie' and receive further instruction. In F1 the soliloquy comes *after* all these exchanges, which affects the play's thematics of subterfuge, suicidal maudlin and apathy.

Prompted by Q1, it is quite possible to produce the 'To be or not to be' soliloquy and the subsequent 'get thee to a nunnery' exchange between Hamlet and Ophelia (in Q1 Hamlet instructs Ofelia, 'Go to a Nunnery goe') in a manner which makes explicit that Hamlet knows all along that he is being spied upon.

This is one of the celebrated problems of textual study in *Hamlet*, and it is not my business here to revisit that particular debate. But the very fact that such details have generated reams of scholarly writing indicates the impact that interpretative decisions have on one's understanding of the play. And those decisions become more difficult, or easier, and certainly show up in starker relief, once the text itself is reshaped. In Q1, the players' 'command' performance is ended when Claudius says, 'Lights, I will to bed.' There is no other indication, as there is in Q2 and F1, of an ensuing general kerfuffle suggesting that Claudius has lost his cool. A production of Q1 could well present this moment as if the King were now bored with the players' entertainment, maintaining the efficient managerial façade which he displays in all other public scenes throughout the play. His dismissive gesture might thus become a mask for his desperation, rather than a giveaway loss of self-control.

Hamlet subsequently confronts his mother in her closet. In Q1 she eventually responds, 'But as I haue a soule, I sweare by heauen, / I neuer knew of this most horride murder'. Her recognition of the fact of the crime is categorical, and there is nothing to suggest that this should not be played as a straightforward statement on the character's part. She then tells Hamlet, 'I will conceale, consent, and doe my best, / What strategem soe're thou shalt deuise.' Q2 and F1 rein back on this – Gertrude merely says that she won't tell anyone else what Hamlet has said to her. In Q1 she explicitly positions herself on Hamlet's side. The wedge between her and her new husband is shown to run deeper when Claudius tells the audience of his plan to have Hamlet put to death on his arrival in England (the King has just despatched him there), whilst he maintains to Gertrude that the trip is for Hamlet's own good. The clarity of this division of loyalties has lots of consequences for the way in which you would decide to play the subsequent scenes. It also helps to suggest a set of clearly vested interests and a spatial pattern of action for the scene in which Hamlet and Laertes duel, which is often extremely messy in performance.

The point to this digression into Q1 is to underline the obvious: there is no definitive version of *Hamlet*. We simply cannot say that there is an authoritative source from which everything else springs. I was excited reading Q1, seeing a play different from that which I thought I knew. We cannot say for sure that Q1, or something very close to it, was not presented by the Chamberlain's Men. As Peter Thomson says, 'It is most unlikely that *Hamlet* was ever performed on the Elizabethan stage in the form in which it has been preserved in Q2 or the Folio. It is too long. The garbled version of Q1 is closer to playhouse norms.'[17] Q1 is only 'garbled' if we are asked to measure it against the presumed authority of Q2 and F1. Different versions of *those* manuscripts have been staged ever since their first publication.

In making use of *Hamlet* for their own purposes, Brook, Lepage and Wilson have not trampled all over a venerable text with their big modern boots. We have no venerable text. And if I am right that Q1 suggests provocative and useful variances from the play that we think we know and love, then by the same token B1, L1 and W1 might serve the same function. They are traces of a set of dramaturgical decisions and theatrical activities designed to give audiences something to chew on.

Actually I haven't had sight of B1, L1 and W1, and I'm not sure that such texts exist. In a further echo of Renaissance theatre practice, the texts 'by' Brook, Lepage and Wilson that I possess were only completed at the end of the rehearsal and development period, and are the result of many working drafts. The text, then, is not the starting-point but the end-point of production. There is no single text for *Elsinore*, but different scripts for each phase of public staging. *Qui Est Là* and *Hamlet: a monologue* have 'finished' texts, but we cannot comfortably assign them an author. It certainly isn't Shakespeare, but nor is it Peter Brook, or Robert Lepage, or Robert Wilson. Nobody can claim that each of the new texts were made entirely by the named director. Marie-Hélène Estienne worked with Brook, Wolfgang Wiens with Wilson, while Lepage developed *Elsinore* in collaboration with his design and technical team. Just as we cannot say for sure that Shakespeare wrote every line of *Hamlet*, so we can't be certain that the three directors selected every line of their own versions for inclusion. Of course they oversaw the selection and sanctioned the final result. I am not trying to deny their central importance to the work. But other hands are evident. These hands were also present in the rehearsal room. They evoke the hands which worked alongside Shakespeare when he first staged his own *Hamlet*-variation in around 1601.

Enduring Hamlet(s)

As Bert States has it, *Hamlet* is something like the tart of world drama and 'has become as promiscuous as the alphabet'[18] Why does the play have so many visitors? Let's start with the central character. To varying degrees, Hamlet can be seen as sensitive, intelligent, devious, unkind, and a victim of circumstance. As someone who is both specially privileged (by his birth and, arguably, by his father's visitation) and especially wronged (by his uncle). As an insider turned into an outsider. As an amateur and a bungler in a world full of professionals.

and a thinker. A melancholic. A toff with a
h. A prototype playboy. A mouthpiece of exqui-
rse. And a lover of theatre and theatrical gestures,
a   ry moment that he is caught up in dramatic representation as a complex theatrical gesture himself.

Of course Hamlet is actually not a person but a *character*.
He is in part a genre figure, a mix of types (revenger and
malcontent). As a cipher for a range of possible embodiments,
Hamlet provides rich pickings for actors and spectators alike.
We can empathise, sympathise and criticise all at once then,
with a turn, enjoy the fact that Hamlet can only ever be
interpreted, never presented *completely*. Perhaps, rather, we
should say that every actor who plays Hamlet makes a whole
by selecting from a larger range of parts. Theatre-makers and
audiences in different periods have responded not just to
diverse facets of Hamlet the potential person, but to different
modes of character, different ways of suggesting the stuff of
personhood.[19]

The play expresses deep and conflicted subjectivity, which
the Romantics found alluring as a register of developed
individuality, and suggests the fractures and multiplicities of
self, exciting to postmodern practitioners. Hamlet has also,
famously, been subjected to psychoanalysis as a kind of Everyman on the couch. Freud and his acolytes saw the deeply
symbolic construction of a story whose protagonist is urged to
break the law by his ghoulish parent, thus dramatising a sub-
strand of the Oedipus complex (horror at transgressing the
paternal Word) and provocatively casting the Father as a
spectral shadow from which one never escapes. The history of
our understanding of selfhood can be traced through the
sorts of self which Hamlet represents at different periods.

Hamlet really became the pre-eminent Shakespearean character, hence the predominant Shakespearean text, during the
nineteenth century. The phenomenon was European rather

than merely English. Goethe seized on the play in
In France, a number of writers and artists consolida   .it
became known as 'Hamletism', in Jules Laforgue's coinage in
1886. As Ruby Cohn explains:

> Nineteenth-century French Hamletism took several
> forms: creating hamletic characters . . . imitating
> Hamlet in life . . . celebrating Hamlet in the theatre . . .
> appreciating Hamlet through the visual artists, notably
> Delacroix and Manet; and finally the elevation of
> Hamlet by the Symbolists to a kind of artist-saint.[20]

He had already been elevated in similar manner in England
by Keats, Lamb, Coleridge (who claimed to have a 'smack of
Hamlet myself'[21]) and Hazlitt (who famously, if gnomically,
observed, 'It is *we* who are Hamlet'[22]). Of all Shakespeare's
plays, *Hamlet* is the most introspective, its soliloquies offering
the most pressing and sustained analysis of self in Renaissance
drama. The Romantic poets were engaged in similar activities
in the rhetorical registers of their own literature. *Hamlet* was
strategically moved by writer-artists into the sphere of the
intellectuals and the chattering class, readers more readily
than playgoers, people who expressed their feeling through
thought. When T.S. Eliot observed, in *The Love Song of J. Alfred
Prufrock*, 'No! I am not Prince Hamlet, nor was meant to be',
he was in part renouncing the construction of characters like
Hamlet, and hence an entire cultural sensibility. Eliot was
dissatisfied with Shakespeare's artistic practice. Too messy, too
fragmented, too multiple, too shifting – the very things which
would excite postmodern practitioners and critics half a
century later.

This reminds us that the play is subject to the ideological
turns of different people at different times, and is in any case
more than its eponymous (non-)hero. *Hamlet*'s discursive range

includes questions about the sanctity of succession, the responsible discharge of public and personal duties, the destabilising effect in personal, domestic, civic and historical contexts of 'unnatural' acts, and the nature of parental affiliation. The notorious theme of uncertainty made *Hamlet* especially appropriate as a late-twentieth-century text. This is a play which swiftly alters its perspectives, which delights in putting utterances in doubt. It is supremely volatile. In *The Tremulous Private Body*, Francis Barker argues that *Hamlet*'s 'incipient modernity' (in the long-view post-Renaissance sense) is figured in the central character's preoccupation with bodily and metaphysical absence, flux, indeterminacy, insecurity. For Hamlet (and his body), read an entire cultural order.[23] A number of critics have found more specific common ground between Renaissance and postmodern formations. Hugh Grady, discussing the structure of Shakespeare's writing, suggests that 'we are dealing with a series of metaphors whose final meaning is endlessly deferred in a play of thought with no obvious terminus.'[24] Several resonant postmodern fancies are evident here: a refusal of closure, a taste for mindgames, a liking for play, and a penchant for metaphor rather than literalism. These are also Renaissance fancies, Hamletic fancies.

We shouldn't forget that *Hamlet* is a good story spicily told. It hooks its spectators with various thriller-like questions (who killed Old Hamlet? Will Hamlet gain his revenge? Will he be assassinated?) It offers its audience three different points at which a ghost visits, scenes involving spying, outbursts of verbal and physical violence (largely directed against women), swearing and explicit sexual innuendo, a failed attempt at assassination, a duel, and a bloodbath of deaths at the end.

Most pertinently for my current purposes, *Hamlet* is saturated with motifs of performance and performativity. It is about a desire to take action, to *do* things. It is also about a need to pretend, to dissemble. It concerns the distinction between falsity and reality, that which happened which is assumed or claimed to have happened. It di fascination with the business of putting on a performance and with the capable conjuring of extreme emotion. It is about questions of perception and experience, and about trusting the evidence of your own eyes. The theatre is not just a metaphorically rich reference-point in *Hamlet*, but is shown to *work* (as evidenced by the Player's speech and the play within the play.) There is a peculiar sincerity to the play's theatricalism, as Peter Thomson suggests:

> Elizabethan playwrights were rarely averse to the cheap laugh, and actors were often asked to speak scurrilous lines about their profession. More often than not, the metaphorical references are belittling – acting is 'seeming', the actor a 'shadow', the play a deception. But in *Hamlet*, the play is the thing, not the thing's shadow, and the passion of the First Player is singularly without deception.[25]

This is Shakespeare's – indeed the Renaissance's – most committedly metatheatrical play.

It is also, arguably, 'the greatest playwright's greatest play',[26] and as such *Hamlet* has become the emblem *par excellence* of the Theatre itself. Anything *in* the play now comes with an additional lashing of meaning which derives from *Hamlet*'s status as a pinnacle of world drama. So this is a text drenched in history and glowing with potency, an icon not just of things Shakespearean but of performance in general. Was there ever a play with more baggage than this?

Elsinore, Hamlet: a monologue and *Qui Est Là* reverberate with the echoes of previous approaches to *Hamlet*. Not necessarily by way of direct influence – they are too idiosyncratic for that – but such a well-trodden text inevitably comes marked with the incursions of previous visits. Other writers have mapped out something of the history of *Hamlet* criticism and performance, so extensive is the play's appeal through the last four hundred years.[27] I am not about to repeat their work here, but it is worth sampling some of the most resonant historical outcomes. Any *Hamlet*-production trails an army of ghosts, some of which throw their own pallid light on the latest progeny.

*

In 1661 Sir William Davenant, who had acquired the play for his company the preceding year (the year the London theatres reopened after the Interregnum) produced a version of *Hamlet* with Thomas Betterton as the Prince. Restoration productions of Shakespeare's plays adapted them to suit the sensibilities and the emergent staging practices of this theatrical dawn. Sections were cut, characters removed and scenes presented according to new realist conventions allowed by the introduction of sliding scenery flats. The plays were produced differently and therefore *experienced* differently, and the introduction of female actresses to the English stage sharpened this alteration. Three generations after Shakespeare's death, his plays were radically remade in order to fit the moulds of a changed world.

Davenant accordingly tailored his production of *Hamlet* to appeal to Charles II and the royalist audience. He changed words in order to make what already appeared a dated language comprehensible (and socially acceptable) to his audience. He purged the play of seemingly tasteless references to pestilence, physical or political, and depicted Hamlet's conflict with Claudius in terms of a straightforward battle over rightful occupation of the throne. The practice, incidentally, was little different from that with which Shakespeare's companies had treated the texts they themselves inherited. Davenant was merely restoring a mode of theatre-making geared around 'derivative creativity', to use Michael D. Bristol's phrase.[28] Nonetheless, it was clear that Shakespeare would only be staged in the Restoration by being rearranged, and Davenant was the first notable fixer of Shakespeare's plays. He claimed to be Shakespeare's illegitimate son. How fitting that the sorts of canny revisionism which Brook, Lepage and Wilson trade in – alert to the exciting possibilities offered by new staging techniques and the tastes of new audiences – should be pioneered by this possibly bastard offspring. After all, the legacy of the Bard is best preserved by continual disbursement on the part of his inheritors.

*

Of all the actors, directors, scholars, critics and tourists who compete for the title of Shakespeare's greatest advocate, few can match the claims of the eighteenth-century actor-manager David Garrick. Entirely a man of his time, Garrick nonetheless made sure to represent himself as the preserver of an authentically Shakespearean tradition. He publicly renounced the versions of Shakespeare's plays in use at the time, in order to return to the Bardic original (even though that original was actually the product of the by-then flourishing editing and publishing industry and was further refashioned by Garrick according to his own predilections). He was instrumental in Shakespeare's institutionalisation, by the middle of the eighteenth century, as a beacon of high art. Nevertheless Garrick understood that this notion of the transcendent genius of Shakespeare could only be realised in staging terms by a ruthlessly focused act of interpretation. The most brilliant actor-manager of his generation legitimised the recuperation of Shakespeare, anew and afresh with every production, according to the parameters of current staging technologies, performance conventions, political sensibilities, and fashions. If Shakespeare was to last at all, it would be because his work was rebuilt for a modern audience every time it appeared onstage. And who better to do the rebuilding than the star performer, reworking the play from the inside whilst organising the event from the outside? With Garrick, the terms 'actor' and 'manager' were not so much hyphenated as soldered together. In his management of the entire production, the centrality of the lead was further secured. The playscript was the vehicle for the star, not the other way around. Audiences would come to see Garrick sponsored (but not eclipsed) by Shakespeare.

Garrick first played Hamlet in 1742 at Drury Lane, adopting the text published in 1718, prepared for Robert Wilks's performance by the poet John Hughes. In 1751, 1763 and most notoriously in 1772 Garrick published his own revised versions of the play. One of the highlights of his production, throughout, was the point at which Hamlet saw the ghost of his father. The apocryphal story is that, recognising the importance of the moment and the advantage of a distinctive effect, Garrick had a wig made whose hair would stand up hydraulically when bidden, thus signalling Hamlet's fright and the performer's panache. His Hamlet might be momentarily terrified, but Garrick was otherwise in full possession of his faculties. His adaptation (hence his performance) ignored anything which smacked of wimpish indecision.[29]

Garrick methodically promoted the impression that he and Shakespeare were kindred spirits, with Garrick evidently the Bard's long-awaited interpreter-inheritor. He built a temple dedicated to Shakespeare in the garden of his Thameside villa. He was painted by Thomas Gainsborough with his arm draped in comradely fashion around the bust of Shakespeare therein. Most notoriously he produced the Stratford Jubilee in 1769, a massive festival of things Shakespearean (apart from a production of any of the plays), more corporatised celebration than carnival, and in the event something of a damp squib. Garrick read 'An Ode upon Dedicating a Building and Erecting a Statue to Shakespeare at Stratford-upon-Avon', bringing off even this act of cultural brown-nosing with characteristic aplomb.

Garrick mounted a new production of *Hamlet* in 1772 – at the age of 55 – with a freshly-prepared version of the text, which he played until his last appearance in the role on 30 May 1776. As Peter Holland recounts, this restored over 620 lines of Shakespearean text which had lain unused for decades, in the process augmenting the importance to the play of characters like Polonius and Laertes and the play within the play.[30] Nevertheless this was again a drastically edited text. Garrick audaciously ripped out most of Act 5, dispensing with the voyage to England, the plotting between Claudius and Laertes, the graveyard scenes and the duel, and 'managing to get from Ophelia's last exit (Shakespeare's 4.5) to the end of the play in only sixty lines where Shakespeare needed over 800.'[31] Garrick informed one of his friends that he 'would not leave the stage till I had rescued that noble play from all the rubbish of the fifth act'.[32] (Peter Brook's *Qui Est Là*, which largely dispenses with Act 5, is similarly brisk.) Revenge was definitely, decisively obtained by this Enlightenment Hamlet.

In some respects, in the matter of *Hamlet*-adaptation Garrick is a direct forebear of Wilson and Lepage. The one an actor-manager who in effect was his own director and adaptor, the others performer-directors who run their own companies. In each case, the text is respected up to a point – Wilson and Lepage, surprisingly perhaps, feature only lines from *Hamlet* in their productions, with no interpolated material. But in each case a kind of highbrow showmanship is the first priority, with Shakespeare recruited to the cause. This is more than simply a matter of displaying the star performer or producing the play. Garrick's work had *flair*. It was serious enough to take on the play and render it meaningfully, and it was cavalier enough to rework the drama according to his own compelling and contemporary perspectives. Garrick produced a sense of stylish specialness, that intangible quality in theatre where intelligence, fashion and performance come together. I wouldn't want to take the comparison with Lepage and Wilson too far, but all three can be seen as arbiters of upmarket theatrical panache. And Garrick's canny exploitation of his hair-raising technology would surely find approval in the workshops of Lepage's company, Ex Machina.

*

Derivative creativity marked the work of that long line of noted actors and actor-managers who followed in Garrick's footsteps. Kemble, Kean, Macready, Booth, Irving, Fechter and Sarah Bernhardt all had their turn. New interpretations were instantly measured against those of old favourites. Clement Scott, for example, observed of the impression made by Henry Irving's performance in 1874 that 'it has affected the whole audience – the Kemble lovers, the Kean admirers, and the Fechter rhapsodists.'[33] Each new presentation of *Hamlet* was an overt reinterpretation, an act of informed decision-making. Playing Hamlet – minting the character anew – was seen as a summit of the actor's ambition and it was certainly the actor-manager's role *par excellence*. Wilson Barrett, who played the part in 1884 at the Princess's Theatre in London, gave a curtain speech at which he told the audience that 25 years previously 'a poor and almost friendless lad' had come to the playhouse to see Charles Kean perform. 'Coming out of the theatre, he swore to himself that he would not only become manager of that theatre, but that in the distant future he would play Hamlet on that very spot.'[34] Of course that poignant lad with the steely ambition was none other than Barrett himself. Hamlet, the role, is a measure of an actor's esteem. In an era of actor-managers it was a necessary calling card.

Barrett's production is interesting in this regard, however, since it seems that the star announced his arrival with an unusual degree of modesty. As Clement Scott reports:

> Mr. Wilson Barrett's rearrangement of the text is in many respects novel, in most judicious, and in all unselfish. By unselfish we mean he has not sacrificed every consideration of the play to the fact that he is himself playing the leading character, and desires to show it off to the best advantage; on the contrary, he discards much theatrical trick personal to himself as Hamlet, and adds prominence thereby to the character of the King, who never before has been allowed to show how dramatically effective he can become when in capable and clever hands.[35]

We would now say that the clever hands were those of the director. In this instance Barrett took most plaudits as the star of the show, but it is clear that he was working as producer, director and dramaturg all at once. In being very selective in his treatment of *Hamlet* Barrett was doing no more than had become the norm, but in other respects his production signals the incipient demise of the actor-manager.

Shakespeare was 'saved from the actors', as Gary Taylor puts it, in the late nineteenth century and the beginning of the twentieth century by the likes of William Poel, Harley Granville Barker and Edward Gordon Craig.[36] Poel used amateur actors in his attempts to recuperate 'authentic' conditions of Shakespearean performance, featuring an open playing area and swift movement from scene to scene. Granville Barker asserted the preeminence of the director as an interpreter of the Shakespeare's text, which would best be served through an observation of the staging disciplines in force when the texts were written. In Craig's terms, theatre production was conceived as a visual and plastic undertaking whose first precepts were to be found in architectonics and the movements of the performers' bodies.

The rise of the director as an independent figure in the late nineteenth century signals the separation of directing from acting. The director becomes the *metteur en scène* – the arranger of the stage – in ways which include the actor's performance but do not uniquely prioritise it. At the turn of the twentieth century the director claimed the rights of interpretation which the actor-manager had previously enjoyed. Rather than oversee productions built around stars, directors like Antoine, Stanislavsky, Poel, Reinhardt and Barker sought a more transparent relationship to the text, and attempted to arbitrate its 'original' meanings. Only after the first flush of naturalistic drama did theatre direction become more explicitly interpretative, to the extent of effectively reauthoring plays through production – as the work of Craig, Meyerhold and Brecht most eloquently bears out. The productions of Lepage and Wilson, in particular, evoke a number of historical glances. They combine the individual flourish of actor-manager theatre, a modernist drive towards interpretation and the theatrical decentrings of postmodern performance.

*

In 1896 Edward Gordon Craig played Hamlet wearing Henry Irving's costume. He had trained under Irving, whose authority he greatly respected. It would be misleading to assume that this situates him as a man of the nineteenth-century theatre. Just over a decade later Craig became involved with one of the most definitively modernist theatre productions of the twentieth century, whose precepts still come over as bold and extraordinary.

In 1908 Craig was approached by Stanislavsky regarding a joint staging of *Hamlet* under the auspices of the Moscow Art Theatre. The concept, designs and staging instructions would come from Craig and the production would be realised by Stanislavsky. The project was fraught with difficulties. Craig didn't speak Russian or French, Stanislavsky didn't speak English. Stanislavsky was a champion of psychologically consistent characterisation, Craig viewed movement and scenography as predominant, and during the course of the project never worked with the MAT's actors. The collaboration brought together two innovators who represented radically different approaches to theatre.

Craig viewed *Hamlet* as a monodrama, arguing that the entire action and its environment could be portrayed as if through the eyes of the protagonist. He devised a staging concept which figured this scheme. A sketch of the first court scene in Act 1 shows a reclining Hamlet downstage, and behind him the massed bodies of the Danish court, with Claudius and Gertrude as the central, highest reach of the swooping shape. Separated physically and by his posture, Hamlet might be dreaming, or remembering, the entire arrangement.

The most striking aspect of Craig's design was his use of a series of proscenium-high movable screens, which were configured differently for different scenes. As Christopher Innes explains, Craig conceived

a different arrangement of screens for each of the twenty scenes in the play. They could radically alter the size and shape of the acting area, changing from a flat wall across the very rear of the stage for the court scene

to a claustrophobic enclosure with corners jutting
forward almost to the proscenium for Polonius's study.
The shape could also provide a spatial representation
of a character's state of mind . . . Or, by moving some
screens while leaving others in the same position from
one scene to another, they could give a sense of
progressive development.[37]

The screens suggest battlements. They evoke the architecture
of church and palace, with towers, aisles and formal halls.
Their monumentalism allows the creation of very 'public'
open spaces and private nooks, crannies and passageways.
Craig's staging creates depth and perspective through the
use of different levels, and choreographed relationships between the huge screens and the much tinier performing
bodies. The screens allow the evocation of literal settings and
abstract, atmospheric structural formations, and they emphasise the formalism of the stage as a place of architecture.
Craig's sketches, and pictures of the production, show a coolly
elegant design, balanced, geometrical and beautiful in its
clarity. The screens are part of a transitional but resolutely
modernist *Hamlet*, touched with symbolism and cubism, and
pre-empting the more severe figural arrangements of theatrical expressionism.

The production, staged in 1911/12, was inevitably compromised.[38] Craig was interested in controlling the scenic
environment in order to manifest his selective reading of the
play's themes, and to affect spectators through their visual
perception. He called for extremely stylised acting, rendered
through movements which were expressly sharp, dynamic and
graceful, depending on the context. Stanislavsky, meanwhile,
was interested in a new realist approach, focusing on the interior life of character (partly drawn out of the actor's imagi-
native and empathic development of role) and a detailed

realism of setting. Critics writing in the Russian papers were sceptical, attacking the concept and the production's mixture of styles. Reviews in the foreign newspapers, by contrast, were very enthusiastic. From an 'international' perspective, Craig and Stanislavsky's production appeared to consolidate a bold new style, built around scenographic daring and the prevalence of a directorial concept. The production – paradoxically, given its otherwise lukewarm reception and the litany of miscommunications between the two directors – established the Moscow Art Theatre as a major European producing venue, its work now of genuinely international stature.

This famous meeting of realist and non-realist approaches provides a vexed but illustrative modernist moment. It emphatically subjugated Shakespeare's text to the interpretative, creative ministrations of the director-artist. It made the stage a place of design rather than acting. And it produced meanings through a machine-like organisation of the stage picture. Craig's screens, repositioned out of sight of the audience (in scene changes which were notoriously cumbersome and long-winded), made for a multifaceted series of images whose new permutations were presented to the audience as automatic.

Richard Halpern includes Craig's MAT production in his quirky discussion of 'Hamletmachines' in the late nineteenth and twentieth centuries. According to Halpern, 'machinery is drawn to Hamlet, and also emanates from him, because he represents in a particularly oppressive form the burden of tradition for modernist culture.' This burden is played out by a variety of modern machine-*Hamlet*s, all of which perform the '"hollowing out" of allegorical subjectivity'. In addition to Craig's production, Halpern examines the clockwork Hamlet and Ophelia in *The Mountebanks* (W.S. Gilbert's musical play of 1892); Cocteau's *The Infernal Machine*; the lectures on *Hamlet* given by the French psychoanalytic critic Jacques Lacan, for whom the play is 'a kind of mechanism . . . in which human desire is articulated'; Heiner Müller's *Hamletmachine* (published in 1977), which posits a 'split' Hamlet caught up in the routines of history; and *The Last Action Hero* (1993) starring Arnold Schwarzenegger, included for its brief *Hamlet* send-up. Indeed the film allows Halpern to reflect on his eccentric collection: '*The Last Action Hero* shares with almost all the other works considered a presumption that *Hamlet* is, in some sense, obsolete.'[39]

It is a nice thought. *Hamlet* can be remade only if the 'original' is already exhausted. In that sense Craig hurried along *Hamlet*'s obsolescence, his own interpretation being more palpable than any attempt to deliver (modestly and neutrally) the Shakespearean source. Craig's work on the play echoes further into the twentieth century. His vision of *Hamlet* as a monodrama anticipates Robert Wilson's treatment, which pursues the idea more implacably through Wilson's solo performance. It also prefigures the machine-based *Elsinore*, which evokes different settings through rearrangements of screens, albeit that these are projection screens rather than abstract Craigian shapes. And in a further twist of coincidence, towards the end of his life Craig met and discussed ideas about the theatre with Peter Brook, who included this eccentric guru as one of the directorial authorities of *Qui Est Là*. His work stands as a beacon of modernity early in the twentieth century, and casts its glow on the three *Hamlet*-projects featured here, over eighty years later.

*

In 1925, just over a decade after Craig's production and six years before Brecht's radio version, Barry Jackson's Birmingham Repertory Theatre toured its modern-dress production of *Hamlet* to London.[40] Modern-dress productions followed in quick succession in New York, Vienna, Hamburg and Berlin, thereby claiming the play for the twentieth century and institutionalising it as a text capable of – indeed ripe for – contemporary setting. One of these – Leopold Jessner's production in 1926 in Berlin, with Fritz Kortner playing the lead – was perhaps the first systematically political production of the play. Two years previously Tristan Tzara had produced *Mouchoir de Nuages*, a surrealist piece taking *Hamlet* as its prime referent.[41] Two poles of twentieth-century *Hamlet* production were established: the one exploiting political resonances in the play, the other tapping it for themes of madness which themselves legitimate a full-scale emptying out of the play's *gravitas*. One of the most bracing examples of the first approach is provided by a familiar figure.

Bertolt Brecht's brilliant interpretation of *Hamlet* is summarised in a passage in his *Short Organum on the Theatre*, and deserves lengthy quotation.

It is an age of warriors. Hamlet's father, king of Denmark, slew the king of Norway in a successful war of spoliation. While the latter's son Fortinbras is arming for a fresh war the Danish king is likewise slain: by his own brother. The slain kings' brothers, now themselves kings, avert war by arranging that the Norwegian troops shall cross Danish soil to launch a predatory war against Poland. But at this point young Hamlet is summoned by his warrior father's ghost to avenge the crime committed against him. After at first being reluctant to answer one bloody deed by another, and even preparing to go into exile, he meets young Fortinbras at the coast as he is marching with his troops to Poland. Overcome by this warrior-like example, he turns back and in a piece of barbaric butchery slaughters his uncle, his mother and himself, leaving Denmark to the Norwegian. These events show the

young man, already somewhat stout, making the most
ineffective use of the new approach to Reason which he
has picked up at the university of Wittenberg. In the
feudal business to which he returns it simply hampers
him. Faced with irrational practices, his reason is utterly
unpractical. He falls a tragic victim to the discrepancy
between such reasoning and action.[42]

How deliciously Brechtian. Hamlet is not the delicately
nuanced, tortured soul of conventional interpretation, but an
'introspective sponger', as Brecht put it in an earlier sonnet,
whose downfall is that he abandons scrupulous hesitancy and
launches into barbarous slaughter. Brecht developed this view
when preparing a radio version of the play, broadcast in 1931.
The script is lost, but for the final lines in which Fortinbras
describes Hamlet 'greedily taking up the battle-cry of unknown butchers . . . in a single horrible maniacal fit he
slaughters the king, his mother and himself'.[43] Not in Shakespeare's play, of course. Of all the versions and approaches
mentioned in this book, Brecht's is the most pointedly
centred around a political reading of the play.

The terms of this reading were clarified in a short rehearsal
scene which Brecht wrote for Helene Weigel, who was giving
acting lessons while the pair were in exile in Stockholm.
Brecht's rehearsal scenes are halfway between workshop exercises and textual interventions, and this particular one is to be
rehearsed between 4.3 and 4.4 of Shakespeare's text – that is,
between the scene in which Hamlet is despatched to England
and the one in which he encounters Fortinbras and his army
marching to defend a scrap of land. In Brecht's interpolation,
Hamlet meets a Ferryman who tells him that since Claudius
has decided not to press the war with Norway the fishing
industry is booming. Claudius, the arch-pragmatist, engineers
prosperity through the strategic avoidance of warfare. Hamlet,

by contrast – pre-empting his final conversion to action – calls for arms to be taken up again 'because the other one started it'. As Brecht noted, the scene 'should prevent a heroic interpretation of Hamlet. . . . Hamlet's hesitancy is explained; it springs from a new bourgeois attitude already disseminated in the socio-political realm.'[44]

What is so arresting about this reading? Firstly, it is mischievously unorthodox, laying about *Hamlet* in order to dislodge it from the plinth on which it is normally positioned. As Brecht well knew, if you really want to make your mark you have to rewrite orthodoxies rather than merely playtexts. Secondly, Brecht's scheme has a ruthless clarity, in pursuit of which Brecht knocks the play around somewhat, chops and changes, and creates new linking and expository material. Shakespeare's work is up for grabs – but also in need of tidying up. Thirdly, there is the smart idea that character can be explored through appended scenes. In this instance the 'Ferry Scene' is designed to develop not a style of acting but an attitude on the part of the actor – robust, sceptical, interrogative, keenly aware of the relationship between political action and economic interests. Such thinking, however, is manifested through theatrical playing. The rehearsal room is where the newly thought text is forged. Fourthly, there is Brecht's liking for fable: narrative storytelling with metaphoric significance. Shakespeare's text is refashioned, but in order for meaning – not style or starriness – to predominate. This rationalist perspective does not characterise any of the productions which form the mainstay of this book. It is here by way of contrast.

*

The major thrust of Shakespearean deconstruction, as opposed to adaptation and interpretation, occurred in the 1960s. Charles Marowitz produced a *Hamlet* collage at the Festival of Experimental Theatres in Berlin in 1966, two years after collaborating with Peter Brook on a twenty-minute version of the play as part of the pair's Theatre of Cruelty season. In a move reminiscent of Craig's approach and prefiguring Wilson's, Marowitz decided that everything should be a figment of Hamlet's imagination, and his collage version lasted only around an hour and five minutes. A year later Joseph Papp staged *William Shakespeare's "Naked" Hamlet* in New York's Central Park – another collage, this one lasting an hour and twenty minutes. According to a note in the programme: 'This production . . . seeks to discover the veins of the living original, buried under accumulated layers of reverential varnish.'[45] The 'real' play, then, was to be accessed by way of the irreverent jangle of the collage.

In 1970 Paul Baker staged *Hamlet ESP* in Dallas, Texas. This was another collage. In his director's notes, Baker suggests that: 'The main action of the play happens inside Hamlet's mind'[46] – another turn to an introspective Hamlet, and to a text which produces interiority. In Baker's version three performers play Hamlet. The central character may be the originating mind of the action, but he is nonetheless decisively split. In 1967 the National Theatre presented Tom Stoppard's *Rosencrantz and Guildenstern Are Dead* (originally produced the previous year at the Edinburgh Fringe Festival by the Oxford Theatre Group). In this showpiece of textual unravelling and interweaving, Shakespeare's eponymous courtiers take centre stage and the events of the play (and the character Hamlet) are glanced as they happen around them.

By the end of the 1960s, then, *Hamlet* had been claimed as a play suited to emergent postmodernism, not least because it could be turned inside-out, sliced up and seen from askew. The productions of the late-sixties emerged out of the cultural and political ferment of the time, when master scripts, whatever their nature, were challenged and part-rewritten. What script could be more masterful than *Hamlet*? As Charles

Marowitz observed at the time, 'Our generation has a thing against the classics. They represent not only what we've been taught in school, but exist as the artistic embodiments of that paternalist society we are rebelling against at every turn.'[47] There is a curious reflex, however, which also characterises the *Hamlet* excursions of Brook, Lepage and Wilson. The collage and pastiche productions of the 1960s also *validate* Shakespeare's *Hamlet*, staging responses to it which require their audiences to know the original text in two senses: firstly, for its story; secondly, for its status. Each production undercuts the play but can only do so by trading on its esteem. *Hamlet* remains unassailable, even where it is most beset. That said, productions of Shakespeare's plays are always laid out along shifting cultural and ideological fault-lines. The Bardic texts are squeeezed, pulled and torn according to the tectonics of culture and history. Regardless of any intrinsic value they might possess, they are always something other than themselves. *Hamlet*, then, is not so much primary source as palimpsest.

The stuff of theatre

In 1952 Herbert Marshall edited a collection of illustrations depicting productions of *Hamlet* since 1709. In his introduction he lamented the absence, even in his own day, of a decent archival tradition where a production would routinely be memorialised, its prompt copy retained, the designer's, director's and actors' notes and sketches collected, along with 'action photographs of the high spots of every scene'.[48] Marshall is right that this is a neglected form of recording. He points to Edmond Malone's Variorum Edition, *The Plays and Poems of William Shakespeare*, published in ten volumes in 1790, which collected writings pertaining to the plays. Two of the ten volumes are devoted to *Hamlet*. Marshall is struck by what he finds: 'there are about 270 pages of literary and philosophical criticism of the text and action from the earliest extant (1710) to date of publication (in my volume 1905); only fifteen pages on actors' interpretations; two and a half pages on costumes; nothing on production or scene design.'[49]

Turning his attention to latter-day productions, Marshall asks for 'a set of photographs to be taken with a miniature camera and a high-powered lens during a performance, recording every episode and sequence throughout the play, contact prints to be made and kept purely for historical and research purposes, letting the publicity and art photographers continue their normal work.' Furthermore, he asks for the following to be preserved:

> the producer's own working copy of the play, with any notes, ground-plans and drawings; the stage manager's recording on his prompt-copy of the moves and business; the electrician's lighting cue-sheet and notes of the lights and colours used; the musical score (if any) properly cued; the original designs of the artists and final ground-plans, or at least photographs of them, any written work done by the actors during rehearsals; any recordings on gramophone discs or tape recorders or television news-reel; any films whether news-reel or documentary; any sound tracks (such as those made on 35mm. film for Gielgud's *Macbeth*), noises-off and music; any articles or interviews with producer, designer and actors; and of course all the write-ups in the Press and publications.
>
> If this sounds impossible, all I can say is that many European theatres have been doing most of this for years.[50]

Most? Certainly not all. Marshall is hardly an obvious authority for a book on postmodern performance, although he does fit within a rather disparate British tradition of performance-centred criticism which can be traced back to Granville Barker's

Prefaces to Shakespeare and which includes the work of J.L. Styan, John Russell Brown and Dennis Kennedy.[51] He is perhaps the most ascetic, and the most utopian. I like his list for three reasons. Firstly because it recognises that the fabric of theatre involves the colours of the gels used by the lighting designer, the cueing of sound effects and the notes actors make in rehearsing a role. Theatre is nothing without this vast background of lived work and tiny detail. Secondly, I admire its train-spotterish zeal for collecting the stuff of production, its passion for the completeness of the record. And thirdly I sympathise with the yearning tone of Marshall's comments. For any such collection of ephemera is already grasping at the air, doomed to evoke a presence which has already left the room. Archival details can only conjure the outlines of an entity which existed more fully for the people who presented it and witnessed it at a particular time and place. Really, any theatrical record proclaims its own inadequacy. Theatre can be traced and scored, but its primary effects are visceral and sensual.

Marshall's list nonetheless captures some of the horizons of my own project. Theatre is an activity involving concrete details, where the choice of a particular lighting unit, for a certain effect, has a bearing on what the spectator sees and feels. Any discussion of this kind must proceed with due caution, in the light of the demonstrations by post-structuralist and deconstructionist critics that we cannot trust what's under our noses, for the present and visible is structured according to absence and lack. What's more, theatre events are subject to differences of interpretation depending on the performing context and the constitution of the audience. One of the more stimulating recent books on performance practice in relation to Shakespeare is W.B. Worthen's *Shakespeare and the Authority of Performance*, a Foucauldian account seeking to show how 'authority' (of text and/or performance) is systematically constructed. Worthen suggests that:

> Performance signifies an absence, the precise
> fashioning of the material text's absence, at the same
> time that it appears to summon the work into being, to
> produce it as performance (remembering that reading
> is as much a performance, a production of the work, as
> stage performance is), a performance that summons
> one state of the work while it obviates others.[52]

My approach takes a different tack. Unquestionably theatre is always defined by the shifting nature of the room and by what's not in it. But as Bert States observes, 'we tend generally to undervalue the elementary fact that theatre – unlike fiction, painting, sculpture, and film – is really a language whose words consist to an unusual degree of things that *are* what they seem to be.'[53] It is time to refocus and look at what *is* in the room and how it got there, by way of that stream of details and decisions which accounts for what's put before an audience. For we can also talk of performance in terms of irreducible presence – not standing for or alongside an originating (authorising) source, but offering particular effects which impinge upon performers, technicians and spectators in various ways at the same moment. (We will still be very interested, of course, in the strategies which produce 'authority' in *Elsinore, Hamlet: a monologue* and *Qui Est Là*.)

On the cusp of the twenty-first century, Shakespeare's *Hamlet* became a springboard for three distinctly original shows. So drastic was the emphasis on the production over and above the play that if you had no knowledge of the text in the first place you would not have been able to reconstruct it out of the spectacle. 'You can't make a *Hamlet* without breaking eggs,' as Lepage punned. He neglected to say that the eggs should also be beaten, mixed with other ingredients and heated up by the chef to make an entirely new dish.

Hamlet in pieces

The chapters which follow are governed by the points which the respective productions had reached when I embarked on this project. *Qui Est Là* had already finished its tour. Although I subsequently interviewed Brook and a number of his collaborators, rather than attempt a second-hand description of the production's rehearsal process I give a briefer account of the development and rehearsal work then focus on the outcome. *Hamlet* is a touchstone throughout, as are the writings of some of the most significant directors in western theatre. Whilst Shakespeare, Artaud *et al.* loom as authorities, their work is ransacked and fused in a brilliant act of theatrical synthesis which occludes as much as it includes. A closer look at the melding of this material reveals some underlying tenets of Brook's theatre practice and suggests the outlines of a Brookian system. All of which casts some light on Brook's full production of *Hamlet* in 2000, which is the subject of my epilogue.

I spoke with Robert Wilson and some of his collaborators during a run of *Hamlet: a monologue* in Amsterdam, where I watched the show again from both the auditorium and backstage. By this point the production was already fixed and complete. A good deal of information regarding its development came to hand by way of interviews and Marion Kessel's video documentary, *The Making of a Monologue: Robert Wilson's Hamlet*. I have used these to describe Wilson's rehearsal process for this show, before looking at the production itself. I became interested, not least, in the hyper-theatricality of Wilson's work, and spend a few words musing upon this.

While Wilson was periodically touring his controlled histrionics to venues around the world, Robert Lepage was planning a revamped production of *Elsinore* featuring an English actor, Peter Darling, in place of himself. The show was rehearsed in three weeks at Lepage's base, the Caserne Dalhousie in

Quebec City, during which time it was extensively remade. I sat in on rehearsals. My account largely considers the company's work during this intensive period and the way in which the rehearsal process bore fruit in variously ingenious stagings.

I am most interested in the 'theatreness' of the three shows, and this is the stuff of Chapter 5. Each of the three directors is renowned as a 'magician' of the stage, especially gifted in exploiting the medium in which he works. Such high craft is practised in an age where electronic and mediated artforms are notably ubiquitous. Theatre often seems a dusty, old-fashioned activity, yet to many the work of Brook, Lepage and Wilson appears modern, modish, sexy. Why is this? What is it about their manner of working which gives their outcomes such a contemporary feel?

The three directors, in different ways, trade in a phenomenological theatre, exploiting qualities of space, sound, movement, rhythm, visual image and the body of the performer. They clarify, for spectators, the theatricality of all these – actual space is also metaphorical space, the actual body is also a pretending body, and so on. Their theatre is lucidly of its moment, formed of myriad configurations of sound, image and movement which work on audiences in the 'now'. Does this matter any differently today than it did for spectators in other ages? The answer, I think, has a lot to do with the way we take our pleasure in late-capitalist culture. This in turn informs the kinds of things that are done to *Hamlet* in the workshops of postmodern practitioners.

Which returns us to our starting-point: three exceptional, theatrical shows launched themselves from an exceptionally theatrical text, and in the process raised 'all sorts of immediate questions of theatre'. Let's look at what they did and at how they did it.

Qui Est Là • Peter Brook

2

Qui Est Là • Peter Brook

'For all his apparent concern with metaphysics, there is no more practical man of the theatre than Brook.'

Richard Eyre[1]

Last words

On the face of it, Peter Brook spent the last couple of decades of the twentieth century fashioning an *oeuvre* of millennial masterpieces which have all the resonance of a closing speech at the end of Act 5. There were productions of canonical final works by celebrated playwrights. In 1988 Brook revived (in English rather than French) his 1981 production of *The Cherry Orchard*, Chekhov's last play. Two years later he presented Shakespeare's last play, *The Tempest*, in French, at the Théâtre des Bouffes du Nord in Paris. On a more expansive tack, there was his version of *The Mahabharata* (1985), a Sanskrit poem 15 times longer than the Bible and, according to Brook, 'more universal than Shakespeare's complete works'.[2] Two productions in the 1990s charted abnormal operations of the human brain – *L'Homme Qui* (1993, presented in English in 1994 as *The Man Who*), a study of neurological dysfunction which took

Oliver Sacks's book *The Man who Mistook his Wife for a Hat* as its starting-point, and *Je suis un phénomène* (*I'm a phenomenon*, 1998), which laid out the unusual mental constitution of the Russian mnemonist Solomon Shereshevsky. What better way to top this collection than with a full production, in 2000, of Shakespeare's *Hamlet*?

World mythology, the workings of the brain, complex social interactions – Brook's work is marked by the grandeur of its embrace. It takes big themes and complicated events and attempts to circumscribe their most inner, most outlying, most primal, most final entities. To use a grammatical analogy, Brook's theatre deals in superlatives, a predilection borne out by the liberal use of superlatives in the director's descriptions of his own work. Brook talks a lot about 'truth', 'essence' and the 'essential'. His fondness for extravagant quintessence found its moment at the turn of the millennium.

Presented in 1995, *Qui Est Là* belongs to this quest for magnificent overview. The production combined edited scenes from Shakespeare's *Hamlet* with the writings of Artaud, Brecht, Craig, Meyerhold, Stanislavsky and Zeami Motikoyo (a Noh theatre master in medieval Japan) – a veritable A to Z of practitioner-thinkers.[3] From the outset this was a superbly summative project. Brook was dealing with the Ur-text of modern drama; with the codifications of the director-theorists who most evidently shaped western theatre in the twentieth century; and with an Eastern perspective which provides a decisively alternative reference point. *Qui Est Là* was posted as the twentieth century's final word on Shakespeare, on modernist drama, on world theatre.

It is not surprising to find that the central text is Shakespeare's. Brook has turned to his preferred playwright at pivotal moments throughout his career. In a speech made in 1991 he observed that 'Shakespeare is always the model that no one has surpassed, his work is always relevant and always contemporary.'[4] In his monograph *Evoking Shakespeare*, Brook celebrates his subject as a playwright who was 'genetically speaking . . . a phenomenon . . . [with] an amazing, computer-like capacity for registering and processing a tremendously rich variety of impressions'; and as a poet, who has 'the capacity to see connections where, normally, connections are not obvious.'[5]

For Brook, Shakespeare uncovers such connections without privileging any single point of view. The poet-playwright amasses scenes of remarkable locational and emotional fluidity, which offer an intensely real image of social interaction and individual experience. His writing leans towards a metaphysical understanding 'related to an order that had nothing to do with political order'.[6] This is Brook's Shakespeare: capacious of mind, even-handed, a master synthesiser, an expert in the flowing dynamics of theatre, and always inclined to offer meaning beyond the merely literal (and indeed political). Unsurprisingly, the subject of this sketch sounds not unlike Brook himself. It is a disputable account, but Brook's impatience with the idea of leaving Shakespeare to fend for himself is appealing. Crucially, 'What we look at [when staging Shakespeare] must seem natural now, today. . . . In other words, the problem is adapting this material to the present moment.'[7] This, surely, is a truism of theatre-making too little understood and applied. Brook, meanwhile, rarely lets Shakespeare escape the present moment.

It appears that Brook's first engagement with *Hamlet* was at the age of seven, when he performed as the solo actor in a four-hour version ('by P. Brook and W. Shakespeare') for his parents, in which he played every part himself.[8] His first production for the Shakespeare Memorial Theatre in Stratford-upon-Avon was *Love's Labour's Lost* in 1946, marking the beginning of a long relationship with the organisation that would, in 1961, become the Royal Shakespeare Company, and which Brook left when it could no longer accommodate his unorthodox talent. His 1962 RSC production of *King Lear*, with Paul Scofield in the title role, marked the passage of both European existentialism and Brechtian minimalism into British Shakespearean production. In 1968, as political uprisings spread across Europe and America, Brook returned from Paris to London to present a one-hour 'work in progress' at the Round House, part-experiment in performance exercises, part-exploration of *The Tempest*.[9]

Nobody needs reminding of Brook's 1970 production of *A Midsummer Night's Dream*, one of the most celebrated Shakespearean productions ever. It is more easily forgotten that at the time this was a surprising choice of text, given Brook's inclination towards the more intellectual and problematic plays. The production's radical anti-sentimentality, its meta-theatricality and its bracingly clean style, which owed much to the white-box set designed by Sally Jacobs, a key figure in Brook's work during this period, consolidated trends which reverberated for at least the next twenty years. When Brook opened the Théâtre des Bouffes du Nord in Paris in 1974, where he has been based ever since, it was with a production of *Timon of Athens*. He returned to Stratford-upon-Avon and the RSC in 1978 to direct *Antony and Cleopatra* as an intimate political study. This remains, to date, his last made-in-England production. His 1990 production of *The Tempest*, with Sotigui Kouyaté as Prospero, marked the integration of the 'intercultural' experiments of the 1970s and '80s into Brook's Shakespearean work.

In spite of the global travels and the search for transcultural theatre forms, you can chart Brook's career through his engagement with England's most iconic playwright. Realist, existentialist, anarchist, early-postmodernist, interculturalist – Brook's Shakespeare is nothing if not a creature of fashion. 'Shakespeare is our contemporary,' observed Brook's friend

Jan Kott. He meant that Shakespeare's work was peculiarly in tune with dark and violent strains of the 1950s and '60s. What's striking about Brook's Shakespeare is that he is *always* impeccably up to date, sometimes even anticipatory of shifts in cultural production.

Brook's Shakespearean work has been underpinned by more consistent concerns. The programme note to the Round House *Tempest* of 1968 is reminiscent of the statements Brook was to make about *Qui Est Là*, nearly thirty years later:

> The present project is intended to bring fragments of evidence and experience to bear on these questions. The questions are: What is a theatre? What is a play? What is an actor? What is a spectator? What is the relation between them all? What conditions serve this relationship best?[10]

Throughout his career Brook has had a sharp eye on the mechanics of his medium. Perhaps more than any other director currently alive, he has structured his career as a discipleship in theatrical craft.

Brook's personal history connects him directly with some influential forebears. He was friends with Edward Gordon Craig. He saw productions directed by Stanislavsky, which were still in the repertory of the Moscow Art Theatre when Brook first visited Moscow. His Russian cousin had been Meyerhold's assistant, and described for his English relative the extraordinary work he had witnessed. Brook first met Brecht in Berlin in 1950, when his Shakespeare Memorial Theatre production of *Measure for Measure* was on tour. His encounter with Artaud's writings in 1959 led him to write avidly on the Frenchman's ideas for the theatre journal *Encore* and to produce, with Charles Marowitz, the influential *Theatre of Cruelty* season of 1964. In 1968 France's pre-eminent *homme du théâtre*, Jean-Louis Barrault, gave the actors appearing in Brook's Round House production of *The Tempest* a class in breathing, based on exercises he had learnt from Artaud.[11]

I am reminded of Roland Barthes' opening sentences to *Camera Lucida*:

> One day, quite some time ago, I happened on a photograph of Napoleon's youngest brother, Jerome, taken in 1852. And I realized then, with an amazement I have not been able to lessen since: 'I am looking at eyes that looked at the Emperor.'[12]

Meeting Brook, you confront a similar amazement. It is not enough that this is Brook himself, guru-appellate of the European stage. The hand you are shaking has shaken the hands of Barrault, Brecht, Craig and Grotowski. Brook stands before you as twentieth-century theatre's most ubiquitous witness.

This authenticating biography is brought to bear in *Qui Est Là*. The contours of Brook's most retrospective project are evident in his work over a good number of years. In 1973 Brook suggested that 'there is a very surprising and very interesting connection between Craig and Brecht' – a connection found in their pursuit of minimalism in, respectively, scenography and the work of the actor.[13] In the same article Brook writes: 'For Artaud, theatre is fire; for Brecht, theatre is clear vision; for Stanislavsky, theatre is humanity. Why must we choose among them?'[14]

The urge for synthesis – dramatised in *Qui Est Là* – is already very much at work. And what better place to reformulate modernist theatrics than in the playground of Renaissance drama? According to Brook, 'The whole of our research work has been to try to make the quality of acting less of a communication through imitation and more a form of natural language, moving towards an Elizabethan model where many

different people of different ages, cultures, classes can respond together.'[15] In 1974 he suggested that 'the best example
of a complete theatre [is] the Elizabethan theatre.'[16] *Qui Est
Là* grapples with major strands of modern European theatre
through the prism of what might be called the first modern
play. In 'Manifesto for the Sixties', written in 1965, Brook insisted, 'We need to look to Shakespeare. Everything remarkable in Brecht, Beckett, Artaud is in Shakespeare. For an idea
to stick, it is not enough to state it: it must be burnt into our
memories. *Hamlet* is such an idea.'[17] Thirty years later, Brook
enacts the fusion that these comments foreshadow. He does so
with yet another turn of the hand, for *Qui Est Là* approaches
Hamlet from the transcendentalist perspective of Brook's work
in the 1980s and '90s.

Starting-points

The subtitle to *Qui Est Là* is 'Une recherche théâtrale de Peter
Brook' – research into theatre on the part of the director. It is
difficult to think of another European company which has
concentrated on research – exploring questions – as a primary
activity over as long a period as Brook's company, the Centre
International de Créations Théâtrales (CICT).[18] According to
Brook and his collaborators, two different avenues of inquiry
led to *Qui Est Là*. The first was an exploration of theatre
directing. Brook collaborated over a couple of years with the
English playwright Nick Dear, who researched the work of
influential European directors with a view to creating a playtext. It was Dear who suggested that *Hamlet* should be the
cornerstone of whatever outcome emerged, since each of the
directors had staged the play or had expressed an interest in
staging it. At this point there was no assumption that *Hamlet*
would actually be performed. It would be a 'control text' in a
project which focused on 'what directing means today'.

Brook gathered a team of actors who, as far as possible, were directors as well as performers, to take this work further. The initial intention was that the actors would 'personify' Craig, Stanislavsky, Meyerhold and so on, but it quickly became apparent that the *Hamlet* material made demands that were impossible to ignore. 'We thought that maybe this was going to end up as two plays,' says Brook, 'that we're going to have a whole workshop of the different directors with perhaps a few flashes of fragments of *Hamlet*, and a condensed version like our version of *Carmen*, an hour-and-a-quarter telescoped *Hamlet*.'

There was then a change of tack. 'It was difficult to get out of the historical-biographical impasse,' Brook recounts.[19] Of course a historical-biographical approach needn't lead to an impoverished form of theatre, but it is not one which you would expect Brook to take, and the crucial decision to renounce both history and biography was probably inevitable. Brook suggests, for instance, that a 'biographical' depiction of Artaud 'as the sort of tragic and crazy guy he appeared to be at the end of his life was just self-indulgent and caricatural, and would cover up the fact that when you take that away, his texts are extraordinarily pure, and they're neither picturesque or crazy. In fact what we did in each case, which perhaps is not the only solution, was to take away everything of the personality of these directors to retain something which is the essence of what they are saying.' This 'essence' is actually rather selective, as I shall suggest later. There was a temporary halt in the project, with Dear's work now finished since there would be no play about the selected directors. The focus shifted instead to their theatrical ideas and precepts.

Brook was already reflecting on related questions of theatre praxis, and these provided *Qui Est Là* with its other major impetus. While touring *L'Homme Qui* in 1993 the CICT gave workshops in Vienna and Berlin for young directors from

Central and Eastern Europe. According to Brook, the theme of the workshops was, 'What are you looking for? When you do a play, what actually is it you want to appear? What do you want to bring to life? If there is an end, it is obviously not just putting on a play.' The practical exercises to which these questions applied was the playing of the Ghost in *Hamlet*. The workshops provided Brook with an early means of probing an issue that was shaping itself more insistently in relation to the *Hamlet*-material: the difficulty of representing the supernatural on stage.

This particular problematic is raised by Edward Gordon Craig in his essay 'On the Ghosts in the Tragedies of Shakespeare'.[20] 'Of all people nobody has been more categorical that if you try to take the supernatural out of *Hamlet*, go home,' says Brook. 'He is absolutely blunt about that. So, starting from that point of view – how do you do it?' It is not surprising that Brook should choose to begin with this challenge. He describes as a 'fundamental theme' of the research period the issue raised by another couple of salient questions: 'What is naturalistic in the theatre? What is real?' It is a short step from this to a desire to find ways of playing the Ghost (unnatural, unreal) with a stamp of authenticity.

The work undertaken in the educational exchanges was directly to inform *Qui Est Là* both in terms of general principle (the pursuit of a form of psychological naturalism in dealing with the presence of the spirit world) and actual staging (the playing of the Ghost in production). When Brook's actors workshopped the Ghost, the director found himself preferring the spirits offered by his non-European colleagues:

> We found that the only people who could give
> something without anything more than what they
> understood themselves of the action were the Japanese
> and the African [Yoshi Oida, Sotigui Kouyaté and

Bakary Sangaré]. With the African actor it was just the way of walking. . . . Where with the Africans it was a fine and noble ghost, Yoshi was on the floor behind some cushions, and as he came out, you saw something of the horror of the corpse. It was a corpse being exhumed. Where there was no fear produced by the African ghost, here the first impression was of awe and terror.

The African ghost eventually held sway, with Kouyaté playing the spectral presence in the production (Image 1). In an early workshop Sangaré and Kouyaté improvised an encounter between a son and the ghost of his father, speaking in the West African language, Bambara.[21] (Brook's starting point puts one in mind of Stanislavsky's 'magic "If"', which asks the actor to explore a personal correlative for what's in the drama – 'How would it be if you saw the ghost of your own father?') Brook found the improvisation 'absolutely magnificent because there was a truth. One saw that the scene had an intimacy, it is a scene between a father and a son.'

This linguistic shift was retained in the production. The Ghost's first words to Hamlet are spoken in Bambara, although he speaks French to convey the crucial information that it was Hamlet's uncle who wielded the poison. He speaks solely in Bambara when he returns during Hamlet's visit to his mother's closet. The mixture of effects which impressed themselves upon Brook were noticed by some of the critics. Odile Quirot observed that 'It was enough for Sotigui Kouyaté . . . to exit as though he was gliding over the ground, rather like the noh theatre actor's means of disappearing: he *is* the Ghost.'[22] According to James Fenton, 'We understand Africa to be a place in which the continued existence of ancestors is a simple fact of life. When Sotigui Kouyaté comes to speak to his son, he is a physical presence, not an immaterial being. And the son accepts the apparition and its physical contact with him.'[23]

The consequence of this staging is double-edged. The Ghost in *Hamlet* needn't be some armour-rattling phosphorescent ghoul, simply the dead father of a young man. The African language works here as a guarantee of that simplicity, relocating the scene to the site of the actor's birthplace. Brook has been criticised in the past for a form of blithe late-colonialism, valorising the Ethnic Other in ways which some critics find misrepresentative and patronising.[24] It's true that the African, in this instance, is used to signify something especially pure. Bruce Myers, a longstanding Brook collaborator and one of the performers in *Qui Est Là*, observes that:

> when the African guys play Hamlet and Claudius and the Ghost, something quite extraordinary is going on as far as I'm concerned. When Sotigui plays Prospero and Bakary plays Hamlet they are really living what they are in those parts, in a way like no-one else I can imagine. People can act, perhaps, with more dexterity and more skill, but there's not that reality of the nature of the human being, which is incredibly convincing.

Language, of course, is a basic signifier of cultural identity. The conversation in Bambara marks the Ghost as a being especially 'authentic', not so much supernatural as super-natural – another superlative of sorts.

The team which went on to present *Qui Est Là* was assembled during the early educational workshops around the company of actors (David Bennent, Sotigui Kouyaté, Bruce Myers and Yoshi Oida) which at the time was touring *L'Homme Qui*. Bakary Sangaré, who had appeared in Brook's productions of *The Mahabharata* and *The Tempest*, participated in the Berlin classes at the suggestion of Brook's assistant Marie-Hélène Estienne.[25] Brook was intrigued and delighted that Sangaré had never heard the story of *Hamlet*, which the

director proceeded to recount to him. One can imagine
the relish with which Brook decided to cast Sangaré as his
Hamlet. A black actor in the role instantly has the effect
of disjointing the show from the mainstream of European
representation. How much more delightful if that actor is
himself learning the play, speaking it for the first time, as he
goes along? The ironies of the situation – the European
magus with the African naïf – hardly need stating. A trace of
this choice also appears in Brook's casting of Adrian Lester, a
black British actor, as Hamlet in his full production of the play
in 2000.

Kouyaté had first worked with Brook in 1985 in *The Mahabharata*. Yoshi Oida first appeared in a Brook production in
1968, Bruce Myers in 1970, David Bennent in 1990. Bennent
was lined up as Horatio. The casting of roles between Myers,
Oida and Kouyaté was to be decided later. Both women in the
company were new to the CICT, although both were related to
established Brookian collaborators. Anne Bennent, David's
sister, who had been working in Austria, was to play Gertrude.
Giovanna Mezzogiorno, whose father Vittorio had played
Arjuna in *The Mahabharata*, would play Ophelia.

A close-knit group. The apparent continuity is a little misleading, however, since the actors are not full-time members
of the company but are contracted from project to project.
Once performances and tours are over they are free agents
(and are not paid a retainer by the theatre). If there is a week's
break between finishing a run at the Bouffes du Nord and
taking a show on tour, the actors are out of contract, and unpaid,
for that week. Bruce Myers gives an actor's perspective:

> It seems to me to be absolutely real that you work when
> you're needed. All of us have not been needed [at some
> point]. It's quite hard. There are no presents given. But
> the quality and the intensity and the reality of the

research that happens during the rehearsals makes it possible to live an up and down life. . . . I know that in a way we look for something where the joy of being together, and being free for a moment of what we have to be in daily life, is around when we play together, unlike any other group I can imagine.

Theatre projects, by their very nature, often induce firm bonds between their participants which last for as long as the production and then loosen as the artists move on to work elsewhere. In Brook's case, the inter-personal dynamics of a close company appear to be perpetuated across a large number of projects. So apparent is this sense of camaraderie, indeed, that a French reviewer of *Qui Est Là* was moved to praise the actors on the grounds that they formed 'an interdependent group, consumed by the same fire: a fire of theatre, a fire of play and a fire of joy'[26] . Whether or not such fires burn with consistent intensity, the fact is that Brook has established close bonds with a number of key performers who are willing to work again and again with the CICT.

The presence of Marie-Hélène Estienne, Brook's assistant since 1974, provides further stability. She is a central (and almost hidden) figure in Brook's work. What exactly does she do? 'Everything with him,' says David Bennent. 'She's writing, she's reading, she's having ideas, she's putting everything together, she's organised the rehearsals, everything.' Her in-volvement extends to participation in more directorial work within rehearsals. 'Yes, she's there all the time,' Bennent ob-serves. 'She says what she thinks, she brings in her experience, her ideas. I couldn't imagine Marie-Hélène without Peter and I couldn't imagine Peter without Marie-Hélène. She's carrying nearly everything.'

Estienne is named as a collaborator on the front of the programme for *Qui Est Là* and listed a little later in the credits as the show's dramaturg. Brook pays tribute to her in his memoirs, stating that 'her talent and intuition [are] a vital part of each new experience.'[27] Critics and audiences, however, can be forgiven for overlooking her immense importance to the work. In artistic terms she is perhaps to Brook what Elizabeth Hauptmann was to Brecht: confidante, co-writer, close collaborator, midwife to the work. Brook has produced extraordinary shows in the past without involving an assistant, but it is evident that his output since the pair started to work together would be very different without Estienne's involvement. In professional terms, she is more than just a director's assistant: she is closer to being a partner in the firm.

Excerpts from *Hamlet* were translated into French by Jean-Claude Carrière, another of Brook's long-term collaborators. This was the pair's fourth Shakespearean collaboration, after *Timon of Athens*, *Measure for Measure* and *The Tempest*. The writer participated in the workshops in Eastern Europe, translating fragments of the play, and he eventually translated about two-thirds of the text for potential use in *Qui Est Là*. 'One of the characteristics of Peter's work is that there is no separation of writing, directing and acting,' Carrière suggests. He means that the three activities are geared around collaboration in the rehearsal room. 'When I'm writing, of course there are a lot of moments of solitude, but Peter is always there looking over my shoulder and advising. . . . So he's always there when I'm writing, and I'm almost always there when he's directing. That's an old habit that we have. I'm not there all day long, but often I love to share the exercises and everything, the training of the actors.'

Mahmoud Tabrizi-Zadeh, the Iranian musician, was involved from the beginning of the rehearsal period and also participated in some of the exercises, leaving his instruments to one side. 'It was important for him to get up and do a movement,' says Brook. Important for Brook, too, you'd suspect, in that the music emerges from a physical relationship with the work. The lighting designer, Philippe Vialatte, was in rehearsals for about the last month, although his task was largely to provide a consistency of illumination rather than a panoply of lighting effects. 'The preference is for bright lights with a minimum of changes,' says Brook. 'I hate darkness. There's a great text of Brecht's about that. Mood and atmosphere, those are all completely out of date, I think, and basically boring. One's seen it all, so I hate it.'

If anything, mood and atmosphere seem decidedly in fashion, and it is Brook's austere mode of illumination which seems redolent of an earlier period. The lighting for CICT shows is sometimes designed by the theatre's chief electrician rather than by a dedicated lighting designer, such is Brook's disavowal of mood-oriented lighting effects. In any case, the lighting design for Brook's productions is usually developed as rehearsals proceed and the lighting plot, such as it is, gradually worked up accordingly. This is out of keeping with the orthodoxies of theatre production, and Brook would shudder at the idea of a 'tech run'. *Qui Est Là* had no technical rehearsal. Nor did the production have a set or costume designer.

Such stringency is a case of artistic choice. Brook has consistently argued the value of a limitation of production paraphernalia, so that focus is devoted to what the actor says and what the actor does. This is not the only way to make theatre, of course, but Brook's minimalist leaning has resulted in a distinctive brand of theatre. The very modesty of means is a CICT trademark, and it sets the company's work aside from almost any other kind of theatre produced at this level by companies which tour internationally. In itself it is a form of product differentiation.

Fusion cooking: Brook's process

Qui Est Là was prepared during three months of rehearsal split into two periods, the first of which began in June 1995. The gap in between allowed ideas from the first phase to settle and other intentions to surface. The process allows for a more measured, reflective relationship to the work than would be possible under the pressure of a single rehearsal period with an opening in view. It is worth stating the obvious: this approach is luxurious in the amount of time devoted to initial workshopping involving all members of the company. The CICT offers a provocative role model. It is not unthinkable for major companies – budgetary and scheduling constraints notwithstanding – to engage actors and production personnel for Research and Development, even if only for a couple of weeks, with a pause for reflection before beginning rehearsals proper. The value of such a process is borne out not only in Brook's work but in that of companies like the Volksbühne and the Théâtre du Soleil in Germany and France. This is hardly a case of continental dissipation. R&D, as commercial companies know, leads to a sharpening of product-distinctiveness.

The first rehearsal period for *Qui Est Là* was deliberately fluid. Brook and Estienne describe a typical day where Estienne would be working on a piece of text – an essay by one of the directors, for instance. The actors would work individually or in groups on segments of text, either from *Hamlet* or connected with the work of the central director-theorists. Brook would attach himself where he thought best. The group would come together, perhaps do an exercise, then begin work on the text which Estienne had been preparing. This might then be developed, disputed or swiftly ditched. The process is geared to sketching and demonstrating, physicalising text and ideas and seeing what sticks.

The actors might be given a few lines from a scene in *Hamlet*, which they would then perform, improvising around this scant material. Sometimes they did so according to approaches suggested by the writings of the chosen directors. Yoshi Oida recalls an exploration of the 'To be, or not to be' soliloquy, in which the actor first gives the speech 'cold', then declaims it, then performs it much more quietly, without any physical movement – an exercise drawn from the company's research into Stanislavsky's writings. Bruce Myers recalls that the company read passages from the documents released by the Russian government pertaining to Meyerhold's arrest, imprisonment and death. The actors tried out Meyerhold's bio-mechanical exercises ('They were much too difficult,' Myers recounts). They watched documentary footage of Meyerhold's production of Gogol's *The Inspector General* on video, then reconstructed part of it, with Myers playing Meyerhold in mid-direction, interrupting the playing and having the performers go back on certain sections. The only element that remains from this particular work is a gesture performed by one of Meyerhold's actors, which Myers echoes (without the audience knowing its derivation) when he voices Meyerhold's words about the nature of acting. So *Qui Est Là* is physically inscribed with elements from the research period without the source of these always being made evident.

Brook's actors report a process which is open and inter-rogative rather than predetermined, and it is clear that they are at least part-creators of the work which results. 'Of course if Peter has to do everything he does it,' says Oida, 'but that's a last security. He waits for something to happen, and things happen. . . . For me, he has the high quality to discover things, but even so he looks for more things to discover, so he lets it happen, he looks at it from another point and then dis-covers.' Brook provides a framework within which the actors themselves make crucial decisions (which are then arbitrated

by the director) and where they are free (within implied parameters) continually to negotiate the detail of their performance. David Bennent observes:

> I don't think Peter Brook has a certain play style. He
> never tells you, 'Don't do it like that, but like that.'
> I can say absolutely that Peter is not the director who
> says, 'Now you come from there, then you go there.'
> No. Absolutely not. He tells a lot, but he never directs
> the movement. It comes from the actor, it comes from
> the work. With Peter I can try to do everything. So in a
> way I have more responsibilities, also in performances
> suddenly if I want to do something, I do it. He directs,
> he helps you when you can't play, when you can't
> understand the play or this phrase. Then he helps you,
> then he's wonderful. But he will not really direct a
> scene. Everything is happening while we are rehearsing.

About two-thirds of the way through the rehearsal period the
company presented a work-in-progress version of the show to
pupils aged around 16 at the lycée Colbert and the lycée
Montaigne.[28] The group decided on a running order in the
hour before the performance began, interspersing scenes
from *Hamlet* with those dramatising the writings of the six
directors. Brook uses the school trip as a customary staging-
post in the creation of a new work, claiming that it has a 'tre-
mendous influence' on the show's subsequent development,
since it gives an early indication of the coherence or otherwise
of the work from the point of view of a 'naive' audience.[29] In
the post-performance discussion the students reported that
they understood the import of the scene in which the Ghost
and Hamlet spoke to each other in Bambara, and that it
didn't matter to them that the play had not been presented in
its entirety. Two cornerstones of the production were thus test-

driven and passed before opening night. This tentative public foray was backed up by a graduated series of previews. A week after the visits to the schools, a revised version of the show was presented at the Bouffes du Nord to drama students from l'École du Théâtre National de Strasbourg. On 4 December, eleven days before the opening night, the company gave its first 'public rehearsal' to an audience of friends and theatre professionals. A more orthodox series of previews followed. The show is still in ferment through this period. According to Yoshi Oida, 'Until the first performance we didn't know the final shape.' *Qui Est Là* opened on 15 December 1995.

The production is only let loose on the public at large after it has been carefully tested and market-researched. Mainstream theatres and companies do this, of course, either through a preview period or by means of provincial tours. During Brook's test period the work is more evidently still in development, still being 'written' explicitly in the light of public response. This aspect of Brook's work, as with many others, is taken further than is usual in most theatre practices. Again we catch sight of Brook *in extremis*.

When the production opened in Paris it received a number of glowing tributes, from English as well as French critics. Michael Billington found *Qui Est Là* 'spare, economical and illuminating: a meditation not just on Shakespeare and the mystery of theatre but on life, death and the transforming power of the imagination.'[30] 'Clean, clear and probing, it is two hours of intellectual magic,' wrote John Peter.[31] Odile Quirot applauded the director in more figurative terms: 'Like an expert cracking the code of a baroque architecture, Brook unlocks the burning heart of *Hamlet*.'[32] Frédéric Ferney praised the show for its sophisticated use of space and sound.[33] In Paris, critics paid respectful tribute.

The melting pot: Brook's production

Imagine that you have visited the Bouffes du Nord, the CICT's renovated-dilapidated theatre near the Gare du Nord, to see *Qui Est Là*. You are issued a free programme, an item with many significations. It contains a short piece by Brook. The director argues that the turn of the century witnessed an explosion of activity on the part of 'visionaries' and 'adventurers' in the theatre, who demonstrated that the medium could deal with both 'known and unknown levels of existence, affirming the dynamic possibilities which the human being possesses.' This account prepares the spectator for a show concerned with the business of theatre-making. Brook doesn't mention *Hamlet*. Nor is there any mention of it elsewhere in the programme, other than the note that the 'fragments' of the play are adapted by Jean-Claude Carrière. Instead there is a collection of short quotes, one from each of the six director-theorists, which further situates *Qui Est Là* within the context of a global, transhistorical exploration of the nature of theatre.

The programme contains no advertising other than a list of co-producers and the logos of France's Ministry of Culture and the mayoralty of Paris. No outright commercial enterprise is given space. It is lean (eight pages in all), clear (red type on glossy white paper) and straightforward. It conveys a certain purity in the face of consumerist culture. Yet its apparent modesty is also part of an audacious wheeze – the confident implication that here is a show engaged with the very essence of theatre as it might reveal itself in medieval Japan, or Renaissance London, or late-twentieth-century Paris. According to the programme, *Qui Est Là* is boldly meta-theatrical from the outset. This is a piece of theatre about Theatre. Take your seats.

A rectangular raised platform covered with a sand-coloured carpet forms the playing area, around which are placed a few plain, straight-backed chairs, painted brown. This particular arrangement – seemingly modest and neutral – is familiar. The use of a carpet to define the performance space has been a feature of Brook's work from the African tour in 1972 onwards. *L'Homme Qui* and *Je suis un phénomène* both used the rectangular platform as their performance area. Brook says that he looked at the set for *L'Homme Qui* at the end of one performance, and thought 'one could do the whole of *Hamlet* with just this platform and these chairs and that table. So that was the style, in a sense. The excerpts were in a consistent style of just using the chairs and the table and the little platform.' The actors perform in bare feet, wearing everyday shirts and trousers. Such apparent neutrality is a kind of costume, signalling the production's avoidance of a period setting and its focus instead on 'transcendent' elements in the material.

Qui Est Là was a bracing two hours long. Around a fifth of its eventual script was composed of fragments of writings by the historical figures. Shakespeare's play contributed the remaining four-fifths. This meant that the *Hamlet*-material took up just over an hour and a half – a series of glances rather than the full picture. Brook and his team certainly took the play by the scruff of the neck. A number of characters have gone entirely, with some redistribution of lines. There is no Barnardo or Marcellus. The plays's opening words are given instead to Horatio. These, incidentally, are more usually translated into French as 'Qui va là?' ('Who goes there?'), so the show's title carries a mild notice of the freshness of its translation and its difference from conventional French Shakespearean practice.[34] What's more, the titular phrase is without punctuation. *Qui Est Là* is a question without a question mark, a light utterance which might mean 'the one who is there'. It is a little mysterious, both more and less meaningful than usual.

Geopolitics are out. The beginning of Act 1, Scene 2, in which Claudius discusses affairs of state, is cut. Voltemand and Cornelius, functionaries of the play's sub-plot concerning imperial rivalries, are dispensed with. There is no Reynaldo, so no trace of Polonius's spying on his son. The scene in which Claudius and Gertrude brief Rosencrantz and Guildernstern is cut. Claudius's later instructions to the pair regarding Hamlet's deportation to England are cut, along with Polonius's subsequent suggestion to Claudius that he spies on Hamlet in the Queen's chamber. The motif of espionage and surveillance (so important to Lepage's *Elsinore*) disappears.

There is no Act 4, Scene 4, in which Fortinbras briefs his messenger, who then reveals to Hamlet the nature of the military enterprise on which the Norwegian soldiers are embarked. Hamlet's soliloquy in this scene ('How all occasions do inform against me, / And spur my dull revenge'), in which he remotivates himself in the face of Fortinbras's zeal for battle, is also cut. There is no Laertes. The duel, along with Laertes' discovery of his father's death and Ophelia's decline, therefore become redundant and are cut.

Claudius is made less complex. His aside in Act 3, Scene 1, for instance, admitting that a comment of Polonius has lashed his conscience, is cut. Nor is he shown at prayer. His invocation of Hamlet's death, alone onstage at the end of Act 4, Scene 3, is removed. There is no troupe of players, just a single actor. One of the two gravediggers is cut. The most startling decision in this adaptation is to end the play in the graveyard of Act 5, Scene 1. A number of lines are interpolated from later in the play and the *Hamlet*-material ends with Hamlet's 'Readiness is all' speech.

A number of these cuts are conventional even in full productions of *Hamlet*. Fortinbras is removed so often that when he does appear it is like seeing a surprise guest. The same is true of the second gravedigger. The deletion of Laertes is

more striking, and of course the absence of the play's denouement marks this as a sketch rather than a full-blown staging.
But this is the stuff of textual exegesis. The Bardic narrative,
even in such streamlined form, isn't the point of *Qui Est Là*.

The interjections from the writings of the director-theorists
continually divert attention from *Hamlet* and focus it instead
on larger questions of performance. The audience is given no
indication of the identity of the authors of the interpolated
material. If you know your theatre-writing you might recognise a few of the passages, but you would have to be a dedicated anorak to identify every quote. This, too, is hardly the
purpose. Instead a range of voices is subsumed into one voice
(that of the Brookian master-questioner) which delights in
interrupting the flow of the tentative, partial *Hamlet*. We can
better understand the precepts of this Brookian system by
focusing on the tissue of carefully edited commentary which
runs through *Qui Est Là*. How are the voices of Theatre Past
posthumously recruited to the cause?

Overtures

The opening sequence to *Qui Est Là* is like an overture,
introducing the evening's subject matter and its performance
registers. It begins not with the first words of *Hamlet* which
provide the show's title but with three pages of disquisition on
the theatre, most of it drawn from the writings of Edward
Gordon Craig, with Stanislavsky, Meyerhold and Zeami also
featured. (Artaud and Brecht must wait until later to take their
bows.) The ground is prepared with great care.

There are three figures on stage. As one speaks, the others
listen. Sotigui Kouyaté, voicing Craig's words, alludes to the
architectonics of space as a key modality for theatre: 'It has
always seemed to me that the starting-point most appropriate
to tragedy is a high, severe doorway.'[35] He points to the speci-
ficity of theatre as a medium: 'If it's a literary treat that you

want – go home'. He then notes the dimensions, in front of us, of 'a place without form, rather a huge, empty square'. This is the empty space for which Brook has become famous. One starts from emptiness and absence and adds essential elements.

Bruce Myers intervenes with Meyerhold's words, 'Look, the curtain's open!' He points to the fabric of the building, the paraphernalia which makes up a theatre and its auditorium. Yoshi Oida as Stanislavsky then arranges the chairs on stage in a seemingly random pattern. 'It must be just as in life,' he says, before discovering that his arrangement looks better from behind – the production's first tilt at the sort of mimesis with which Stanislavsky is most readily (and most mistakenly) associated. 'Copying' gives way to theatrical pragmatism.

Oida, now voicing Zeami's words, observes that, 'All the phenomena of the universe develop according to one progression . . . birth, life, death; death, birth, life'. This pronouncement of continual circular development will recur as the final statement of the show. Kouyaté, as Craig, then asks a pertinent question. 'From a practical point of view, if you had to advise a young man who wanted to direct Shakespeare, how would you set about it?' (A knowing joke, of course. Brook, who visited Craig, is always that 'young man' to the senior theatrical guru, whom he has nonetheless displaced in terms of public recognition.) The answer, he says, is that you get him to take the play scene by scene, looking for the 'latent spirit' in each of its sections – a search made more delightful given the presence of the supernatural in Shakespeare. At which point the company begins its treatment of the *Hamlet*-material.

The opening sequence does several things. Firstly it displaces *Hamlet*. Secondly, it presents statements but not characters. Meyerhold and Stanislavsky are not played as individuals. Their words are voiced by actors, with no sign of characterisation, of role-playing. We are not interested in the historical

Stanislavsky, the co-founder of the MAT who (mis)directed the plays of Chekhov, championed the work of Maeterlinck, had differences of opinion with Meyerhold and so on. He is only relevant as the author of certain textual fragments used in an attempt to outline an ontology of theatre. Biography is dismissed.

The sequence makes philosophical opening gambits. It privileges the Brookian idea of the empty space and the consequent minimalist aesthetic. It relates theatre-making to a buddhistic notion of the impermanence of all things, within an endlessly repeated cycle of existence. Thus nothing is final, nothing has absolute value, everything can be remade. Theatre is a part of a natural universe of growth and diminution, rather than a social act which does particular things for particular people at specific times.

The use to which Zeami is put in *Qui Est Là* underscores this approach. His book *Secrets of Noh* is cited as one of the production's key sources. As Brook points out, each of the director-theorists was interested in Eastern forms. In 1935 the celebrated Chinese actor Mei Lanfang performed in Moscow, where he was seen by Stanislavsky, Brecht, Meyerhold and Craig.[36] Lanfang's specialism as a Jingxi actor was the performance of women's roles, and he developed solo performances from a blend of dance and martial arts which evidently appeared entirely foreign but shockingly – theatrically – clear to his western audience. His visit set a benchmark for a certain kind of oriental performance: mannered, graceful, androgynous and presentational. Its vein of non-illusionism had a profound influence on Western understandings of Eastern performance disciplines. In addition, both Craig and Artaud studied the Balinese theatre, and their articulate fascination helped to develop a mythology around the beneficial differences between western and eastern modes.[37] As Brook observes, their work was conducted through 'personal investigation and first-hand impressions, but Zeami is the only written source' for traditional Eastern practice.

Zeami's writings were translated into French by Ionesco, and there is no indication that the other directors who feature in *Qui Est Là* were familiar with his work. So you might expect the show to redress the balance and present a good sample of this Eastern stage scripture. In fact Zeami's words appear hardly at all in *Qui Est Là*, and when they do it is to express the buddhistic belief in life as a cycle of developments, rather than a set of codified theatre practices, or even provocations to distinctly non-Western modes of performance. Zeami does not appear as Brook's Mei Lanfang, providing the shock of a drastically different tradition. He is mobilised for ideological as much as theatrical purposes. He functions as another sign that *Qui Est Là* melts history in its questionings relating to theatre, as it transcends both time, reaching back over 500 years, and place, travelling across the Pacific to Japan. Zeami, too, is a dweller within the global village.

The prologue asserts the theatreness of theatre, its reliance on space and its relationship to its audience. In this it is notably concrete. It establishes a discourse for the production. It has the air of a masterclass. Even the actors onstage, when not speaking, listen reverently to the words uttered by their colleagues. The scene doesn't suggest some lively post-show disputation, voices raised in contention about the work. A respectful, indeed devout, atmosphere is established – one best suited to allow the immediate acceptance, as common sense, of the words spoken. (The show doesn't include any of Brecht's warnings regarding the dangers of common sense.) *Qui Est Là* is open and questioning, yet it also recommends an essential mystification (the 'latent spirit').

Repetitions (the hand of the director)

The *Hamlet*-material begins with David Bennent bounding on to the platform and shouting 'Qui est là?' Yoshi Oida, hovering downstage, just off the platform, shakes his head and says, 'Non ce n'est pas ça' ('No, that's not it'). Bennent withdraws, then somersaults on before delivering the line again. Oida gives the same judgement. Bennent retires for another attempt. The somewhat jokey atmosphere is changed by Mahmoud Tabrizi-Zadeh providing a hollow knocking sound. Bennent slowly, cautiously steps on to the platform, edges under an imaginary rampart and gingerly looks about him, before half-whispering, 'Qui est là?' When I saw the production the audience was entirely silent at this point, hanging on the action. Bennent then speaks to and about the Ghost, in an edited speech which combines the lines of Horatio, Barnardo and Marcellus.

From the outset it is made clear, albeit lightly, that there are different ways to play a scene – but some are more appropriate than others. 'You do it in all the ways possible,' says Bennent, 'and the last of them – in a certain way without playing fear, without playing aggression – is more the way of theatre that Peter [Brook] is for.' The options which are spectacularly wrong merely underline the exquisite rightness of the one which is 'right'. The staging, then, helps the audience to agree that the correct choice has been made.

Part of the pleasure lies in succumbing to the organisation of the sequence. Tabrizi-Zadeh does not provide his tentative, reverberating accompaniment to Bennent's first two attempts. The sound-effect cues the 'proper' version. It is offered as a touch, a sudden punctuation which alerts the audience to the change of register, the evocation of something other than normal. It sounds a quality for Bennent to play into. The sheer difference in the nature of the actor's movement – tense, slow, tentative, where before he had been lithe, confident, impulsive – starkly dramatises the difference between 'right' and 'wrong'. The same is true of his quality of voice, at first breezy and loud, now timorous and soft. 'Proper' performance is a matter of precise bodily and vocal discipline, a measured control of movement and voice to suit the context.

Bennent's mimed ducking under some imagined battlement is a shrewd touch. The performer's action suggests a physical environment. The production will rely on the minimal, significant gesture to colour its locations, rather than elaborate sets or other means of placement. The scene's repetition also tells the audience that the *Hamlet*-material will be stopped and started, scrutinised, played over if it appears not to work. Shakespeare's text is subject to the business of theatre-making. And the staging implicitly promises to make everything alright. With a simple but showmanly flourish it states that the right solutions will be found, that the play will not escape from the company and that the audience can prepare to enjoy the evening.

Much later in the show: the scene in the Queen's closet. Bruce Myers holds a green curtain between his body and the audience to indicate the arras behind which Polonius hides (Image 3). When he is stabbed, he falls to the ground and lies still beneath the curtain. He leaps up once the Queen has replied to Hamlet that this is not the King. 'In the Japanese theatre,' he says, 'if the hero dies onstage the koroko quickly covers the body with a cloth, so that the actor can exit very discreetly.' This interlude is trumped at the end of the scene when Hamlet goes to remove Polonius's body. Myers returns, to compare a 'contemporary' manner of dying (which, he suggests, entails a 'very primitive' naturalism) and that of the ancient Chinese theatre, where the actor 'threw his body in the air like a tightrope artist and only allowed himself to collapse in a heap on the stage after this joking about – which is quite appropriate to the theatre.' He then performs this leap in 'dying' once more. According to Myers:

> The very nice idea of having Polonius dead and getting up again and saying, 'In the Japanese theatre the way of dying is this,' and then dying again a different way, was what Peter saw for the end of the rehearsal period as something that suddenly needed a very sharp change of mood. In that when Hamlet kills Polonius it's a terrible act. He's not a man who kills easily, and one senses in that a kind of despair. It's a terrible, rash action. So it was good if, at the end, it suddenly becomes something funny. That was Peter, of course.

The interpolations, which are from Meyerhold's writings, change the rhythm of the scene at two different points. Both dwell upon a familiar problem for theatre direction: how to clear 'dead' bodies from the stage. They indicate that such solutions are bounded by staging conventions: the Japanese theatre allows a 'discreet' exit, the Chinese delights in the decisiveness of death – a golden opportunity for the performer's final flourish. The first interpolation allows Myers to make his own discreet exit, at which the scene between Hamlet and his mother continues; the second allows him to close the scene with a grace note which delivers a familiar Brookian trope, recognising different conventions and at the same stroke gathering them into the melting pot.

The 'replayed' deaths answer Brook's need for 'a sharp change of mood'. They make the obvious point that the job of direction is in part about the organisation of pace, rhythm and tone. These are notoriously difficult quantities to analyse. It's easy to assume that there is always a 'right' rhythm and a 'correct' pace. It might be better to suggest that there are a variety of options, the fine-tuning of which depends upon a

complex interrelationship of elements: the audience's acculturation, the actor's capacities, the dominant modes of the
production. The texts of *Qui Est Là* do not include any consi-
deration of the science of rhythm, pace and tone (which
Brook practises very adroitly). Brook himself has said a little
on the matter:

> Questions of visibility, pace, clarity, articulation, energy,
> musicality, variety, rhythm – these all need to be
> observed in a strictly practical and professional way.
> The work is the work of an artisan, there is no place for
> false mystification, for spurious magical methods. The
> theatre is a craft. A director works and listens. He helps
> the actors to work and listen.[38]

Of course *Qui Est Là* is not intended to function as a
handbook for theatre-makers. The absence of any discussion
in the show of the likes of pace, rhythm and tone, however,
naturalises these as part of the underlying mechanics of
'good' performance. In fact the show is not *about* directing as
an activity or a craft – rather about the ideas of particular
directors in relation to the work of actors. In many ways this
is a show about *acting* rather than directing. Brook, the
director, has given us the slip yet again.

Actors and acting

The cast list simply names the performers in alphabetical
order. No roles are indicated. It is a subtle but important
gesture, for the programme implies that acting is not exactly
a question of the mere playing of parts. The actors in *Qui
Est Là* do not just perform as Gertrude or Guildenstern
or whoever. They are *agents-provocateurs*, coolly watching the
activities of their colleagues, nimbly commenting on their
work and slipping easily in and out of character as though

trying on jackets for size. The programme lists them as 'interpreters' and the word seems carefully chosen. The cast interprets the play, interprets the writings of the director-theorists and mediates between this material and the audience. It seems a splendidly generous enterprise. The relaxed manner in which the performers go about their business – wearing casual shirts and trousers, observing attentively when not involved in the action, performing with unfussy precision – aids their transparency as filters for the show's meanings. For Michael Coveney, 'Longtime Brook collaborators Myers and Yoshi Oida now perform with an explicit candour that seems to challenge the whole idea of "acting" itself.'[39]

Fabienne Pascaud uses the terms *compagnonnage* and *artisanal* when discussing *Qui Est Là*. Brook's working relationship with his actors, she suggests, is based on a form of companionship, and the resulting work is artisan-like in its emphasis on craft.[40] Brook's actors, as we have seen, report a sense both of enablement and of challenge in their work with the CICT. The director makes room for the actor's offerings but systematically questions, provokes and trims such input. As Myers says, there are 'no presents'. Familiarity – *compagnonnage* – breeds a refinement of craft-skills, which are geared around acting *tastefully*.

Brook has a clear affinity for a certain sort of actor: graceful, modest, transparent and mercurial. Those most associated with his work – Myers, Oida and Maurice Bénichou, for example – are players rather than stars. They perform not with the indelible stamp of personality that governs most top-billing theatre performance, but with a careful erasure of flamboyant egotism. This is actor-as-vessel. Brook's work with his performers is in part a job of stripping and refining. What's left is an embodiment of moments, a limpid display of situation-in-action rather than the forceful presentation of

77

character. This might lend itself to an auteur's theatre, where the actor is the director's puppet. Brook's more recent productions, however, have matched the scrupulous openness of its performers with interpretative even-handedness. At this stage of his career Brook's work with actors does not seek to fill the now-celebrated 'empty space' but to keep its contingencies in play. We are made to *notice* the emptiness of space and the multiple possibilities of embodiment. So when Pascaud points to an artisan-like company diligently working away, this is not quite in the honest-to-goodness sense of the carpenter making the wardrobe. Brook and his actors are honing a sophisticated restraint which is meant to put notions of place, presence and persona continually in jeopardy.

Qui Est Là confronts dominant ideas about acting in similarly destabilising ways. Brook speaks favourably of Craig's observation 'that it is a complete misunderstanding to talk about characters in a play of Shakespeare – that the notion that there is a character is not true to the reality of these texts, which is a conclusion I've reached in a different way over the years.' The alternative (Craigian) view is that characters have different functions at different points of the play, in relation to the whole – a conception of character which is close to that of Brecht, who insisted that actors should not smooth out character traits but should play any contradictions for maximum textual effect. As Brook says:

> The extraordinary thing is that a character reveals
> himself moment by moment and the way the actor and
> director develop a character in a play is moment by
> moment following its life and accepting its contradictions.
> Whereas if you work the other way, which is to work
> from the psychological analysis of what the character
> seems to be, you actually block many of the doors.

The actors in *Qui Est Là* certainly treat their characters dextrously. Being or pretending? The question is addressed in relation to one of *Hamlet*'s hottest metatheatrical zones: the arrival of the players. Rosencrantz informs Hamlet that the players are in town. 'He that plays the king shall be welcome,' says Hamlet. This cues an extended 'discussion' between Meyerhold, Stanislavsky, Zeami and Craig on the nature of theatrical playing. David Bennent as Meyerhold notes that if he wants to cry he uses a 'short cut' which provokes the appropriate reactions, and that this is a question of triggering a nerve – a physical trick. He ends on an aphoristic note:

> I see a bear, I am afraid, I tremble.
> That's not how it is.
> I see a bear, I tremble, I am afraid.
> We are machines.

Oida, as Stanislavsky, then tells an anecdote about finding that he was more moved at the sight of an Italian grieving over his dead monkey than by witnessing a road accident in which an old man died. Then comes the key passage: 'I cannot raise an emotion at will. I can't play love or hate without falling into the easiness of clichés, but I can direct my body. According to the situation, I look for the physical action which will raise the emotion without forcing it.'

This suggests an approach which (to oversimplify) is based on gesture and corporeality rather than on the emotional state of the actor. Stanislavsky is thereby repositioned, in a move which evokes Meyerhold's emphasis on the bio-mechanical and Brecht's espousal of gestic performance. In each case the actor very precisely produces a range of physical attitudes which 'sign' the role s/he is playing. It is a decisive shift back to a European model of physically-inscribed realism and away from the American school of Method acting which, since Lee

Strasberg's work with the Actors Studio in the 1950s, has become the dominant Stanislavskyan inheritance. The passage renounces the naturalistic strain of bastardised Stanislavskyan acting in favour of a more coolly intellectual and corporeal version. To make the point, Oida continues by dwelling on the 'energy' within isolated body parts – the elbow, the forearm, the wrist, the fingers, and so on around the body. His performance becomes an actor's exercise – but one to do with sheer physical self-awareness, not with any of Stanislavsky's more familiar meditations on emotional memory or empathy.

This tour of the body ends at the index finger. Yoshi Oida points out beyond the audience. 'Look at the moon,' he says to his colleagues. Like novices following a master, they copy his gesture and look out to where they are pointing (Image 4). 'I can show you the movement,' he continues, 'but from there to the moon is your responsibility.' The audience laughs. An actor has conjured the moon merely by raising his finger and arranging his posture and focus. The sequence stages one of Oida's favourite anecdotes about Kabuki actors. Brook relates the story in his foreword to Oida's book *An Actor Adrift*: 'And Yoshi added: "When I act, what matters is not whether my gesture is beautiful. For me, there is only one question. Did the audience see the moon?"'[41] To which *Qui Est Là* suggests its own answer: bodies in action make meanings.

The section ends with a number of short questions and answers taken from Craig's writings, the last exchange being:

> [I am asked] what are your methods, your means of investigation?
>
> I respond: Elimination. I know everything that the theatre shouldn't be.

The sort of thing that theatre should be is implicitly proposed in the company's treatment of the Player's speech. When

Yoshi Oida appears as the First Player he is deferential, full of self-effacing courtesy towards his royal bidder. Hamlet cues him to present the speech recounting the slaughter of Priam, and he suddenly becomes a professional in a room full of amateurs. This is the performance of a craftsman at work. He sits cross-legged, with Hamlet sitting on the floor nearby (Image 2). The pair are suddenly reversed in status. Oida gathers his focus, then speaks in Japanese. There is no hint of the ham parody to which many modern actors and directors resort. Instead the speech is performed with gravitas, with fine-tuned observance of rhythm and measure. It builds to a superbly controlled crescendo. The very fact of its foreignness (hardly anybody in the audience could be expected to under-stand Japanese) emphasises its status as a turn. It is a rhetorical *tour de force*. As with the exchanges in Bambara between the Ghost and his son, the distant foreign language is used as a stamp of validity.

'We transposed [the speech] into Yoshi doing this in Japanese so that he could play it as well as possible, with the greatest intensity, in his own language,' says Brook. 'Because I've always seen that in *Hamlet* it's a complete travesty to play it as a sort of camp joke, and that when you really see actors going on the stage to play badly it's so stupid.' Brook's actors *never* go onstage to play badly.

The various segments dealing with acting, in this part of *Qui Est Là*, are compounded as a unitary theory of perform-ance. The basic principle is that the actor must present, not emote. Through careful physicality and artistic control, the actor engages the spectator in a shared play of meaning. The work is intensified through pruning, stripping away anything unnecessary. Later in the show, when Hamlet orders Ophelia to a nunnery, her response is from Artaud: 'When I live, I am not truly alive. But when I act, I feel I exist.' Michael Coveney suggests that 'Ophelia's "madness" is here a resurgence of strength, a definition of self, not a whimsical decline.'[42] This isn't simply a choice about characterisation. It implies a metaphysics of theatre, in which acting is distilled existence. The actor arranges her *presence*.

Performing words

A quiet polemic runs through *Qui Est Là*, deprecating a 'literary' understanding of theatre. The case is made partly in relation to the 'wordy' Polonius, played by Bruce Myers. Polonius tells the King and Queen that he has found the 'true cause' of Hamlet's madness. Myers continues with a couple of lines of Polonius's longwinded meditation upon madness before bringing himself up short with 'A foolish figure'. At which point he delivers Meyerhold's observation, 'Words in the theatre are drawings on the backcloth of movement'. He then continues with Polonius's line: 'But farewell it. / I have a daughter . . . '

The interjection is an ironic actor's aside. It undercuts Polonius's verbal doodling. Meyerhold's figure of speech, moreover, conjures a visual image. Words in the theatre are not a matter of exquisite literary provenance but are part of the larger machinery of performance, which is movement-based. The single line is inserted as a counter to verbosity. It asks the audience to accept the self-evident truth that a predominantly verbal theatre is the stuff of fools and dotards. The line comes as a swift interjection. What it demonstrates – dramatises – is a permanent state of qualification, of quick-witted self-reflection on the part of the performer. It does so in a quintessentially theatrical manner. What better way of inviting the audience into your confidence than through the aside, a guarantee of direct communication?

This theme of the banality of mere words is picked up a little later. Polonius has just exited, with Hamlet bemoaning 'These tedious old fools'. Before continuing the Shakespearean scene, Sangaré launches into Craig's anecdote in which he describes seeing a sign backstage at the Düsseldorf Stadts-theater which read 'Speaking absolutely forbidden'. The delighted Craig declares, 'At last they have discovered the secret of the Art of Theatre! . . . the key to this Art rests precisely in this "Speaking absolutely forbidden".' At which Sangaré turns back into the action, as Rosencrantz and Guil-denstern greet Hamlet politely and with seeming warmth. The interpolation is neatly edited between the exit of one celebrated gabbler and the entrance of the notorious double-speakers. It is a nice joke, then, but it also conveys another Brookian 'truth': theatre is about showing, not saying.

Yet in *Qui Est Là* this sort of 'truth' is shared through a speech-act. The show's staging does not entirely follow the advice that the writings appear to recommend, reducing words to some supporting role for movement, *mise en scène* and scenography in a Meyerholdian or Craigian or indeed Wilsonian sense. Instead, words are used to articulate the untrustworthiness of words. *Qui Est Là* cannot *quite* escape the literary-linguistic framework which its utterances challenge.

The *Hamlet*-material ends at Ophelia's funeral in 5.1, and dispenses with the rest of the play's denouement. According to Brook, 'At the end of the graveyard scene some of the most vital things are expressed. A whole act of piling up corpses, which can be very exciting if it's done well in the theatre, is nothing to do with what we're doing.' Brook and Estienne retain much of the dialogue between Hamlet and the grave-digger. The grave is indicated by a couple of chairs on their sides, covered with a throw. Giovanna Mezzogiorno sits serenely amid this bier (Image 5), and utters text by Artaud, expressing a vision of rebirth from dust, death and small bones. Sangaré then speaks Hamlet's lines (in the play they come before he goes to his duel with Laertes):

There is a special providence in the fall of a sparrow. If it be now, 'tis not to come; if it be not to come, it will be now; if it be not now, yet it will come. The readiness is all.

There are three closing utterances. Firstly, Craig asserts that the words 'today', yesterday' and especially 'tomorrow' are beautiful, 'but the word which binds and harmonises them is a word more than perfect: this is the word, "And".' Artaud then states that a rigour for abstraction and purification, a sort of loss of self, is essential in order to 'learn to give again each gesture of theatre its indispensible human sense.' The final words repeat the buddhistic cycle of existence, voiced by Zeami, quoted towards the beginning of the show:

Beginning – Middle – End

Death – Birth – Life

Jo – Ha – Kyû

What is being staged here? Partly, I think, a respect for the meaning of words, the signness of the sign. *Qui Est Là* closes on a note of sober contemplation, by way of some would-be straight-talking about the metaphysical, rather than the gameful scoffing at language-(mis)use which occurs earlier in the show. The prevailing thrust of modern literary and cultural criticism has demonstrated the untrustworthiness of language as a stable means of communication. Brook flies in the face of this and asserts language's transparency. Individual words, however, are valuable where they are suggestive rather than dogmatic. Craig's virtually spiritual 'and' – which is connective, a conjunction rather than a definite article – echoes the principle of indeterminacy which runs throughout the show's closing section. I am reminded of E. M. Forster's resonant advice at the head of *A Passage to India:* 'Only connect'. This liberal-humanist urge, expressed in 1924 at the height of the modernist era, derived from Forster's engagement with the Asian 'other'. It might also be Brook's personal mantra.

Part of the connective strategy of *Qui Est Là* is to create a Voice of World Theatre which reaches all the zones – topical, historical, performative – which the show visits. Brook suggests that one of his overriding concerns throughout the project was the notion of Hamlet as a man in quest. 'What has made *Hamlet* great and touched people for so long is above all the dramatising of an intense, passionate and anguished questioning. . . . I think that that is the one thread that links Hamlet with what is cogent and totally valid immediately in all the pioneers of theatre . . . this passionate questioning.' Brook reiterates the point in his programme note.

'The readiness is all' stands as the conclusion to the questionings of *Qui Est Là*. 'Readiness', here, implies an openness to fate and an acceptance of circumstance. Such beatific quietude is placed within a context of continual rebirth. Death is put off, cheated, through the assertion that it is merely a staging-post in an endless round of births and flowerings. Thus even the *Hamlet*-material is not closed. The burial ground features an Ophelia who speaks of gathering together 'a new human body'. The play, famous for its litter of corpses, ends at a graveside which is a site of suspended animation, a scene of meditation upon the impossibility of closure, a place filled with bodies, none of them dead, all of them 'ready'.

Brook's gathering of materials from the heritage of European theatre direction results in a poised, serene defiance in the face of closure. It is tempting to see this as the consequence of the director's lifelong engagement with theatre, and a partial resolution to his own particular work. The final utterance of *Qui Est Là* is in Japanese.[43] The last word is foreign. The ultimate connection, Brook might say, is transcultural.

First principles

Brook claims that 'In a way there is no system, there is no method, there is no school, no technique of directing theatre or of acting that can last for all time. These are all things that make everything in the theatre come and go, come and go. So that what is interesting is . . . the questioning and the different horizons that that opens.'

This is easy to agree with. Nonetheless, if *Qui Est Là* explores 'immediate questions of theatre', to use Brook's phrase, these are resolved through the sway of Brook's aesthetic.[44] The show is Brookian throughout, rather than Artaudian, Brechtian or Craigian. What's more, major pre-occupations of the respective directors have been discreetly ignored altogether. There is no mention of the übermarion-ette, Craig's notion of the actor-as-puppet. Nor of Craig's interest in the material stuff of scenography, in particular his abiding passion for screens. Nor is there any attempt to restage – to utilise in performance – the bio-mechanical exercises which became part of Meyerhold's theatrical signa-ture. There is nothing in *Qui Est Là* on emotion-memory, objectives and super-objectives, which now form part of the orthodoxy of Stanislavsky-based teaching.

And what of Brecht? In 1973 Brook argued that 'the danger in misunderstanding Brecht is to take a completely analytical, unspontaneous, anti-acting approach to the work in rehearsal, to think that you can sit down in cold blood and define intel-lectually the aims of a scene.'[45] As John Fuegi in particular has shown, Brecht was nothing if not opportunist, spontane-ous even, in rehearsals, and adept at exploiting the skills of actors, the plasticity of space and rhythm, the architectonics of blocking and *mise en scène*.[46] Brook recounts that on their first meeting he found himself disagreeing with Brecht's ideas about the nature of illusion in the theatre, although in 1965 he found the Berliner Ensemble 'the best company in the world'.[47] Brook's use of Brecht is Brechtian by virtue of being critical and selective, a good deal less Brechtian in the nature of that selection.

Anne Bennent utters Brecht's words: 'While she showed everything that was necessary, she didn't change her personality; she played, as if she was occupied in reflection, as if she continually asked herself, how does it happen like this?' This text is spoken just before Gertrude encounters Hamlet in her closet, a notoriously difficult scene both to interpret and for the actress to play. (How much does the Queen know of Hamlet's suspicions? To what extent is she on the side of her new husband?) A Brechtian approach to the scene entails the actor explicitly placing herself in a meaning-context rather than resorting to emotional absorption. The quote also indicates the prime value of Brecht's writings for Brook: as a reflection upon the work of the actor (cool, intelligent, controlled). This is the Brecht (and indeed the actor) that Brook most admires. The Brecht who argues for dialectical materialism and who 'treats social situations as processes, and traces out all their inconsistencies'[48] is absent from *Qui Est Là*.

And what of Artaud, who called for a spectacular, libidinous, emotionally abandoned form of theatre? *Qui Est Là* is restrained, polite, cool, controlled. It expresses its ideas through language and is predominantly text-driven, certainly in the passages which quote from the director-theorists. Artaud's impatience at a verbal theatre is overlooked in favour of a treatment which is like taking tea with an eminent philosopher. That said, Artaudian precepts concerning engines of live performance – the suggestive effects of rhythms, sounds, colours, shapes and movement – have become so ingrained in Brook's theatre practice that they are now internalised in his productions as part of the inevitable business of staging.

Artaud's claim that the theatre is a place for the generation of primal passions, shared by the spectator as much as the performer, is not acted upon in *Qui Est Là*. The auditorium remains a place for reflection (very Brechtian) rather than entranced excitement in the face of a bombardment of spectacular effects.

Not that we are offered cast-iron conclusions. For the audience, Shakespeare's most luminous play is glimpsed through the mist. It is enticingly incomplete, a mere suggestion of some distant (actually future) production. Sometimes the staging is modified in accordance with the interpolated voices. Everything appears dependent on the game-plan (which is to keep playing the game), endlessly refigured according to proffered theatrical principles. There is no definitive *Hamlet*, only permutations of possibilities.

This suggests a radically modern show. *Qui Est Là* continually advertises its incompleteness, and the staging undercuts any notion of arriving at a coherent interpretation of the play. In fact it is not Shakespeare's *Hamlet* that hoves into view, but a series of *Hamlet*s coloured by the crayons of Artaud, or Brecht, or whoever. Sliced into suggestive fragments, the play is a site of perpetual irresolution. This sort of meaning-effect is not new to Brook's work, as David Williams's account of his 1990 production of *The Tempest* makes clear:

> Brook's scenography eschews closure at every level –
> thematic, moral, political and representational . . .
> The 'open' performative idiom here is self-subverting,
> endlessly remaking itself as it evolves to meet the
> demands of the moment. Much of the production's
> intellectual and affective impact stems from the discon-
> tinuity of its discourse and its rigorous rejection of any
> formulaic stylistic criteria. Brook's syncretism offers an
> elegant and compelling correlative to Shakespeare's

textual (and textural) non-homogeneity . . . Arguably
this is a post-modernist theatre, in its multi- and intertextuality, its deferral of all closed 'meanings', its auto-
citation [Williams means the recurrence of elements –
bamboo sticks, for example – across a number of Brook's
productions] and apparent relativisation of cultural
sources through decontextualisation and hybridisation.[49]

You could make precisely the same points about *Qui Est Là*.
The form of the show suggests as much: its different sorts of
statement, its stopping and starting of the *Hamlet* story, its
repetition (restaging) of parts of that story, the fact that it does
not 'finish' the play. It evokes absence and lack. It stages
possibility, not certitude. In so doing it offers an extremely
subtle response to one of the dominating themes of the play
(the effect of doubt) and marks itself as the product of an era
in which uncertainty and relativity have been central modes.

And yet with that one word, 'arguably', Williams sounds a
note of caution which applies just as readily to *Qui Est Là*. Is
Brook's theatre really *that* postmodern? *Qui Est Là* betrays a
master-narrative of sorts. The phrases which originate in the
writings of the director-theorists are taken out of context.
They appear not in relation to the argument sustained over a
chapter, or through a particular essay, but are truncated and
transplanted. This selection of sound-bites presents the prob-
lematics of theatre as a single field, to be resolved practically
and philosophically through the agency of the super-skilled
(rational-and-intuitive) practitioner. Who other than Brook
himself? As Patrice Pavis says, qualifying David Williams's
view, '[Brook] isn't a postmodernist at all, in spite of certain
stylistic approaches and ingredients which often constitute a
kind of "postmodern" dressing. . . . Brook is the last of the
humanists. His discourse is "profound" on the level of his per-
sistent return to an essentialist vision of humanity.'[50]

Brook is certainly alert to 'the structural principle of discontinuity',[51] but *refunctions* it. The structure of *Qui Est Là* is fragmentary but its many parts combine to make a whole which expresses two principles of continuity. The first of these is the continuity of theatre tradition (from Noh to Russian Realism). The second is a continuity of human sensibility, shared by all people at all times. In this sense *Qui Est Là* betrays a yearning for coherence, for the presence of one gathering, authoritative voice rather than many conflicting utterances.

Brook's interpolations and omissions point to a highly strategic use of the mountain of writings at his disposal. To all appearances the writings of Brecht *et al.* have been usefully distilled by Brook and his team. In fact they have been ruthlessly interpreted – *synthesised* – in order to promote a coherent aesthetic. This is the stuff of an entire system of theatre-making – and it is Brook's system. Shomit Mitter suggests that Brook's urge for synthesis turns him into a brilliant magpie, capably plundering other people's styles without ever quite attaining an original style of his own. In spite of his extraordinary talent, Brook 'does not have a distinctive legacy to hand down to future generations' – although Mitter concedes that his work 'does eventually find that unity of indiscriminate amalgamation, the hallmark we most admire in Shakespeare.'[52]

Only time will tell whether Brook's legacy is lasting and influential. *Qui Est Là* does appear to answer some of Mitter's doubts, however. It demonstrates Brook renouncing received systems in favour of a fusion of influences which we might describe as '*discriminate* amalgamation'. Brook's system may be derivative in that it borrows (very selectively) from the ideas of other directors. But it is certainly systematic. It is geared towards the production of a consistently metaphorical and phenomenal brand of theatre. We are asked to see what the drama is standing for, but also to see it in the business of standing for something else. Brook's theatre is knowingly caught in the act.

This demands consummate control of the medium. Brook certainly knows the precise value of a pause, or a shift in tone, and there is a clear distinction to be made between the transcendentalist Brook, whose tenets are disputable, and the craftsman Brook, whose work has a lucidity and 'felt' effect largely unrivalled by other practitioners. Pavis broaches this peculiar situation in his discussion of the 1990 *Tempest*:

> The entire production was steeped in concrete thought. Nothing was said or thought which was not also signified by a visual or tactile materiality of signs: sand, light, the musical and vocal decor. The abstraction of this parable, its hermetic symbolism, was redeemed by a concrete use of the stage and a warm simplicity in the acting.[53]

Re-enter Zeami. According to Brook, *The Secret of Noh* is

> one of the astonishing pieces of the theatre because it really links the most practical things – the difference between playing at two in the afternoon when people are bright, or at eight in the evening when they've just had something to eat, or a little later on when they've had too much to drink. And from that through to the actual relation between images that flow through the theatre and the images that flow through all living processes. It's a totally comprehensive work, thoroughly illuminated by the Japanese way of seeing the world.

That's to say, it is grounded in a deep understanding of materialities in and around performance. And this is Brook's own disposition, as revealed in *Qui Est Là*. For all its mystifying tendencies, the show exploits the special attributes of theatre with unerring skill, in order to excite the spectator and have her excited at that excitement. According to Brook, when theatre works, 'you are sharing an experience that at the moment that it is happening is real. It is real to you, and therefore it stimulates you in a way that touches the whole of you, and that doesn't put you to sleep, that wakes you up.' This simple formula reveals the quest at the heart of *Qui Est Là*. Not 'What is *Hamlet*?' nor 'What is directing?' nor even 'What is acting?' but 'How do we get to the audience?' You have to admit, it is the best question.

Elsinore • Robert Lepage

3

Elsinore • Robert Lepage

'It's a sport. You don't know anything about Shakespeare until you've performed it.'
Robert Lepage[1]

Base camp

The story goes that Robert Lepage turned to *Hamlet* with a significant personal loss very much in mind. 'I found myself, in a certain way, haunted by the ghost of my own father, and I was called to question my relationship with my mother, my brother, heredity and so on.'[2] Lepage's father died in 1992. In 1994 Lepage established Ex Machina, a new theatre company based in his home city, Quebec, with himself as artistic director. His *Hamlet*-reappraisal came at a time of momentous personal and public redefinition.

The new project was intended as a one-man show in the manner of *Vinci* (1986) and *Needles and Opium* (1991), both of which had featured Lepage as the solo performer. But other shadows loomed, as Lepage recounts:

> At the start of 1993, a few weeks after beginning the project, I met Bob Wilson by chance over breakfast in

Toronto and he told me that he was planning to direct
Hamlet as a one-man show. Like me, he intended
to play all the characters, and his show was due to
go on only a few months before mine. And then,
during a meeting I had with Peter Brook in Munich,
he told me that he was also interested in *Hamlet*,
especially the whole question of translation. Given
their projects, I suddenly found myself in an awkward
situation and I put my *Hamlet* on ice to start working
on another project [a show based on Serge Gainsbourg's
L'homme à la tête de chou (*The Man with the Cabbage
Head*)].[3]

When it's put like this – imagine the horror! But *Hamlet* would
not go away. Gainsbourg lost, Shakespeare won. Lepage turned
back to the enticing task of rendering Shakespeare's best-
known play as a one-man show.

The story is repeated various times and there is no reason
to disbelieve it.[4] But the care with which Lepage recounts his
reservations about continuing with the project once he learns
that Brook and Wilson are embarked on similar endeavours is
instructive. The three artists appear at the same international
festivals, are mentioned in the same newspaper features,
scholarly articles and theatre textbooks, are acclaimed in
similar breaths as masters of avant-garde theatre. In fact their
biographies, styles of working and artistic outputs are very
different, but the international theatre circuit has an homog-
enising effect. How tawdry and embarrassing, to appear to be
copying someone else's good idea – especially in this hothouse environment where the marketability of the artwork
depends upon its claim to uniqueness. No wonder Lepage was
at pains to impress upon everybody, retrospectively, his reluc-
tance to press ahead with an idea closely shared in particular
with Wilson.

Be in no doubt that a kind of sibling rivalry exists. Ex Machina's producer, Michel Bernatchez, observes that the company's identity and its production values go hand in hand – and that both exist in relation to a kind of peer pressure. 'Robert was reaching a level of touring which had more and more prestige. Obviously he wanted his shows to be on a par with what Bob Wilson produces, or small shows from other European directors who are invited to the same festivals as he is.' Product differentiation – ensuring originality of approach and execution – is therefore of prime importance. If Lepage was to press ahead with his own *Hamlet*, it would have to be different – *really* different – from anything anyone had seen before.

Lepage is now celebrated as a director of devised work created through extensive collaboration with groups of performers.[5] Lepage explains the difference, as he sees it, between directing a group-devised show and creating his own one-man pieces:

> If you work for a long period of time with a collective, if you work with actors who are also writers, you have to have a certain humility in what you do, and there are certain themes you cannot explore in a group. There are certain *formel* ideas – *formel* means just the aesthetics of theatre – you cannot explore with a collective, you can only explore on your own. . . . The difference is that in this case I have a big machine behind me, and I play around with the machine and the machine answers back very different things than a group of people.

In this instance the machine is literally a machine, more of which later. As this suggests, Lepage develops his solo shows alongside a design and technical team. The work is still collaborative in important ways, and still developed from the ground up in the rehearsal room rather than primarily at the desk or the drawing board. Indeed Ex Machina's new base at the Caserne Dalhousie provides a bespoke home for this kind of craft-based workshop-development. The building testifies retrospectively to the way the company had operated prior to taking residence in June 1997.

A converted fire-station situated in the spruced-up old port in Quebec City,[6] the Caserne is a dream come true. It comprises two rehearsal studios – one large enough to house complete sets in the dimensions of the stages for which they are destined – along with offices, design and construction workshops, and computer rooms for video capture and editing. It is a flexible, multidisciplinary space. Lepage occasionally gives public showings of work in progress, testing nascent productions in front of a local, non-paying audience of up to two hundred people. The Caserne's situation in Quebec City, an airplane journey from Montreal or New York, with no direct flights from London, means that Lepage works in a more tranquil, indeed rather backwaterish environment. Quebec is the heartland of the French-Canadian separatist movement, from which the internationalist Lepage maintains a polite but studied distance. In a way he is a little out of kilter even in the centre of his home city, itself on a periphery. Collaborators on all projects are increasingly brought to work at this outpost/ base camp, as Bernatchez explains:

There is now a company strategy at work. . . . we noticed at some point that whenever [Robert] was directing a show in Munich, for instance, the Munich people were making money with that show. Robert had a fee, of course, that was nice, but this company was losing him for two or three months and was not benefiting from that work. Robert came to realise at some point too that big structures, the ones who could pay him well and who invited him, were not producing his shows the way he wanted them to be produced. Generally speaking they were expecting developed concepts prior to rehearsals, which is not his way of working. So what we now say to people who want Robert's services is that Ex Machina and Ex Machina's production space have to be involved in one way or another. So most of the time we end up with co-productions. We're involved in a way that we can bring over the artists for at least part of their rehearsals. Robert's collaborators, set designer, image designer, assistants, are also automatically working with him . . . Ex Machina is part of everything, and Ex Machina also has control over his schedule.

In order to secure sufficient finance for Lepage's projects, Ex Machina enters into co-production agreements with foreign festivals and theatres. The 'client' buys a presentation of the show in question, paying a certain amount of money up front and making a further payment once the show has been presented. Ex Machina must, of course, deliver the work at the due date. But at the point of commission the show may simply be a gleam in its makers' eyes – and when the app-ointed moment arrives it may still not be fully formed, as Bernatchez admits:

We have to be ready when they are, when they want us, especially in the case of the festivals. We have to fit our production into their schedule, and that is slowly becoming a problem. Sometimes Robert now has the feeling that he's delivering half-baked cakes, and that was probably the case with *Elsinore*. So now for his new productions he's trying to convince our agents that he needs more time. We're asking presenters for money a

year-and-a-half in advance, so that we can develop
shows slowly. And as you may have noticed there's a
notion of organic process and very gradual development . . . And that needs time.

Elsinore comes at a pivotal moment in Ex Machina's early
history. It was made according to the workshop principles described above, which underlie the acquisition and configuration of the Caserne. The show was developed elsewhere in
Quebec city, although it was revamped in 1997 at the Caserne
as one of the first projects in the building.

About 70 per cent of Ex Machina's income derives from
abroad – a substantial proportion. At the point when *Elsinore*
was initially mooted, co-producers were given the possibility
of seeing a 'first draft' – not a copy of a script but a public
rehearsal. This was presented at the Monument-National in
Montreal in November 1995, using the nineteenth-century
French translation of *Hamlet* by Jean-François Victor Hugo,
whose father wrote a volume of critical essays on Shakespeare.
(More famously, of course, he penned *Les Misérables*.) This
'draft' was three hours long. Lepage would subsequently trim
the production to around an hour and 40 minutes.

Initial investment was supplied by ten production partners
from Quebec and from abroad, each of whom put in around
40,000 Canadian dollars. Eventually the show in its first
incarnation cost nearly one million Canadian dollars, much of
it swallowed up in the process of building, testing and revising
Elsinore's mechanical set. This single element, so crucial to the
project, was allocated a further 100,000 Canadian dollars
when the show was remounted to allow the company, according to Bernatchez, 'to make corrections to the whole thing to
make it work without any risks.'

The extreme riskiness of the endeavour had been confirmed
when the company had to cancel or delay performances in

Chicago and Toronto, and was most strikingly demonstrated when the entire run of performances at the 50th Edinburgh Festival was cancelled on account of technical malfunction. To make matters worse, *Elsinore* had been billed as the highlight of the first week's theatre programme. Local indignation was further aroused given that the company had spent a week at the Tramway Theatre in Glasgow (where the show was to be presented in December) to make final preparations, with no indication at that stage of any difficulty.[7]

'One very small piece broke,' says Bernatchez, 'and it fucked up the computer, and that created another series of problems. So from one small thing we ended up with five problems at the same time. With no spares. It was a pure catastrophe. We've certainly lost credibility over there.' No spares! Such poor preparation seems culpable in the extreme. Yet Ex Machina's calculated risk was to offer a one-off – a new and previously unseen approach to the play whose very uniqueness meant that the budget was stretched beyond the point of affording spares in case of breakdown. With *Elsinore* Lepage was going out on a limb in more ways than one.

Game, set . . . *Elsinore*'s first coming

Lepage has staged a handful of Shakespeare's plays (*A Midsummer Night's Dream*, *Macbeth* and *Romeo and Juliet*, for instance) a number of times, returning to them in the light of previous excursions. 'If you want to know what *The Tempest* is and do a good *Tempest* one day,' he proffers, 'you have to do zillions of them.' *Elsinore* was his first engagement with *Hamlet*. Lepage's tilting of the play is not dissimilar in principle to the interpretative turns performed in his other Shakespearean productions immediately prior to this. In 1992 he staged his notorious 'mudbath' production of *A Midsummer Night's Dream* at the National Theatre, London. The usual division between court (domain of humans) and forest (realm of the super-natural) was renounced in favour of a setting which deter-mined the entire action, a central muddy pool surrounded by muddy banks – a 'dreamscape' which meant that a good deal of action (human and fairy) was inelegant and messy. Spec-tators sitting in the first three rows of the auditorium found plastic macs on their seats to protect them from the inevitable splashing.

The following year Lepage staged a trilogy of Shakespeare plays in French in Montreal.[8] Each production depended upon dislocations of setting and perspective. *The Tempest*, for instance, was staged in a rehearsal room, opening with actors sitting around a table engaged in a reading of the play under the eye of a director who went on to play Prospero. The room's mirrored walls facilitated a number of the revelations and discoveries in the play. For *Coriolanus* the front of the stage was walled off from the audience, with a letter-box aperture opening on to the playing space behind. The production, set in 1930s Rome, offered a series of peep-show-like plays with perspective (puppets one moment, the lower half of human torsos the next; one scene was played below a mirror at 45 degrees to the audience, which therefore showed, in effect, a cinematic top-shot). *Macbeth*, set in the Middle Ages, featured panels of slatted wood which were positioned variously as walls or platforms. The scene in which the ghost of Banquo appears to Macbeth was presented in shadow-play behind a large screen, and shown as if from the ghost's point of view. The light source moved in keeping with Banquo's move-ments, so that the silhouettes of the diners veered grotesquely in different proportions as he moved among them.

Each treatment sought to offset the literal suggestion of set-ting and usual assumptions regarding spectating positions. Together these productions suggest a consistent attempt to turn spectatorship into a recognised, conscious engagement rather than an unthought mode. 'Looking at the stage' is turned into a reflexive pleasure, since what's on the stage is arranged to emphasise its surprising, unorthodox, unexpected relation to actual proportions, spatial relationships and to the spectator herself. *Elsinore* has the same ambition: Shakespeare to be *seen differently*.

The real work on *Elsinore* seems to have begun once Lepage decided to stop work on the Serge Gainsbourg story. Initial preparation took place over a period of five or six months. During this time Lepage and his designer Carl Fillion read different versions of the text and looked at films. Fillion made a drawing of a potential set in response to their initial discussions and produced two or three more before settling on the agreed design concept. After this research work Fillion made a prototype of the machine which would eventually form the show's set. In June 1995 the company embarked upon two weeks of workshop-development, after which Fillion commissioned various items and constructed the set himself. The rehearsal period started at the beginning of August and lasted for two-and-a-half months. *Elsinore* had its first performances in Montreal in the Autumn, and Lepage presented the show in Berlin, Brussels, Helsinki, Limoges, Milan, Oslo and Rotterdam (to name but a few staging posts on the international festival circuit) in 1996.

According to Fillion, Lepage knew that he wanted to create a show similar in its ambience to *Needles and Opium*. The same dynamic – one performer in close relationship with a moving set – underpins both pieces. In *Needles and Opium* Lepage played a film director who comes to Paris to escape a failed affair and to research settings for a new movie, and who becomes fascinated with the work of Miles Davis and stories of Jean Cocteau. The central scenographic element was a rotating screen which Lepage pressed against and indented, softening its 2-D starkness.

Elsinore, too, featured a moving screen, but in more technically sophisticated configurations. An early seed was planted by Lepage's interest in a piece of film in which the entire wall of a house falls, like a toppling book, on a character who remains unharmed since one of the window frames passes around him. The image is from Buster Keaton's film *Steamboat Bill Jr*. 'Robert found that interesting, he didn't know why or how,' said Fillion. Perhaps Lepage saw in the simple image of Keaton's unwonted escape an emblem for Hamlet's unwittingness as his world tumbles around him.[9] In the film, a raging storm topples the wall of a nearby house, which falls on (or rather around) the stationary Keaton. The image distils the paradox of Keaton's unsentimental filmmaking. It presents the 'chance' of human survival in the face of a catastrophe which needed painstaking rigging by Keaton and his production team – the triumph, you might say, of art over accident.[10] With the falling wall in mind, Fillion proposed as a working principle that the actor could stand centre-stage and have the set come to him, rather than the other way round.

This idea was consolidated in a moving flat, which became what the pair described as the 'monolith': a plane surface held at its four corners by industrial wires connected to a set of motors. Thus the monolith could be lifted horizontally, tilted backwards or forwards, stood upright, and flipped (relatively slowly, of course) through a plane of 180 degrees. It could be floor, wall or roof, and present its front or its back to the audience (Images 6 and 7). Lepage also customarily referred to the set as 'the machine'.[11]

Fillion then introduced a circular, rotating disc into the middle of the flat. Inside this he put a rectangular opening – a hole which could look like a door, or a grave, or a large letterbox, depending on the alignment. 'It's more interesting to have a square in a circle inside another square,' he suggests, 'for the form and the symmetry between each geometrical shape.' The aperture – about the height of a man – was fitted with mechanical bolts to hold additional scenic elements built onto 'tablets', which would stay in place as the monolith was lifted.

During the workshop-development fortnight the prototype was manually operated by a team of stagehands. This period yielded a number of ingenious uses of the machine. Fillion explains:

> We worked with the different settings and asked, for instance, what we wanted to do with scene 2. We tried out ideas. We thought it would be a good idea to have a chair on the wall. How? So I looked at how you would start with a chair on the floor [with the monolith horizontal] and finish on the wall [with the monolith vertical]. I built, with tubes and screws and wood, a support for an ordinary chair, we moved the monolith and saw, yes, that's interesting.

The prototype chair swivelling on a prototype frame is fitted to the prototype set. None of this is suggested by the text. The intention is to make the set work in different ways which might be useful in staging specific scenes. The playing, rather than the play, is the thing.

At this early stage the company was already considering the integration of slide and video projections. Experiments were made with a video camera and projector, a miniature camera and a moving light (a computerised lighting unit that allows you to change focus, intensity, colour and 'target' at the press of a button). The company mounted the mini-camera on the handle of an épée, an experiment which resulted in the eventual depiction of Hamlet's duel with Laertes and the play's notorious sequence of deaths by way of a huge projection of the view from the duellers' rapiers (Image 10). Fillion researched possible projection images involving Renaissance decorative motifs and tapestries, and 'set-dressing' images such as the bricks of the castle wall. These were finessed by Jacques Collin, Lepage's multimedia designer. Images were projected on the central monolith and two large screens, one at either side, hinged at the edge of the stage so that they could swing in and back like huge barn doors. These were covered with spandex.[12] The result, generated from early in the production process, is a pictorial evocation of Renaissance motifs laid onto – and thus reimaging – a structure made out of metal and cloth.

By calling his show *Elsinore*, Lepage designates a place rather than a person as the hub of the piece. The setting promises to be as important as the central character. The new title observes Shakespeare's geographical limitation. The play's concerns extend to Wittenberg, Paris, Norway and England, none of which provide locations for the drama as Shakespeare arranged it. We hear of the activities of Laertes, Hamlet and Fortinbras in these more or less distant reaches, but the characters themselves are always brought back to the place that matters. For all its length and breadth, *Hamlet* has a geographical tightness, a unity of place which Lepage exploits scenographically by suggesting the kinds of spaces which constitute Shakespeare's Elsinore. Actually, Lepage's Elsinore is a multi-positional set, and certainly not a strong-hold on the coast of Denmark. Its location matters less than its metaphorical significance. In *Elsinore* space as well as per-sonhood melt in a series of theatrical transformations. This is a place (and a set) which gradually stamps its own personality: restless, shifting and implacable.

Hamlet features a number of self-evident settings, including the throne room, the Queen's closet and the plain on which Hamlet meets Fortinbras. In *Elsinore* Lepage makes some of these more specific and adds a good few more. The show depicts a library, Ophelia's bedchamber, the stage and (separately) the auditorium of a theatre, the area *behind* the arras in the Queen's bedchamber, the cellar in which Hamlet stows Polonius's body, a dining room, a number of the castle's doorways and passages, and Hamlet's quarters on the ship which carries him towards to England, along with the deck and a cabin in which the crew are engaged in offstage conversation.

We are taken behind the scenes of the play we think we know. Public spaces are offset by a range of secret, private or subterranean ones. This alteration of perspective is accompanied by new angles from which some scenes are viewed. Laertes and Claudius meet at a long table, the top of which is revealed upstage, standing up on its vertical axis. Lepage (playing Claudius) lies on his back at the bottom end. It looks as though he is sitting at one end of the table. Laertes' hand (or rather a stagehand's hand) casts a shadow along the table from the top end. The audience's view is, in filmic terms, a top shot. Ophelia's grave is seen from below, as I shall discuss later. The duel is viewed in part, as mentioned, from the handle of one of the duellers' rapiers. Elsewhere proportions are altered to create unorthodox effects. When Polonius reveals Hamlet's love-letter to Ophelia, the letter descends at the back of the stage as a huge backdrop which Polonius examines, pointing out words with his cane as if he were giving a public lecture (Image 9). The scene between Hamlet and Gertrude in Gertrude's bedchamber is played as if the entire stage is the King and Queen's bed – kingsized, perhaps.

The combination of the moving set, continually creating new relationships between the performer and the space, and the depiction of a range of 'backstage' areas configures a number of the play's themes. *Elsinore* is about instability, about a whirl of activity around a central figure, about continual tensions between a human figure and a piece of machinery (which one could express, metaphorically, as a tension between individual and state, or even the human and the cosmic). The *mise en scène* elaborates *Hamlet*'s discursive play with ideas of personal, psychological and political disturbance, the potency (or otherwise) of individual agency, and the turbulence of illicit action. 'In theatre,' Lepage has argued, 'the audience has to be immersed in the show's argument, and to be immersed in the argument every sense has to seize it and so the form has to become an incarnation of the subject and themes.'[13] According to this view, then, the production 'writes' the play, rather than the other way round.

The singular performer

Lepage claims, rightly, that his presence as performer in *Elsinore* was not the show's most interesting aspect. He talks engagingly of the show as a 'sketch-pad' for a 'full-blown production of *Hamlet* with real actors' that he might essay at some point in the future.

> I'm a bit burdened by people coming to see Lepage play Hamlet – and of course there's absolutely no interest in seeing me perform Hamlet. What's interesting is to see how I cut up the story and devised theatrics out of that, and to see how you can tell the story of *Hamlet* in different ways and how to use technologies to try to tell a story – how does it change the story, how does it bring insight to some parts of the story? So it's . . . an experiment, and I'm always burdened by people thinking that I'm coming to do this big actor's thing. I think, 'My God, go and see Daniel Day-Lewis do *Hamlet* if you want to see an actor play Hamlet.'

Lepage observes that he was interested in *Hamlet* partly through the filter of painting, adding that 'Hamlet is a Romantic hero in a certain way.' His own rendition of the Prince was reminiscent of the images produced by Delacroix in his lithographs and oil paintings depicting scenes of the play. Delacroix saw Kemble and Smithson's production which toured to the Odéon theatre in Paris in 1827 (Victor Hugo was also in the audience).[14] Delacroix's Hamlet is fine-featured and elegant (he apparently modelled the character on a female friend). He is also a man of action, depicted in moments of decision: about to follow the Ghost, unsheathing his sword as he sees Claudius at prayer, standing alert over the dead Polonius, wrestling with Laertes in Ophelia's grave. He is a Byronic type, sensitive but swift. And this is the kind of Hamlet Lepage plays. What's more, he performed in a capacious white shirt, black leggings, high boots, a wig of flowing black hair and a pointy Renaissance beard. His Dane was a performing type rather than an overtly modern figure – a dashing adventurer out of a theatrical heritage, something like a revamped Kemble, operating at the borderlines between fantasy, irony and caricature.

Playing that sort of figure might be reason enough to star in your own show, but there are other benefits. Lepage talks of a developmental line in his 'one-man' work, from *Vinci* to *Needles and Opium* to *Elsinore*, through which he explored the question 'how do I express myself as a solo artist compared to how do I express myself as a collective writer?' You could certainly argue that the fabric of the piece is best experienced from the 'inside' by its solo performer, who evolves his own distinctive brand of theatre even as he works the playing of it himself. Lepage's one-man shows involve fluctuating relationships between the human body, the set, the space and theatrical-narrational tropes. The performer isn't the sole focus: he *interacts* with the *mise en scène*. In which case the director-as-actor is likely to be more neatly ingrained in the production – able to inflect his performance strictly in relation to the staging.

Lepage was well aware of the performative contours to his solo turn:

> To do a one-man show allows you to explore in depth certain themes and completely avoid others. So of course there's no political aspect. . . . But things like incest and schizophrenia become extremely incarnated in the fact that you're alone, that you get to play all the characters. When I do Ophelia, there's a bit of Hamlet speaking, there's a bit of Gertrude, and there's an advantage to that.

The presence of a single performer doesn't *necessarily* elide political concerns to do with usurpation, territorial dispute and civic duty. But it does help concentrate the play's discourse of isolation and loneliness. Lepage also had a keen eye on the possibilities offered to the one-man show by a play renowned for its soliloquys. He exploited this mode of performance – talking-to-yourself (to the audience) – to counterpoint utter privacy with all the public exposure intrinsic in the theatrical moment.

Lepage was solo but not alone. *Elsinore* featured the appearance of Pierre Bernier as a double. Bernier is a Quebecois mime performer, maker of gadgets, all-round man-of-the-theatre and engaging eccentric. (One day he turned up to rehearsals on his penny farthing. On another he drove to work in his pristine blue converted hearse.) 'Robert always uses someone to help him, like in *Vinci* or *Needles and Opium*,' he recounts. 'There's always someone else, like when you've got shadows of hands, it will be the hands of the second performer.' This shadow presence gives the lie to the understandable misconception, voiced in one preview piece, that Lepage 'works best alone'[15] and to the observation that Lepage is 'seul sur scène'.[16] In fact the opposite is true.

Bernier was a key presence in the workshop-development of *Elsinore*. He suggested ideas, performed stunts so that Lepage could watch and facilitated bits of business that were eventually used in the show. During performances he coordinated the backstage activity – the loading of various elements of set, the movement of the screens on either side of the stage, and the arrangment of various props and items of costume. He appeared as a double in order to create neat illusionistic effects which playfully traded on the show's one-man status – as, for instance, when Lepage impossibly kept up a conversation between Hamlet and Polonius with the aid of some careful sleight of hand involving a moving ladder, falling papers and Bernier's adept silent doubling and redoubling.

Bernier also appears as both Hamlet and Laertes in the duel scene, as the peformers swap weapons at strategic moments (only one épée bears the camera which films these final exchanges). The fencing masks and kit of the two protagonists make slippages from one character to the other possible, whilst the trickery reinforces the enjoyable impression that Lepage is super-ubiquitous as the soloist.

The show's effects of outlandish singularity are pleasurable but also thematic, for they suggest what Michael Coveney described as 'the absorption of events into one man's identity crisis'.[17] In Lepage's performance, however, Hamlet's loneliness and vulnerability were compromised by the bravura nature of the playing. As an actor Lepage reminds me a little of Chaplin in the facility with which he manipulates props and objects. In *Vinci*, for instance, he performed a comic routine with a retracting tape measure with Chaplinesque dexterity. He spent part of *Needles and Opium* suspended in a swivel-jointed trapeze harness, performing in mid-air with easy élan.

In *Elsinore* he conveyed the members of the court watching *The Mousetrap* (the play within the play) simply by rolling a crate along the stage. Each turn of the box, made with a thud with his hand or foot, punctuated the exchange, cued a new posture and signalled the speech of a different character. The scene was played with panache.

Such aptitude has its limits. Perhaps because of the way the work had been developed, Lepage moved ultra-capably from one moment to the next without suggesting a larger arc for the character, a developmental journey from beginning to end. His facility with devices (scenic or technological) produced a segmented mode of playing – and in this Lepage is expert. But such an approach runs a grain of self-possession through the performance which goes against the devastating uncertainty of the protagonist. Lepage's Hamlet capably manoeuvred around objects and set, running the show even as the events of the play undercut his authority.

Many observers felt that *Elsinore* was greater in its parts than as a whole. At its heart was a deeply paradoxical figure: a skilful, resourceful showman, fully in command of his environment whilst the action displays a man knocked out of kilter, an intelligence deprived of autonomy and control. There was something at odds in the combination of Lepage's consistent surefootedness and the character's fraught insecurities. This is in part a question of acting. Not that Lepage is a 'bad' actor – but his performance perhaps derived too clearly from the show's creative process. His relationship to his own set was so inscribed with a physical grammar of mastery, that the resulting presentation ran counter to the very things the staging was attempting to convey. On one level (the surface, indeed) this was a performer taking sheer pleasure in his set, like a boy on a stunt bike. What would happen if he gave the bike to someone who wasn't used to riding it?

Revision

The possibility of a new tour of *Elsinore* led Lepage and Bernatchez to contemplate a revamped production involving a different performer. Initial soundings were made, in particular amongst North American promoters, until a tour began to take shape, including visits to Ottawa and New York (the esteemed Brooklyn Academy of Music), with around 25 performances mooted – enough to make the project viable. Further venues were approached, with the result that the revised production toured in addition to Stamford, Dublin and Madrid, playing for 27 performances. The rehearsal period cost around 100,000 Canadian dollars, with the production on tour costing around 350,000 Canadian dollars.

The new soloist was the British actor Peter Darling, who had appeared in Richard Eyre's production of Shakespeare's *Richard III* at London's National Theatre and had also worked with Declan Donnellan, one of Britain's most exciting directors of Shakespeare. Lepage had been advised by Rachel Feuchtwang, one of the co-producers of his tours to Britain, to check out Darling's work. He watched him in *MSM* in Montreal, a dance-theatre piece about cottaging and male sexuality presented by DV8, a leading British dance-theatre company. Darling, then, was a classical actor who mixed it with more avant-garde work as a 'physical' performer. This blend of skills seemed enticing. And he was not a star. The director remained the guarantor of the show's marketability. Nevertheless, the presence of a new performer presented fresh possibilities. 'It's a great thing to decide that you do a clean-up in a show, that you only keep what's essential,' says Lepage. 'Take out a lot of the razzmatazz, really go to the point. But you need to know what the through-line is emotionally and psychologically. . . . Peter really takes the characters on board, he really forced or helped me to clarify that through-line.'

Elsinore was reworked in three weeks of rehearsal at the Caserne according to an unusual daily schedule. Lepage generally attended to the show from about 9.30am to 12.30-1.00pm. For the first week he spent this morning session at a table with Darling, working through the edited text and discussing nuances of meaning and interpretation, whilst in the main rehearsal studio the technical team installed the set and carried out initial modifications and repairs. In the afternoon Lepage moved to the smaller rehearsal studio at the top of the building to work with the Italian company Segnali, which had bought the rights to co-produce a tour to Italy and Spain of *Needles and Opium* featuring the Argentinian actor Nestor Saied. Lepage's technical team, meanwhile, continued working on the *Elsinore* set in the main space. In the evening, from about 6.30pm to 9.30pm, Lepage joined them.

For the first week he introduced Darling to the set, working through the settings as they existed, experimenting with new ideas and trying alternative stagings. From the second week onwards rehearsals were more directly oriented, at times opportunistically, to what 'worked' on the stage, without direct reference to the conversations at the table in the first week. Individual scenes, then, were not staged in relation to an agreed conceptual approach but were determined according to their efficacy in the rehearsal studio. This puts me in mind of Peter Brook's comment, 'I have always been very dubious of the idea of the value of a view or an interpretation. One doesn't in that sense work from an idea, one works in trying to bring moments to life.'[18] Of course a notion of what 'works' is governed by aesthetic and ideological preferences, although these can operate fairly loosely. The driving impetus to the rehearsals consisted in a search for theatrical 'moments' – a search which could only be undertaken by trying out ideas and hunches on the set itself.

The unorthodox nature of the schedule had beneficial consequences. Darling had time during the day to relax and to digest the morning's work. He was busy during what might otherwise have been rather quiet evenings. The technical team had sole use of the performance space in order to build and try out new props or refinements, to make adjustments suggested by the ongoing rehearsal work, and to integrate the various technical elements. The importance of this can hardly be overemphasised. Ordinarily, the technical paraphernalia of theatre production is developed secondarily to the director's work with the actors, who move into the theatre only in the last few days of pre-production, at which point the show has lighting and sound added, with little time for alteration as opening night approaches. In this case, however, set, sound, lighting, video and slide projections were given dedicated time in the space and finessed accordingly.

Technical equipment was installed by the second week, so that rehearsals were conducted with the full array of lights and projections. As Darling rehearsed scenes by running them more or less in their entirety from the second week onwards, the designers and operators were able to set lighting positions, lighting and sound levels and cue-points as they went, and adjust and fine-tune as the rehearsals continued. Darling found the process a little disorienting. 'It's like being in a tech from the beginning of it,' he observed. 'You haven't had that incredibly private rehearsal of scenes. People milling around, moving lights or whatever – and that means it's very difficult to focus on what the scene might be.'

In fact the entire programme seemed dizzying. Darling only knew of his schedule once he had arrived in Quebec City and rehersals had actually started. On the second morning of the first week Lepage announced that he had to fly to Montreal later that day, so would not be able to take the rehearsal that evening. Darling should instead go through certain physical business in the show with Pierre Bernier. This might have made Darling conscious that he was, after all, merely a cog in a much larger set of wheels, which themselves turned only in relation to the central cog, Lepage himself. That said, Lepage's style of interaction with his lead actor was not so much to keep him in his place but to foster a sense that the show was open to all manner of revisions to suit his particular qualities.

One aspect of the work was to determine what, from the original production, was within Darling's capabilities as a performer and what might be changed either because Darling brought additional skills or was constrained by particular limitations. To state the obvious: the work is likely to be stronger for paying attention to the particular strengths of the actor. There is a philosophy of directing at stake. 'If I ask an actor to take up a challenge, it has to be within his capability,' says Lepage. 'It's not a question of compromise for me. You can't treat everyone the same way, make the same demands of them. If an actor can't do a particular movement, the ball is back in my court and I have to find a new way to accomplish what I want.'[19]

As a priority, Darling needed to familiarise himself with the set and to feel comfortable clambering over it as it moved and turned beneath him. One sequence, for instance, placed Hamlet in the central aperture discoursing on 'this goodly frame the earth' as slide projections form and melt around him. Lepage had initially performed the scene standing still. He decided to make it more spectacular by having Bernier turn the aperture manually from behind, with Darling lying down on the frame in order to be turned almost upside down, climbing up and swinging like an ape from the top. This took a good deal of rehearsal. Lepage never forced the scene, and it was clear that the idea could be abandoned if needs be, but as Darling became more used to the movements the scene grew as a surprising theatrical turn – quite literally, as the actor-acrobat performed inside the vertical revolve.

In other places the ease with which Lepage had 'played' his set was never quite recaptured. In one scene, for instance, Claudius interviews Hamlet shortly after the latter has disposed of Polonius. Lepage performed this at a revolving table, playing a bullish Claudius one moment at the head then swinging the table through 180 degrees to play a louche Hamlet seated at the foot. This scene was something of a *tour de force*, culminating in a bravura series of table turns and changes of attitude, with Lepage fixing the character's posture precisely as the appropriate end of the table arrived. Darling never achieved such dextrous playing, and the scene lost much of its dynamic as a result.

In other respects, however, the change of actor gave the show an added dimension. Darling's Hamlet was more contemporary, less decided than Lepage's. Balding and shaven-headed, he wore a black designer shirt and tight black trousers, sightly flared at the bottom, a single black loafer and a red woman's court shoe. His appearance was classless in a post-modern way, simultaneously elegant, awkward, cropped and weird. And you might expect that Darling's cautious, *hesitant* relationship to the set might enhance this sense of volatility, where the central character is more evidently acted upon by things around him. This turned out to be the case.

*

The revised production of *Elsinore* opened in Ottawa on 9 September 1997. Anyone who had already seen the show would not have recognised the opening scene. The pre-set lighting illuminates the metallic frame of the set and the red curtains at the back of the performing area. The monolith lies flat on the floor, with five white mini-spotlight circles visible just outside its four corners and front edge. The houselights and pre-set go out, leaving just the mini-spotlights. Peter Darling enters from upstage and settles into position on the throne, in a brooding, foetal huddle. His costume creates an edgily transvestite image which anticipates the cross-dressings later in the show. A black curtain closes unseen upstage, so that there is no plush red for the opening scene. The mini-spotlights creep onto Darling from the four corners of the stage. When they reach him they fill out and become a cold blue. The overhead frame, which houses a square of spandex forming a small roof, is illuminated light-blue, with a kaleido-scopic droplet effect slowly turning.

Darling begins speaking probably the most famous words of Western dramatic text: 'To be or not to be, that is the question.' He reaches the line, 'And lose the name of action.' The downstage edge of the monolith starts to rise, until eventually it forms a steep cliff-like slope. Darling moves to the edge as it rises, looking out over the audience as though standing on the edge of a sheer cliff. The monolith continues to rise, until Darling slides down the back, only his head visible as he clings on to the top. A video image, in negative, of the Ghost of Old Hamlet is projected on the centre of the monolith. The Ghost, played by the pre-filmed Darling, starts with the line, 'I am thy father's spirit,' and continues to des-cribe the details of his own murder at the hands of his brother. As he does so, two further projections (again in negative), on the screens either side of the monolith, show close-ups of the phial of poison, and of the poisoner (played by Darling) crawling over the top of a huge ear in order to pour the poison into its aperture. The Ghost bids Hamlet to revenge his murder and announces the arrival of the dawn.

The monolith pivots in order to reveal Darling seated on the throne, fixed to its centre and now suspended under-neath. As the monolith comes into position along the plane of the downstage curtain, Darling is in mid-air, seated on the throne which has swivelled to allow him to maintain his equilibrium. He performs as both Claudius and Gertrude (his magnified voice electronically altered for each), welcoming Rosencrantz and Guildenstern, pronouncing on Hamlet's strange behaviour and bidding that they spy on him.

The monolith tilts back until it is flat on the floor. As it does so, Darling melts from his stiffly regal posture as the Queen to the brooding figure of Hamlet with which he started the show. Seated in the throne, he speaks Hamlet's lines about 'guilty creatures sitting at a play,' ending with the lines, 'The play's the thing / Wherein I'll catch the conscience of the King.' The light melts away, reconstituting into mini-spotlights which reduce and glide in the reverse movement to the opening of the show. As they do so, Robert Caux's music swells, the monolith rises to vertical and the side screens slowly close, until a fourth wall is formed across the front of the stage – an effect exaggerated by the projection of a continuous image of granite blocks, giving the impression of a huge castle wall. As the monolith ascends, it leaves the tablet holding the throne on the stage. Darling catches hold of the aperture as it lifts over his head, so that he is swinging in the empty frame. Once the monolith is vertical, he writhes in the frame, now backed by white material, as if pushing against a trap. A series of projections laid over the granite image bear the credits for the show.

This extraordinary sequence, which packs surprise on top of surprise, gives some indication of the way *Elsinore* works. It displays the show's most overt themes in very muscular ways. There is the theme of theatrical performance, for instance, signalled in the use of the spotlights from the outset. The red plush curtains at the back of the set evoke – 'quote' – the standard paraphernalia of proscenium arch theatres, an icon not of the theatre of Shakespeare's time but of Theatre generally. Hamlet's speech about the play-within-the-play is taken out of context. Perhaps Hamlet, in a flashforward, muses on the Player's impending performance; on the other hand, the lines give the audience a taster of the production's flagrant metatheatricality.

Darling's doubling (trebling, quadrupling) flamboyantly underscores the Prologue's theatrical fabrication. His video appearances mean that he is simultaneously present as Hamlet, the Ghost and the dastardly poisoner (Claudius and/or the murderer in *The Mousetrap*). He then plays Claudius and Gertrude, evokes the presence of Rosencrantz and Guildenstern and returns to his embodiment of Hamlet to complete the circle. It is as if, whilst the King and Queen have welcomed and briefed their spies, Hamlet is brooding alone on fratricide, revenge and performance.

The frisson of opening with the words 'To be or not to be' underlines *Elsinore*'s bravura sense of (the) play. The production is luminously Shakespearean – and it is definitely *not* Shakespeare's *Hamlet*. Echoes of a fascination with this soliloquy sound from Lepage's previous activities. He delivered it as part of his performance as an actor in Denys Arcand's 1989 film *Jesus of Montreal*. In the film and theatre versions of *The Polygraph* it is delivered in French. In both works it is presented as an icon of earnest theatrical endeavour, something which no self-respecting actor would approach 'straight'.[20] Placing the soliloquy at the very beginning of *Elsinore* likewise bathes it in dramatic irony – whilst jolting it into a drastic new perspective. Interestingly, Lepage comments that 'when I was doing *Elsinore* on my own I was looking for approval too early, so I didn't restructure [the play] really. So now to start with "To be or not to be", that was one of the first ideas I had that I never dared do.'

A statement is made: Shakespeare's play has been rejigged. What more audacious edit could one conceive than dislodging, and opening with, the most famous soliloquy in history?

The germ of the idea was sown when Lepage heard at a conference that the soliloquy may have been presented as a Prologue in early productions of *Hamlet*.[21] When Peter Darling joined Lepage to begin work on the revival of *Elsinore*, he suggested that the show's opening sequence could usefully be altered:

> Robert wanted [the show] initially to be an examination of someone's head, but he didn't have time to really explore that very fully. My thing was that at the beginning of the play you had to do something that explained to the audience what the show was about . . . I just said that at that point there ought to be a speech or something that gave the audience a hint as to what the general framework of the show was, and sort of 'set' it.

At which Lepage proposed beginning with the soliloquy. This immediately delivers another theme: that of the lonely individual considering the possible termination of existence. As it turns out, Hamlet's suicidal tendency does not feature large in *Elsinore*'s schemata. His isolation does, however. The exigencies of doubling immediately point up the paradox: the single actor embodies a range of characters, in order to illuminate the fervid psychological turmoil of the central figure.

The Prologue has another function, which encompasses all the above. It establishes that the show is, to use a favoured Lepagean term, 'poetic'. Whenever Lepage uses the word it is to suggest that there is a frisson in two or more things happening at once – a theatre of metaphor or simultaneity. *Elsinore* begins with Hamlet on the throne. If this is an actual setting he is in the throne room at a time when it is empty. But of course putting the actor on this resonant prop has all sorts of reverberations. The setting is instantly metaphorical rather than literal. Hamlet, for instance, temporarily reclaims the seat of power which has been usurped, albeit like a child sitting at the wheel of his father's car. This reflex – to evoke an abstract state at the same time as suggesting a concrete setting – is characteristically Shakespearean (or, better, Jacobean). It is characteristically Lepagean as well: the actual is also metaphorical.

The Prologue opens and closes with the image of Hamlet alone in the throne room/seat of power. His musings might take place at any point in the play up to the presentation of *The Mousetrap*. In other words the image floats free of strict chronological positioning. Hamlet's encounter with the Ghost might therefore be presented as a flashback, or perhaps as a memory. Either way, it locates the event within Hamlet's consciousness rather than in the run of the story. The scene between Claudius, Gertrude, Rosencrantz and Guildenstern is potentially a flashback. Claudius sits on the throne, but so too does Gertrude. This place with two thrones might be the throne room in which Hamlet broods. Perhaps not. What's important in this staging is the speed at which the action moves from one scene to another, the means by which it melts between scenes, and its capacity to return to a place/event already in motion. We are concerned not just with chronology but with layerings which embellish metaphor and theme. The material – Shakespeare's text – is manhandled in order to produce these meaning-effects, which nonetheless emerge directly in relation to the play.

You don't have to be an expert in film to find this kind of storytelling and scene construction cinematic. A storyboard of the Prologue might appear as follows: 1) Spotlights on edge of stage surround empty throne. 2) Spotlights on Hamlet on throne. 3) Hamlet stands on the edge of the precipice. 4) Ghost appears in the middle of everything. 5) King and Queen on throne (raised in mid-air). 6) Hamlet on throne (returned to floor). Evidently the *mise en scène* is cleanly pictorial. This is a sequence of visually striking stage-images. The show cuts extremely quickly between different locations, different chronological moments, and even different qualities of time (between, we might say, real time and interior time).

Elsinore is continuously in flux. In 1901 Strindberg wrote about his new work, *A Dream Play*:

> Time and place do not exist; on an insignificant basis
> of reality the imagination spins, weaving new patterns;
> a mixture of memories, experiences, free fancies,
> incongruities and improvisations. The characters split,
> double, multiply, evaporate, condense, disperse,
> assemble. But one consciousness rules over them all,
> that of the dreamer.[22]

Raymond Williams suggested that Strindberg, elsewhere, 'was imagining a single word-and-scene medium – in effect the patterned control of film – which did not yet exist.'[23] The point was to be able to transform and combine multiple images without breaking the flow of dramatic action. Nearly a century later Lepage achieves this representational flux, albeit with a greater array of theatre technology at his disposal. He evokes the plasticity of cinema – theatrically. Of course Shakespeare's *Hamlet* was written for a Renaissance stage, not a postmodern performance space. Liberties must be taken.

Revamp until ready

Lepage and his team reworked some parts of *Elsinore* and left others intact, so the revamped sections especially concern us here. Let's begin with a sequence set in Ophelia's bedchamber. This scene does not exist in the play. At least, there is no indication in any of the published editions of *Hamlet* that the audience should witness Hamlet break into Ophelia's bedroom, rifle through her effects and ponder the nature of face-painting and the authenticity of emotion. Nor that this infiltration should be followed by two intercut scenes in which Ophelia recounts to Polonius the details of Hamlet's visit 'with his doublet all unbraced', whilst Hamlet urges Ophelia to 'get thee to a nunnery'. Lepage has conflated the fact that Hamlet visits Ophelia in her closet with an interpretative decision (supported in the text) that he should be sexually obsessed with her, and followed this by intercutting two scenes in order to detail the consquences of his obsession.

The company works on this section on the evening of Day 5 of rehearsals. The monolith is tilted to form a garret-like roof, with its aperture suggesting a skylight. Hamlet enters through this window into Ophelia's bedchamber. He steps onto Ophelia's bed – the central tablet, with a sheet draped over it – and then interests himself in Ophelia's make-up, at the front of the stage. In the previous version of *Elsinore* Lepage had delivered the 'To be or not to be' soliloquy at this point. Now that the soliloquy has been moved to the top of the show, this scene is open for development. Lepage and Darling decide that Hamlet, after putting on make-up, should segue into Hamlet's soliloquy following the Player's impromptu performance ('Is it not monstrous that this player here, / But in a fiction . . . ').

Darling runs this scene three times. Each time Lepage augments. The first time through, Darling comes through the window and onto Ophelia's bed. Lepage suggests that he step off the bed quickly and carefully – it is a special site. Lepage moves onto the stage himself and runs some possible actions. He strokes the sheets and the mattress, and slides his hand down to where Ophelia's genitals would be. He lies his head back on the pillow, where he notices Ophelia's nightshirt. He holds it up. Lepage indicates that Darling can hold the shirt in such a way that it forms the body-shape of Ophelia from the point of view of the audience. Darling runs this action. He smells the nightshirt. He takes his own shirt off and puts the nightshirt on, as if to inhabit it as fully as possible. At this point he tries on Ophelia's make-up, some blusher and some lipstick. He mimes the brushing of hair. He slips the night-shirt off his shoulder, part-lascivious, part-feverish, and lies back on the bed.

Darling performs a fetishising of female space and accoutre-ments, but also an insidiously masculine violation of that space, hence a metaphorical possession of the female body. It is not especially subtle. 'What's nice is that [Hamlet's] so en-dearing,' says Lepage to Darling. 'It's a completely different side to him.' A side, of course, that is made concrete by the invention of a completely new scene which offers a glimpse into Ophelia's private space – the bedchamber that ordinarily we never see. It is also a glimpse into Hamlet's private reverie. He plays out a male fantasy of dressing like a woman, femi-nising his body and his appearance. What becomes evident – and this is characteristic of Lepage's layering of potential readings – is that this might also be a glimpse of Ophelia herself. There is an inevitable shadow of the character as soon as the actor performs Ophelia-like mannerisms. Darling presents, fleetingly, a narcissistic, girlish teenager, a vision of both Hamlet and Ophelia at one and the same time. The audience is given a 'privileged' view of an intensely private realm, the space of adolescent self-exploration.

Another performative element accrues. The character 'pre-tends' at being somebody else: so the scene is partly concerned with modalities of *performing*. This motif is made literal when Darling puts down the blusher and launches into the 'Is it not monstrous' soliloquy, in which Hamlet berates himself for lack-ing the means to act through 'authentic' emotion, whilst the Player has just produced a compelling performance through the contrivance of acting.

The section ends with the line, 'O, vengeance!' Lepage's direction is that Darling finishes the scene back on the bed, under the skylight, with both arms raised – the melodramatic revenger's gesture. In fact this is necessary, since the next scene begins with the descent of the monolith, 'dressing' Darling in a lacy latex sheet which covers the whole monolith, and which stretches down from his shoulder to form Ophelia's nightshirt. His arms must be raised in order to fit through the small armholes above him. This is – and looks – contrived. The further difficulty, after today's rehearsal, is that there doesn't seem to be any time for the crew to get the sheet over the aperture, unseen by the audience, once Hamlet has climbed into the bedchamber through the open 'window'.

Four days later, and the crew have found a technical solution to the problem. The latex sheet is rolled up at one end of the monolith, its bottom corners fixed to a small pulley system which runs the length of the monolith. It can be tracked from top to bottom by the pulley operated from behind the upstage curtain by one of the stagehands. Once Hamlet has stepped through the window into the bedchamber at the start of the scene he mimes closing a blind. As he does so the sheet/dress, which from the audience's point of view looks like a curtain, slides to cover the aperture.

This second rehearsal of this scene on the morning of Day 8 yields a number of other improvements. Lepage suggests to Darling that he applies lipstick, then starts the soliloquy about the Player, explicitly motivated by the sight of himself in 'slap'. He should then break off the soliloquy in order to sing a verse of the song that Ophelia sings, later in the show, when she has become 'mad'. After this verse, Hamlet should chide himself for his lily-liveredness, as before. Then Darling, as – potentially – the mad Ophelia, should finish the song, at which point Hamlet, despairing of his own inaction, rouses himself to vengeance.

This instantly alters the performance register. The actor is now explicitly *playing* both Hamlet and Ophelia, shifting from one to the other in a display of Hamlet's fantasia and Ophelia's fancy. The chronological position of the scene is complicated. Hamlet is in Ophelia's bedchamber, but 'remembers' the Player's speech – this is close to flashback, but doesn't quite have the same crystalline status – and at that point (not, as in the play itself, once the Player has delivered the speech) decides to stir himself to action. Meanwhile there is a flashforward to the 'mad' Ophelia singing her song.

Not surprisingly Darling finds it difficult to find a through-line in the scene. 'It's as if Ophelia comes into the room as well,' he observes. Lepage instantly replies, 'Let me give you a context. Hamlet is on his way to spy on the King, with his dagger, walking past Ophelia's window. His eye is caught by Ophelia's room. He looks in. He makes to go again, but decides to enter.' This, needless to say, flagrantly rejigs the play's chronology and the apparent motivations presented by the revenge narrative. 'This scene is multiplex,' Darling observes, with good reason. It is indeed, and today's rehearsal has added to its multilayering of meanings. 'This scene intoduces a lot of things,' Lepage observes. He reminds Darling that it should be a sexual scene. Hamlet is not just 'dressing up' – he plays out tropes of fascination and possession.

The explicitness of the doubling is similar to the scene, later in the show, in which Gertrude recounts the details of the death of Ophelia. Darling enters, wearing the Queen's heavy black mourning dress. As Ophelia he sings a verse of one of the songs from Ophelia's 'mad' scene. He then reverts to the performance of the Queen, to speak the lines detailing Ophelia's drowning. He lets the black dress slip off his shoulder, and cradles it in one arm as it does, so that suddenly it evokes the limp body of the drowned girl. Darling is wearing a woman's nightshirt underneath the dress. He moves to the middle of the monolith, which lies flat on the floor draped with a blue cover. The monolith rises, so that Darling, standing within its central aperture, is gradually swallowed by the blue fabric which lifts and spills around him. The short sequence rolls the actor's performance as both Gertrude and Ophelia into a phantasmagoric rendering of madness, fragility, grief and death. The mode (plangent loss) is more important than the story-event. It veers between – and thus virtually melts together – the 'present' of Gertrude's account with the 'flashback' to Ophelia's drowning, and concludes the whole with another striking visual trope (the body sucked into the blue – drowning!) which emphasises again the fluidity of the moving set and the simultaneities of the performance.

According to Lepage, the continual doubling, redoubling and shift through different roles in *Elsinore* is in itself an unorthodox experience for the performer:

> It's a strange feeling, physically, to be performing a woman, then her son, then the girlfriend, then the father. Physically what happens to you in this play is really interesting. . . . I think that you have to be extremely eager to explore your own ambiguities.
> It's a great opportunity to explore that, because *Hamlet* is extremely ambiguous at all sorts of levels, whether it's mentally, physically, sexually.

The effect is to melt character difference – hence gender difference – into a continuum of performance. Fixed roles, whether they be parts in a play or sexual identities, slip into indistinctness. Is there another Renaissance echo here? In their discussion of boy actors in Renaissance theatre, David Scott Kastan and Peter Stallybrass suggest that 'on the stage a "single" gender was split into multiple sexualized roles, and gender was treated as itself a masquerade, a teetering performance.'[24] *Elsinore*'s *mise en scène* certainly underpins a 'teetering performance' of the quotability of gender. What is staged is a subordination of gender difference to the synthesising skills of the actor-artiste. Certain orthodoxies remain in place, however. Hamlet is pictured, still, as the brooding malcontent, Ophelia as the fragile victim of male fantasy. The staging erodes some boundary lines, but still depends upon stereotypical images (the sexually obsessive young male; the narcissicistic teenage girl) which it sustains almost as archetypes.

The scene in Ophelia's bedchamber is rehearsed again on the evening of Day 12. Robert Caux is now in place, and his contribution makes a vivid difference. The grandeur of the music makes the staging seem more spectacular. It turns what had previously seemed overheated and hammy into something more portentous. The scene ends with the descent of the monolith, clothing Hamlet in Ophelia's nightdress. The intercut scenes which follow, featuring Ophelia with Polonius, and Hamlet with Ophelia, end with Ophelia's 'O what a noble mind is here o'erthrown!' (continuing to 'O, woe is me / T'have seen what I have seen, see what I see!'). Darling then steps out of Ophelia's dress, comes to the front of the stage, puts on Hamlet's shirt, takes the dagger, then walks across the front of the stage and off stage-right.

As he does so Caux plays music, underscored with a sample of lines which he has captured live as Darling delivered them, and which he plays back on one note. As Darling calmly dresses as Hamlet, he is accompanied by insistent phrases from the preceding scene: 'Why wouldst thou be a breeder of sinners,' for instance, and 'The observed of all observers – quite, quite down!' The one-note playback makes these utterances sound chanted, ritualised and melancholic. Their repetition underscores the sequence's allusions to madness, fascination and betrayal.

Lepage directs Darling to take time over the simple don-
ning of his shirt at the end of the scene. It allows the staging
to resonate and builds a pause for breath, in order to finesse
the rhythm of the show. Hamlet calmly dresses after his illicit
and traumatic visit to Ophelia's bedchamber. The actor
Darling dresses again as Hamlet after his hyper-performance,
in preparation for the next scene. Once Darling has exited,
the music swells into the major key. The monolith lifts and
tilts into its vertical axis and the side-screens are pushed into
place, making a fourth wall across the front of the stage. The
music makes the flow from one scene to the next seem omi-
nously momentous and machine-like. The moving set evokes
a visual grammar which is virtually cinematic. Rather than
new visual compositions being formed by a moving camera or
post-production editing, however, they are made as the set
moves. Technology is subjugated to staging in a plenitude of
effects at once cinematic and theatrical.

The stage picture is augmented when the sequence is run
again on the evening of Day 15. A projection onto the sloping
monolith shows a wood-carving pattern, suggesting an elaborate wood-pannelled room. The projections on the two outer
screens, swung open like bookends, show the night sky with a
moon on the stage-right flat. These are highly conventional
images, but effective in quickly setting an environment. When
Hamlet enters at the beginning of the scene – perhaps walking across the roof, or along some gantry – his shadow falls on
both side screens. The projections keep the exterior continuously in play, even as the scene shows the interior of Ophelia's
chamber. Whilst the content of the sequence trammels and
overlays time, the *mise en scène* trammels and overlays space.

*

Photographs of early versions of *Elsinore* show Lepage, rather comically, leaning on a short section of crenellated battlement or popping up from the grave in the floor with a skull in his hand. As the show went through different phases of production, so Lepage developed less literal stagings. In the graveyard scene, for instance, he had performed as Hamlet, grave-diggers and members of the court in the funeral train. By the time of the Darling production the scene had been slimmed down so that it featured Hamlet alone, pondering upon existential questions. This scene was reworked on Day 10.

The monolith stands vertical upstage. Lepage wants to raise it to form a roof above the stage, so that the audience views through the aperture, as if watching from the underside of the grave. How is Darling to get on top? Darling suggests standing in front of the vertical aperture, as if he is lying on the ground looking down into the grave. The nature of the picture becomes clear as the monolith moves – Darling remains in position, and eventually comes into 'true' relationship with gravity, lying on the flat surface looking down. Lepage suggests that Darling holds the gravedigger's shovel in his right hand, in view of the audience, and the skull of Yorick in his left hand, hidden at first. As the monolith tilts into position, Darling can make the motions of wrenching the skull from the side of the grave.

The few lines of the text which are retained are those in which Hamlet memorialises Yorick and expresses his love for Ophelia. Darling delivers these once the monolith is in its high horizontal position. Lepage suggests that he throws the skull back into the grave after the section dealing with Yorick. This means that it falls the entire vertical height of the playing area before hitting the floor. Darling tries this. The rubber skull bounces ridiculously. Lepage suggests that Ophelia's nightshirt should follow, and then possibly some flowers. One of the crew is instructed to carry to the top of the grid a bucket of sand, another to lay a dark green floorcloth over the stage. Lepage suggests that, as the final action of this scene, Hamlet shovels stones and sand into the grave. Darling tries this. Dust fills the space as the sand falls.

Lepage asks Claude Cyr to position a floor microphone to amplify the thud of the falling items and to provide a reverberating echo. He asks the lighting engineer to light the scene directly from above, through the aperture. As the different elements are tried again, the space is transformed. Dust from the sand, illuminated in the shaft of light, billows drily in the air. Towards the end of the scene the monolith descends again, horizontally. When it is at the top the entire floor of the stage is lit, since the aperture is near to the light source. As the monolith descends, the illuminated area of the floor tightens in a contracting rectangle. It is as if the dimensions of the grave are inexorably closing in, diminishing entirely as the monolith reaches the ground. 'Wow!' says Lepage.

The new scene provides a drastically altered point of view, with the lip of the grave seen from an impossible depth. The perspective is not that of Hamlet, nor is Hamlet foregrounded. Instead the *mise en scène* makes the grave itself the object of the gaze. The reverberating sound effects endorse this focus and the illuminated dust, hanging in the air, evokes a stifling dryness. The contracting rectangle of light helps to relocate the scene in proper perspective, offering as the monolith descends the image of the actual size of the grave forming. It works metaphorically as well. This is the inevitable snuffing out of the light, the closing of the lid. Hamlet doesn't actually ponder any of this in the lines left to him in this scene. He finishes by shovelling dirt. In another compounding of the play's figurative elements he has become both gravedigger and graveyard obsessive, in the midst of a dynamic *mise en scène* which emblematises the tomb.

The scene has taken about an hour-and-a-half to rework and the new version again depends upon happy conjunctions of movement and meaning. It is next developed on Day 14. Lepage directs Darling to start the lines, which begin with, 'This [the skull]? Alas, poor Yorick!' as the monolith ascends, rather than waiting for it to reach its final position. The scenic transformation, then, flows smoothly over the action. The pace of the show is not allowed to lag. Robert Caux provides an undercurrent to Darling's speech whereby Hamlet's lines are played back, simultaneously, on one note, Caux changing the pitch as the speech continues. The falling skull no longer appears gratuitous and takes its established place as an icon of death (and indeed of the play itself), which plunges through theatre-space. This is now a virtuosic scene, an arresting combination of voice, music, sound, light, movement of set, physical gesture and textual editing.

The director was certainly pleased with the result.

I was interested in this play mainly through people
who painted. It's a play that has been painted a lot . . .
It's a play that refers to painting also. There's a murder
that happens behind a painted curtain. [Hamlet]
deliberately says, 'Look upon this picture.' . . . The
Queen comes in and she 'paints' Ophelia. So I haven't
been pictorial enough. There's a lot of imagery and
visual stuff, but it's not painting. It's starting to happen.
When the Yorick scene takes the shape it does right now
it's closer to the painting I would have done than what
I used to do, where I tried to do every character. . . .
But I had to go through all of that to end up doing
this thing which is very simple where there's nothing
else involved. Now it's one spot, the machine we've
been seeing – that piece of set – an actor and a skull,
and it's just the way they relate to each other and move

that creates different points of view or dimensions to
a scene.

Such a process of distillation is not a solitary pursuit. 'It's
really strange how Robert works,' observes Carl Fillion. 'He
takes the ideas and the generosity of all the creators around
him. . . . After one or two years, when somebody asks me "Who
had the idea of whatever" you don't remember, it's part of the
process.' For Pierre Bernier:

> *La force* of Robert is to be surrounded by people who
> know very well their technique and make confidence
> in them. It's like a conductor ready to put all the
> energy of people in the right place. Everyone is happy
> to work in that, because they can bring ideas and be
> sure he will listen to them. Sometimes he can laugh
> about the idea, sometimes he can ask more questions,
> because he needs to have more explanation. Very
> interesting.

I don't remember Lepage saying 'No' at any point during
my three-week stay in Quebec. His strategy was to say, 'You
could . . . ' or 'It would be interesting to . . . ' He would tend
to work from what had already been presented, often accepting, at some level, the first inclinations of the actor. He might
then suggest shapes or nuances to the work which responded
to or developed what had already been sketched. Peter
Darling was certainly enthusiastic, despite his difficulties with
some of the material and the speed at which the show was
remounted:

> He's fantastic to work with because he's so relaxed.
> Ideas just flow from him. And you feel completely
> integral to the process of those ideas, in the sense that

> if I didn't like the staging I'd feel quite easy about
> saying, 'I don't like that bit.' You do have a sense that
> anything is possible with him, because there's always
> going to be a way to make what you want to happen,
> happen. And the fact that he doesn't mind you saying
> what you want to happen is very liberating.

Where the actor overtly participates in the creation of the show, we are close to Lepage's notion of the performer as a 'writer' of theatre. The crucial principle is that theatre-making is an act of primary creation rather than secondary interpretation.[25]

Just as the rehearsal room, rather than the writer's study, is the place where the theatre-work is created, so the video of the show, rather than the text, becomes its authoritative record. This was made evident during an afternoon rehearsal of *Needles and Opium*. The Italian company reached the section which depicts, by way of the overhead projector, an exchange across the counter of a pawn shop along with the preparation and injection of heroin. The various items are placed on the surface of the OHP and their shapes appear two-dimensionally as a back-projection on a screen. The audience watches a shadow play of hands and objects. The company can't quite remember the sequence. Nor can Lepage, so everyone gathers round the video of Lepage's production. The visual document (the video cassette), not the literary one (the script), is the final authority for restaging. We *watch* theatre.

The Ghost in the machine: *Elsinore* and technology

The modernity of works of art often derives from their use of contemporary technologies. Lepage keeps a sharp eye on the opportunities which a digital culture presents for a 'technological' theatre practice.

My growth as a human being and as an artist is accompanied by machinery and technology, and technology undergoes as many revolutions and transformations as I do as a person of this era who goes through new ideas and trends in society. It's like growing up with a partner. It's very difficult to dissociate myself from that machinery which is evolving with me because it's an expression of my stage vocabulary and it's as if from that I understand many themes . . . Theatre is always a big problem, how you are heard, how you are seen, how you can tell this story that everybody knows but in a different way, how you can change a point of view, in a cinematic way, in a televisual way, in a multimedia way, whatever it is, the next trend. . . . So even if *Elsinore* never really found its shape many things were found out.

Critics wrote of the show's overtly technological nature.[26] But what is this exactly? Fillion's set is an ingenious construction, custom-built and therefore unique. But other technological components of the show were hardly ground-breaking. The technical itinerary of *Elsinore* combines orthodox theatre kit with some state-of-the-art equipment. The ingenuity here – the apparent technological wizardry – lies in the use to which the relatively ubiquitous machinery is put. Robert Caux accompanies the show live, as he observes, 'like in old cinema when you have the piano player in front of the screen.' This is exactly right, and there is a precise fit between musical accompaniment and action that would otherwise be impossible to achieve. Caux sits at a keyboard, but this is more than an orchestra pit organ. Everything goes through a MIDI (musical instrument digital interface) system. Caux's sampler allows multiple treatments of notes and effects, enabling more sophisticated colouring of the design concept – an interface between a palette of period sounds (lute, flute and viola da gamba, for instance) and a tight, modern scoring. Caux also plays two additional synthesisers. When Darling speaks as Polonius, his voice is fed through a vocal harmony processor programmed to produce a particular pitch, timbre and reverberation. Darling wears not just one radio mic but two, so that Caux and sound engineer Claude Cyr can switch rapidly between vocal sources and treatments.

What of the show's vaunted multimedia elements? The three screens were sites for projection, but the images themselves were from slide projectors, paired so that they could be cross-faded. A single video projector was focused on each screen, playing a feed from one of four onstage cameras or from a video cassette player. The vision mixing was done by Éric Fauque, the stage manager. The two side screens, which moved into different positions with seemingly computerised smoothness, were in fact pushed by stagehands supplied by the respective venues to which the show toured, who were rehearsed during the get-in and cued by members of the backstage team during the show.

Much of the effect of slide and video images in the theatre depends upon neat operation – fading in and out of black, for instance, and achieving an appropriate rhythm to cuts and cross-fades. The operators' work makes a great difference to the finesse of the production, and time spent in the rehearsal room with technical operators in place is crucial to the polish of Lepage's style of mixed-media performance. In terms of sound, lighting and image design, much of the work can be pre-treated. Equally, whether pre-set or not, the designs only come into play as an organic component of the live event. As Fauque observed, each department (sound, lighting, music, multimedia, set-remote-control) is responsible for its own cueing and operation, rather than everything being called by the stage manager or deputy stage manager. This is unusual, but it means that each technical element is 'played' by its operator in (ideally) complete synchronicity with the rhythms of any particular performance. It also means that integrated theatre (performance/design/technical operation) can be sketched and developed as an entity in the rehearsal room, rather than suffer from the late addition of complicated technical operation.

Consider an interpolated transition-effect developed during the re-rehearsal period. After the play within the play, Hamlet is discovered buckling his sword on a small flight of stairs rising to the monolith's central aperture. Caux provides a musical accompaniment. As Hamlet ascends, Caux dips the music and sounds a bell chime. Darling begins Hamlet's lines, ''Tis now the very witching time of night', in which he announces that he will visit his mother. Lepage asks Darling to call 'Mother', and repeat the call twice, as soon as he has ascended the stairs. This is a transition effect. The monolith lowers once Darling has exited through the aperture – to reveal Darling in the Queen's costume, standing on a raised platform upstage, a tableau of anxiety. Lepage asks Caux to loop Darling's last 'Mother' with an echo, so that it becomes the sound which plays over this image of the Queen. Hamlet calls, his mother perhaps hears, or in any case is suddenly viewed.

Brecht might have called this a gestic moment: a tableau suggesting potentially a mother's concern for her son and/or regal guilt at an 'o'er hasty marriage'. The monolith is raised again to obscure Darling, and a curtain pulls to reveal a table, hung vertically upstage, at which the next scene takes place. So the segment showing Gertrude is a piece of pure theatrics – or we should perhaps call it cinematics, a flash-cut from Hamlet's decision to seek out his mother to the object of his affection/affliction. The looped word 'mother', incidentally, loses its initial context with repetition, and the replay has the effect of evening out Darling's accentuation. By serendipity the word sounds increasingly like 'murther', the Elizabethan spelling of 'murder'. Another happy accident – in a process which continually chances its arm with the technical equipment at its disposal.

The reconceived Ghost is another case in point. Lepage was unhappy with his previous version of the Ghost's appearance to Hamlet. Work on this scene begins on the evening of Day 8.[27] The monolith is set at a 45 degree angle, its position for Hamlet's first ascent to the 'cliff edge'. Darling is in position at the top of this extreme incline. A video projector is placed in the recess in the middle of the stage, pointing up at the monolith, to which is fitted the breastplate from a suit of armour. A live feed from the camera projects the image on to the breastplate, so that the company can see immediately and *in situ* what it is making. Pierre Bernier, the double, stands to one side and the camera frames his face and upper body. Lepage then has the projector moved to the downstage edge of the stage and asks the stage manager, Éric Fauque, to make the image 'fit' onto the breastplate, so that the head is on top as if emerging from the armour. This entails fitting a piece of white material across the top of the breastplate so that the image shows clearly. The effect looks clumsy and contrived.

Lepage asks that the breastplate be removed and that Bernier put it on. A larger piece of white material is fitted over the monolith's central aperture, replacing the breastplate, to show the video image. Now, simply, there is an image of Bernier wearing armour – nothing particularly ghostlike or exciting about that. Fauque flips through various effects on the camera, making the image black-and-white, washing it in one colour and then rendering it in 'negative'. The image suddenly looks interesting, a dark head on a whited-out breastplate. A white screen is quickly rigged up behind Bernier, so that the background to the projected image is black (the negative effect reverses light and dark, of course). The group discovers that if Bernier looks up, lit from below, the movement exaggerates the shadows in his eye sockets, making the negative image appear to gaze with milky (you might say ghostly) intensity.

Lepage directs Darling to look down at the image projected on the monolith 'underneath' him, while Bernier looks up, creating the impression that the Ghost looks up at Hamlet. Lepage suggests that Darling reaches his hand down, trying to touch. He then asks that the monolith be moved, so that its top edge continues upwards. As the monolith moves the image extends and thins out along the ever-flatter plane of projection. It looks as though the Ghost is being sucked downstage, slipping away from Hamlet as the top edge of the monolith tilts away.

There is now a technologically-driven representation of the Ghost, providing an unusual image which works thematically. What could be more fitting, more *obvious*, than this figure from the nether-world appearing in negative, the register of the not-living, the reverse of the actual? The harsh black-and-white, its seeming phosphorescence glowing out of the darkness, evokes memories of cinematic graveyard zombies. The chance configuration of projector and moving screen means that the image slides away, as if the very movement of the terrain – the earth spinning, perhaps, as dawn approaches – enforces the separation between the living and the dead. Hamlet appears powerless in the face of his spectral father. He is unable to touch, unable to prolong the encounter.

The creation of this small scene has taken a little less than an hour. Its generation lies in three essential elements. Firstly, the capacity to move swiftly from the initial attempt, which seemed over-literal and clumsy. Secondly, the engaged participation of the crew, whose suggestions were always taken seriously and often instantly tried out. Thirdly – and most simply –

the fact that the scene was developed onstage, with technicians in place to light Bernier's face and body, wield the camera and projector and move the set. The scene couldn't have been devised by, say, the director, designer and actor alone. And it is difficult to imagine that it could have been conceived, in the mind, in advance.

On Day 17 the Ghost's words are recorded so they can be treated and played back. To make the recording Darling goes into a small room off the main rehearsal studio, with Claude Cyr, the sound engineer, at his desk in the rehearsal room. The company's staff are informed that they should keep away from the ground floor whilst recording is taking place – a nicely homespun procedure for an outfit deemed to be at the cutting edge of high-tech theatre production. Cyr treats the recording to make Darling's voice deeper, with a good deal of added reverberation and echo.

Once this and another couple of voice recordings from other parts of the show have been completed, the next step is to record the image of the Ghost on video. Darling dons the armour and is filmed in negative. The video projector is set up with a live feed so that Lepage can view the image on the set itself, exactly as it will appear once the recording is played back. Lepage directs Darling to make extremely slow hand movements and to look up slowly, to animate the image of the Ghost 'speaking', in tandem with the lines which Cyr now plays back. There is no attempt to have the Ghost 'lip synch' to the lines. Lepage then asks Fauque to zoom in on the cross embossed on the breastplate. The Christian icon of suffering, death and deliverance looms out of the image as Hamlet and the Ghost part. Again a chance detail – the decoration on the armour from the *Elsinore* props store – is exploited for its thematic reverberations.

The image of the Ghost will be projected onto the central monolith. It will be accompanied by projections onto the side screens. These are filmed next, both in negative. The stage-hands set up a small phial – poison! – on a box covered in white material. Pierre Bernier then reaches his hand around the phial, pauses for a millisecond, and lifts it silkily out of shot, with the camera remaining stationary. (Darling is not asked to do this. Bernier, the mime artist, is more gesturally deft.) The crew carry in a slab on which is mounted a large foam ear. This was originally a fitment for the monolith in the days when Lepage performed almost the whole of the play. In early versions of *Elsinore* the Ghost would crawl out of this enlarged orifice. The company finds the optimum position for filming – ear standing upright. White fabric is draped behind the earhole (which is, literally, a hole) so that it reads black when filmed in negative. The ear is then illuminated from the front. Darling climbs over the top of the body part, leans down, and pours liquid from the phial into the earhole. He looks like an infesting insect.

The projection sequence is then run. The Ghost appears on the central screen. As he speaks the poison appears on the screen stage-right, to be lifted by the anonymous hand. The image is faded out and the stage-right screen swung by the crew to align along the front of the stage. The contamination of the ear appears on the stage-left screen. This image too is faded out and the screen swung into its new position face-on to the audience. The Ghost continues to the end, after which the monolith moves and his image slips away. The monolith continues its movement until it completes the fourth wall across the front of the stage.

*

Lepage can be seen as a thoroughly traditional practitioner. There are parallels between the sort of theatre he makes and the scenic fluidity of Renaissance staging, the visual transformations of the late-eighteenth-century stage and the spec-tacular effects of nineteenth-century theatre. Of course the theatrical conjuration in *Elsinore* is carried out through tech-nologies and strategies appropriate to latter-day mass media. Lepage utilises the rhetorics of cinema, television and video – flash-back, flash-forward, intercutting, cross-fade, image flow, multiple imaging – and underscores it with a cinematic sound design which combines melodramatic flourish, postmodern pastiche and New Age ambience. We experience his theatre with the eyes and ears of cinemagoers in a video age, even as it trades in showmanship reminiscent of previous kinds of theatre.

The overt use of technology creates a nice tension between the domains of modern machinery (cinema/TV/video) and the live, human performer (theatre). The actor is more vulnerable, as he works within evident parameters set by the machine. But he is simultaneously empowered, since he acts with and for technology. Apart from riding the set, he relates to the audience by means of performance on stage and to the camera. When Hamlet meets Horatio in *Elsinore*, he does so by way of a simple configuration of live and mediated images. Hamlet sits in the monolith's aperture, in profile to the audi-ence. A camera upstage conveys his image, which is projected live on the central screen. Since the camera films from 'behind' the actor and the projection is 'in front', the image is reversed. Hamlet's body faces a larger image of a seated figure (Image 8). When Lepage and Darling rehearse this scene, Lepage suggests that Darling stroke the image facing him as though greeting a friend. The actor talks to himself-as-other.

When Hamlet greets Rosencrantz and Guildenstern, he does so standing in the doorway-like aperture. This time he is filmed by two cameras placed either side of the opening, behind the flat plane of the monolith (out of sight of the audience). The image from one camera is projected on one side-screen, the image from the other on to the screen on the opposite side. We imagine Rosencrantz and Guildenstern either side of Hamlet. As he turns to one, so the entire configuration alters and the screened figure 'behind' is now looking directly at the corporeal performer. In this way the actor triples as Hamlet and his two slippery friends in conversation. The *mise en scène* underscores the liveness of the staging precisely by placing the actor alongside his own (doubled and tripled) screen-image, which is mediated, two-dimensional but still most evidently live – the same body, but different.

This raises the intriguing question of how as an actor you perform for the camera and a theatre audience at the same time. As J. L. Styan suggests, in an earlier discussion of not dissimilar issues, 'A character in soliloquy, seen alone on some 1,000 square feet of platform space, is *not* the same as in a film close-up, as is often maintained. The film captures the intimacy, maybe, but not the simultaneous quality of isolation.'[28] In *Elsinore*, on the other hand, Lepage and Darling can have their cake and eat it. The figure of the lone actor onstage in a 'solo' show suggests isolation, whilst the camerawork allows the spectator moments of intimacy with the actor-as-character. The fact that this is theatre, where the videoed body is staged alongside the actual actor, means that the screened image is *always* the image of a performer-in-mid-performance rather than, uncomplicatedly, the character (Image 10). Lepage's use of video technology is metatheatrical here, too. On a more mundane level, the use of the live camera, snooping and spying, evokes contemporary security-video surveillance and lends a modern texture to the depiction of Hamlet's anxiety.

Barbara Hodgdon suggests that Lepage's work 'is grounded in the materiality of actors' bodies'.[29] Given Lepage's fondness for live video projection, 'presences' might be a more appropriate term than 'bodies', for performance is also delivered through the screen as well as the stage. The tension between

3D and 2D, the live and the mediated, the corporeal and the mechanised impacts upon the spectator's experience of the show. Technology isn't just a means to an end, or a handy tool-kit for modish experiments. Its use suggests a broader thematics. We watch not only an articulation of *Hamlet*, but an articulation of the meeting between theatre and electronic technology. The production is about – it *stages* – the interface between the human and the technological.

(Meta)Theatre and transformation

To what extent was *Elsinore* improved in this revamped production? Critics found the show more compelling than its earlier incarnations, although the reviews were still decidedly mixed, as the following examples bear witness. For Alvina Ruprecht, interviewed on CBC Radio 1 after the production's opening night in Ottawa, 'The play . . . becomes a projection of Hamlet's troubled mind, performed as a psychodrama right up to the final moments, when Hamlet drops all his personality and curls up into total withdrawal. I found this really very, very powerful. Lepage has, on his own, created a new play.'[30] For Peter Marks, writing in the *New York Times*, *Elsinore* offered 'an uninterrupted succession of stage stunts, some as clever as the best moments in "Seven Streams," others as hokey as the pseudo-solemn theatrics of David Copperfield.'[31] Nor was Marks alone in conveying reluctant admiration mixed with suspicion at what appeared to be gaudy razzmatazz.

Of all the critics who reviewed the revival, Jocelyn Clarke best conveys the flavour of *Elsinore*'s modernity.

> Lepage's staging liberates both the performer and
> the text by constantly and dynamically reconfiguring
> the relationships between the various elements of his
> production. The audience gasps at moments of

astonishing simplicity and beauty – Darling revolving
in a video-scape of stars or . . . playing Hamlet and
Ophelia simultaneously by raising and dropping a body
veil – because they recognise the visual and narrative
idioms, and see and hear the text and the actor in new
and exciting ways.[32]

Clarke observes, rightly, that 'where traditionally all elements of a production "serve" the text, in *Elsinore* the text is now presented as another element of the production.' This causes its reviewer a little discomfort, although she has hit on the luminous truth without which there would be no show. Lepage doesn't jettison Shakespeare's *Hamlet*. The play remains a recognisable and authoritative source. But it is boiled down according to the decisive interventions of late-twentieth-century theatrics. The playtext? That's hardly the central concern. The *contemporaneity* of the production in front of its audience matters more. According to Lepage:

> Kids who would never read *Hamlet* for pleasure can
> come to *Elsinore* and immediately feel at home with the
> visual vocabulary that it uses, because of TV influences.
> They're used to flashbacks, jump-cuts and zapping.
> This is a very interesting moment: now theatre and film
> tend to clash, but they are going to have to really meet
> and merge.[33]

I don't believe that Lepage's embrace of emergent technology and current visual rhetoric stems merely from a desire to be with the kids, an implicit suspicion of more sceptical observers. The spectator takes pleasure in the 'new and exciting'. This is a question of theatre form – *how* you get from moment to moment, *how* you shape material which is otherwise well-known. It is also a case for innovation. These imperatives point us back into a metatheatrical theatre – a theatre which makes its audience conscious of the (new) way in which it operates. The spectator's pleasure really takes wing when the staging itself rather than, solely, the show's over-familiar content becomes available for enjoyment. This is part of the novelty, the excitement, that we seek. In this instance, the novelty is theatrical. The *mise en scène* figures the story and *at the same moment* signals its élan as theatre. (It also defamiliarises the material, another source of pleasure.) It offers a visceral *experience* of the theatrical.

When Don Rieder saw Lepage's 'first draft' presentation of *Elsinore*, he found that 'Any kinesthetic experience we have is given by the staging, the moving planes of the on-stage structures or objects. We remain intellectually engaged, curious about the next scenic transformation and always delighted by its originality and ingenuity.'[34] Staged events are not simpl[y] enjoyed because they find neat ways of illustrating or e[m]blematising the text. They convey a *capacity* in theatre-mak[ing] (hence image-making, meaning-making, surprise-monger[ing].) This mode of theatre raises expectations (I am *curious*[:] What neat device, what new trick, will be employed to [make] the stuff of this scene, or to shift from one moment to th[e] next? A desire to be delighted is hardly new in theatre audiences. But the means of producing delight will need refreshing from time to time, and in Lepage's case they involve novel theatrical-technical configurations. This is still theatre in all its phenomenological force, stirring the spectator through continual shifts of time, place and persona. We return to principles of flux and transformation.

'I'm very drawn to plays in which the characters are transformed,' says Lepage, 'but also to plays in which the sets are transformed and matter is transcended. . . . So rather than just being a mode of working, the transformation becomes the whole basis of the work.'[35] In all Lepage's shows there is a continuum between the content of the performance (concerned with a series of changes which take place to characters, to social groups, and to situations), the presentation of that performance (in which actors change themselves into characters and theatrical events enact change) and a philosophy of mutability. There are political implications. On one hand it becomes less pressing to take a stand on anything, since everything is subject to the cosmic truth of endless flux. A settled opinion is nothing but banal and illusory dogma. This is a rather caricatural extreme and Lepage has never articulated anything as reductive as this. Even so, his work avoids recommending specific political perspectives in favour of a pervasive sense of the 'truth' of change.

There is, on the other hand, a Brechtian insistence that things are unfixed and subject to alteration. This gives Lepage's theatre a certain clarity: characters are depicted as people who, for now, have made a certain set of choices, which are always contingent. (It's no coincidence that Lepage doesn't deal with blue-collar characters, whose choices are a good deal more restricted). In terms of production process, a philosophy of change – very difficult to hold on to in the pressure-zone of rehearsal – makes easier the reimagining of things that don't work or that impose constraints.[36] The Ex Machina rehearsal room is indeed a place of constant development and reformulation. Lepage's taste for transformation has deep theatrical roots in another sense, for transformation is basic to theatre production. It is at the heart of a medium which routinely evokes, conjures up, stands for something other than its mere presence.

The pursuit of transformations also means the production of difference, which contributes to Lepage's identity as a liberal postmodern theatre-maker.[37] Perhaps his special talent is for metamorphosis, knowing how to turn this into that, how to make that suggest the other. Where two things exist in the

1. *Qui Est Là.* Hamlet (Bakary Sangaré) and the Ghost (Sotigui Kouyaté)

2. *Qui Est Là.* The Player (Yoshi Oida) gives his performance

3. *Qui Est Là.* Gertrude (Anne Bennent) in her chamber, with Polonius (Bruce Myers) behind the arras

4. *Qui Est Là*. 'Look at the moon' (l to r) David Bennent, Bakary Sangaré, Bruce Myers, Anne Bennent, Yoshi Oida, Sotigui Kouyaté

5. *Qui Est Là*. The graveyard (l to r) Anne Bennent, Giovanna Mezzogiorno, Bruce Myers

6. The set for *Elsinore* installed at the main rehearsal studio at Ex Machina's base. The monolith, with its central aperture inside a circular disc, is in the middle. The two side screens are hinged at the scaffolding frame. The plastic sheet – an experiment, here – was not used in the performances which I saw. Pierre Bernier (left) and Robert Lepage stand in the foreground.

7. The set for *Elsinore*. The monolith held horizontal, with composer and musician Robert Caux's station in the foreground.

8. *Elsinore.* Hamlet talks with Horatio (Robert Lepage, doubled by the projection of his own image on the monolith)

9. *Elsinore.* Polonius (Peter Darling) reveals Hamlet's letter to Ophelia

10. *Elsinore.* Claudius (Peter Darling) poisons the cup, as emphasised by the live projection on the central screen, filmed by the camera in the jeweller's rapier handle

11. *Hamlet: a monologue.* Hamlet on the rocks.
   (See storyboard 1, 'The sleep of death', page 159)

12. *Hamlet: a monologue*. Wilson shows the lining of his jacket .
   (See storyboard 5, 'Get thee to a nunnery', page 159)

13. *Hamlet: a monologue*. The Player. (See storyboard 7, 'For Hecuba', page 159)

14. *Hamlet: a monologue*. The Player Queen and her dummy King.
(See storyboard 8, 'The dumb-show', page 159)

15. Wilson lines up the costumes.
(See storyboard 15, 'This sergeant, death', page 159)

16. *The Tragedy of Hamlet*. Adrian Lester as Hamlet. ('To be, or not to be')

same breath, or where one entity morphs into something else, you are provoked to make the connection. Lepage's theatre is brilliantly synthetic – it puts things together through delightful fakery. It is also intrinsically fluid and unstable, always about to take a new turn. Which makes it sound not a little Shakespearean.

Hamlet: a monologue
Robert Wilson

4

Hamlet: a monologue
Robert Wilson

'At some point a dilettante has to arrive who does something that the learned can't do because they've all learned not to.'

Heiner Müller[1]

All for one

The very title emphasises the singularity of this production. There is one performer in *Hamlet: a monologue*. This – as if you didn't already know – is Robert Wilson, who is also the show's director and designer.

Faced with such a polymath, you could be forgiven for not noticing the many other hands involved. Wilson's touring company comprises 20 people, including his co-director Ann-Christin Rommen, composer and sound designer Hans Peter Kuhn, stand-in and prompter Thomas Lehmann and personal assistant Rupert Wagg. The tour's producer and project manager are both present, along with five people in the technical and stage management department, five people looking after the lighting and electrics, a sound engineer, a make-up artist and a wardrobe assistant. To this cavalcade we must add the 13 local technicians provided by the host theatre (stipulated by Wilson's company), including two fly operators and six stagehands. Eight further local crew are added to help with the get-in and get-out, unpacking and packing the company's 17 flight cases – its items of set, stage carpet and assortment of laths, pipes and lighting equipment. Clearly this production is modest only in the number of performers onstage.

On Days 1 and 2 of the get-in the containers are unloaded, drops and flying items hung, lights rigged, sound equipment installed and the stage carpet rolled out. The lights are focused on Days 2 and 3 and cued on Days 3 and 4, while the stage areas are prepared. The sound is checked on Day 4 during breaks and during the night-shift before Day 5. The sound technicians will have equalised and patched the system during a previous night-shift. On the afternoon of Day 5, according to the company's workschedule, 'Bob looks at lights'. There is a walkthrough of the show between 7pm and 11pm, a run-through the next afternoon, and the show is ready to open that evening – Day 6. The time is tightly scheduled to include rehearsals of the venue's crew.

Any get-in involves intensive work, but Wilson's shows raise the stakes because of the detail lavished on visual elements, and the scrupulous care with which they are lit. Abbie Katz, stage manager of *Hamlet: a monologue*, estimates that she calls around 325 cues for lighting, set shifting and for Wilson's entrances. The sound cues are handled separately by the sound operator, who is so busy that he is in effect an ardent accompanist.

The host theatre must be well-endowed in order for Wilson even to consider a visit. It must supply 370 lighting units, for instance, although the company brings its own additional kit. Ten fluorescence units provide the illuminated backdrop which has become a characteristic of Wilson's theatre. Black drapes (legs at the sides of the stage and borders along the top), a blackout drop and a traveller (a curtain which opens along the stage) are amongst the company's bespoke masking material. Its drapes are made in Germany and Katz explains that they provide a greater degree of 'blackness' than ordinary masking, reflecting no light whatsoever. In addition there is a black gauze, downstage, which flies in during blackouts between scenes. This expensive curtain provides an additional degree of control. It allows complete concealment of a number of Wilson's entrances and exits and a number of scene changes, since the audience is unable to see through the scrim when there is no light behind it.

What kind of artist is at the hub of such a fulsome production number? Wilson has received some glowing notices. For Susan Sontag, 'His is the great theatre career of our time.' For John Rockwell, arts critic turned director of New York's Lincoln Center Festival, 'He's the most original director of this century. He's offered a totally new idea of what theatre is.' For critic Robert Enright, Wilson's career 'has changed fundamentally the way we look at and hear plays and operas. I can think of no other director – other than perhaps Peter Brook – whose effect has been as profound.'[2]

Peter Sellars, the American theatre and opera director, re-dresses the balance.

> In the age of Hollywood movies, television and Robert Wilson, the image is a source of singular fascination. And I suspect that it is Hollywood movies, television, and Robert Wilson that have rendered theatre temporarily obsolete and forced many of us who are interested in theatre to take refuge in the realm of opera and redeem our tattered selves.[3]

What can this mean? Can Sellars really associate the fastidiously avant-garde Wilson with America's populist entertainment industries? Both, he implies, combine a command of presentation with blandness of content. Wilson's works have themselves been called 'operas' – large-scale spectaculars combining music, movement and stylised utterance. Are they really as empty as Sellars suggests?

Contradiction and downright confutation lie at the heart of Wilson's artistic output. On one hand it is fiercely formal and organised, on the other, spontaneous and instinctive. It stands aloof from the mass but depends upon assiduous courting of society patrons and wealthy theatre angels.[4] Its difference marks it out as radical, its abstractness makes it seem politically conservative.[5] Wilson's theatre is the apogee of many definitive twentieth-century artistic developments – surrealism, anti-psychologism, the free-form styles of the 1960s, the chic minimalism of modern design disciplines. This same extra-ordinary oeuvre is still uncelebrated in large vistas of the theatre industry itself, certainly in Britain and even in Wilson's American homeland. And Wilson himself is deeply paradoxical. On the one hand the subject of risible anecdotes which describe the antics of the primadonna director. On the other, the object of goggle-eyed veneration in cities in Europe and America as a theatre artist without equal.

Like the Cheshire Cat, Wilson often seems to be in two places at once. His pieces frequently revolve around polarised categories, instanced by Michael Vanden Heuvel as 'vocabulary/language, performance/text, freedom/determinism, innocence/experience, and dreaming/science'.[6] We might add individual/ensemble, movement/stasis and culture/instinct. There is nothing intrinsically baffling about paradox. It is quite possible to think two mutually opposing things at the same time, which is the state of mind I find myself in when considering Wilson's seizure of *Hamlet*.

Back to base

There was a period in the 1980s when it was rare for anything new by Wilson to be premiered in the country of his birth. By the mid-1970s he had rehearsed and opened shows in France, Italy and Germany, and these three countries in particular formed a friendly axis for his work. Berlin, Bordeaux, Cologne, Lyon, Milan, Rome, Spoleto, Stuttgart . . . the list of cities which hosted the peripatetic director reads like an intinerary for an upmarket culture-crawl. With continental esteem came relatively lavish financial support, and Wilson increasingly located himself in Europe rather than America. Arthur Holmberg somewhat dramatically states that 'Wilson flourished because Wilson fled America,' the artist leaving his homeland directly as a result of the cancellation of his *the CIVIL warS: a Tree is Best Measured When it is Down*, which had been commissioned as part of the Arts Festival attached to the Los Angeles Olympics in 1984.[7] In equal measure he was welcomed in European theatres comfortable with modernist traditions and able to accommodate his extensive, expensive production timescales. (Unsurprisingly, London rarely features as a port of call.)

Wilson seems to have desired a homecoming of sorts. In 1992 he acquired the Water Mill, a disused electronics and communications laboratory in the woods in Long Island, and turned it into a base for artistic workshop and rehearsal activity.[8] The centre is expressly devoted to the production and perpetuation of Wilson's aesthetic. 'Bob has created a shrine for himself – his own Bayreuth,' says John Rockwell. 'What was good for Richard Wagner was good for the rest of the world; Bob's thinking is along the same lines.'[9]

Work on Wilson's *Hamlet* project began in July 1993 with a two-week workshop at Water Mill, followed after a break of some months by a four-week workshop. The project lay fallow for just over a year. There was then a rehearsal period of four weeks at Houston's Alley Theatre followed by two weeks for technical rehearsals.[10] *Hamlet: a monologue* was premiered at the Alley Theatre in May 1995.

Wilson was born and brought up in Waco, Texas, so his association with the Alley was some kind of return to roots. In 1990 he premiered there his adaptation of Ibsen's *When We Dead Awaken* (a co-production with Robert Brustein's American Repertory Theatre at Harvard). The following July Wilson agreed to become an Associate Artist, and his adaptation of *Danton's Death* in 1992 was produced under the theatre's auspices. The co-production arrangement with the Alley for *Hamlet: a monologue* provided a friendly host venue for premiering a new work and afforded Wilson the relative luxury of rehearsal space and resources (human and technical) for part of the development of the show with someone else footing the bill.

And back to the drawing board

Wilson's creative process for *Hamlet: a monologue* began, as with so many of his projects, at the drawing board. 'Bob always works with a structure first,' says co-director and long-term collaborator Ann-Christin Rommen. 'He needs to have a visual book first and the text does not interest him. That's not the first thing.' Wilson first 'storyboarded' a production in 1976, making a series of sketches of the stage pictures of *Einstein on the Beach*, his collaborative project with Philip Glass. These drawings governed the construction of the piece.[11] Since then the visual book has become the central 'text' of Wilson's productions, expressing their structure in spatial and imagistic terms and supplanting any written source.

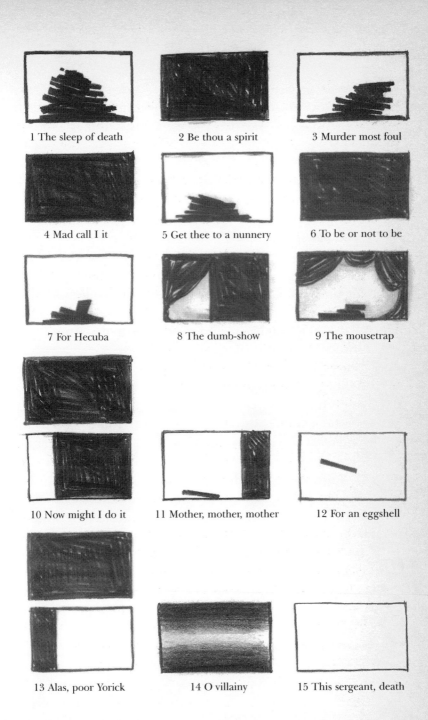

1 The sleep of death 2 Be thou a spirit 3 Murder most foul

4 Mad call I it 5 Get thee to a nunnery 6 To be or not to be

7 For Hecuba 8 The dumb-show 9 The mousetrap

10 Now might I do it 11 Mother, mother, mother 12 For an eggshell

13 Alas, poor Yorick 14 O villainy 15 This sergeant, death

Robert Wilson's storyboard sketches for *Hamlet: a Monologue*, May 1995
(Robert Wilson, courtesy of Byrd Hoffman Foundation)

The 15-scene structure of *Hamlet: a monologue* was suggested by the dramaturg, Wolfgang Wiens. 'I think that just came out of the plot of the play,' says Wiens, casually. Wilson describes his response.

> I made very quickly in one day a kind of sketch, with
> an idea of what it could be, and it stuck . . . this pile of
> rocks that diminishes. I don't know where it came from
> but one day it happened. I thought of the colours,
> mostly of black and white making a formal space, and
> the rocks being dark, and a space in back of the rocks,
> and a kind of blinding light, to suggest different times,
> darker and lighter times. And I really saw that often the
> piece was black on black, and sometimes more light
> and other times more dark.[12]

The storyboard figures the flow and movement of the production in graphic terms (page 159). The pile of rocks diminishes, until the final frame is drawn as an empty white space. I'm reminded of Wilson's airy suggestion, in an interview a year or so before beginning the *Hamlet* project, that 'the furniture can be very large and through the course of the play it can be reduced until it's sometimes very small. There's some kind of structure.'[13] The whittling down of the pile contrasts with the five black frames (two of them paired with an accompanying frame which shows the stage curtain open to different positions). Wilson's first visual gestures, then, outline a diminution from a massed organic structure to nothing; and alongside this a massy blackness which is finally resolved as pure white. You can speculate on the evident relationship to the themes of *Hamlet*. Black is the colour most associated with the play – references to death predominate and Hamlet is initially in mourning for his father. The seeming extirpation of the 'rottenness' of Denmark through the deaths of all the major characters (very) arguably constitutes a movement to 'purity' and emptiness. Deliberately or not, Wilson evokes part of the play's thematics through related (but not literal) graphic representation.

The storyboard also shows the use of the stage curtain to create smaller segments of open stage (scenes 10, 11 and 13), to frame the pile of rocks in an evidently theatrical manner (scene 9) and to stand, precisely, as a stage curtain for the dumb-show section (scene 8), as well as functionally closing off the space in the scenes depicted as black. This familiar item, which usually merely opens and closes to signal the beginning and end of things, is positioned within the set and accordingly *staged*. It offers a constant reminder of the performative nature of the production.

'[A]ll Shakespeare's plays turn, right in the centre,' Wilson observes, with gnostic certainty.[14] His own storyboard for *Hamlet: a monologue* places 'the dumb-show' at the middle of its scheme. If this production turns right in the centre, it does so in a scene depicting speechless playacting.

Wilson also envisaged the presence of two 'columns' representing Hamlet's lover and mother. 'For me there are two pillars in the way I have reconstructed the text,' he says. 'The one is the Ophelia section, and in the mother text.' He refers to Hamlet's 'nunnery scene' exchange with Ophelia – scene 5 in this adaptation – and his exchange with Gertrude in her bedchamber – scene 11. The first is one-third of the way into *Hamlet: a monologue*, the second one-third from the end. The two scenes are located roughly according to their position in Shakespeare's text. In the eventual production Wilson performed repeated actions in both scenes, so that in this respect, at least, they parallel one another more closely. In the final scene he pulls costumes relating to various characters out of a large box. Those of Ophelia and Gertrude he hangs from the pillars of the proscenium arch either side of the stage, making their joint equivalence in his scheme of things and, you might say, their 'column-ness' yet more apparent. In spite of all this it is difficult to imagine that an audience would identify this particular structuring principle. But it is characteristic of Wilson's method: to be governed by pre-determined logics, some of which become evident to the audience only obliquely, if at all.

Wilson suggests that his structures are usually 'classical constructions'.[15] That's debatable – but what he perhaps means is that structural elements in his work can usually be understood according to classical principles of unity, juxtapostion, balance and proportional relationship. They are not designed to produce clear meanings or even to tell stories, which is partly why they seem postmodern rather than classical. The Wilsonian production is certainly organised according to dominant principles. It's just that these offer a different dish than is usually put before us in the theatre.

It's worth emphasising: there is nothing here, on the surface at least, which suggests an interpretative response to the play in terms of its themes, historical resonances, character psychologies or the thousand and one nuances of meaning which usually concern directors. Wilson serves up lashings of form instead. What are the main ingredients? A manner of performance which renounces characterisation, and a visual system which depends upon light, line and colour. The latter derives from what Trevor Fairbrother terms Wilson's

vocabulary of forms . . . The block, the cube, the shaft, the pyramid, and the curtain of light appear either as solids, or, more frequently, as bodies of light defining the darkness. These forms recur in endless variations of scale, mood, and subject, communicating the monolithic solidity of a wall, a room, or a building; the punctuation of space by tree trunks, columns, or giant figures; or the openness of a lake, a desert, a sky, or a window.[16]

This comment is made in connection with Wilson's drawings, but it applies no less readily to his stage-aesthetic. In *Hamlet: a monologue* Wilson presents a massy block upstage centre, a lighted rear cyclorama, shafts of light, and a black curtain which either creates a wall of darkness or, when partially opened, a rectangular segment of light and depth. We are not asked to imagine what Hamlet is suffering or plotting at any particular moment – rather to recognise the way the show is moving forward through its visual and architectural system.

When Jonathan Kalb asked the playwright Heiner Müller whether Wilson could be seen as 'directing' his work, the answer was, 'No, no, he just "utilizes".'[17] This is a nice way of looking at it. Wilson doesn't do anything as obvious or banal as interpret the text. But nor does he ignore it completely. He uses it, just as he 'utilizes' Shakespeare's *Hamlet*. It hardly needs stating that this projects the director as the key creative arbiter, more than merely a fellow traveller with the writer. He works with and alongside (but never according to the dictates of) the written resource. This is one way in which the identity of the director as auteur is guaranteed. In fact it was only in 1984 – after nearly twenty years making his own work – that Wilson first directed a piece conceived independently by another artist, when he staged Charpentier's 1693 opera *Médée*. Since then he has worked on a number of more or less canonical playtexts and operas, including Shakespeare's *King Lear*, Ibsen's *When We Dead Awaken*, Euripides' *Alcestis*, Wagner's *Parsifal* and Puccini's *Madame Butterfly*. In each case, however, the individual stamp of the auteur-director is especially evident. Wilson doesn't so much visit the classics as have them visit him. And when they do, they are quickly laid out on the drawing board.

In the (quiet) rehearsal room

Wilson accorded a certain 'respect' to Shakespeare's text by handing responsibility for its editing to his dramaturg. 'He's a man who has read a lot of books,' says Wilson, 'and we complement each other. I can do something that he can't do and he can do something that I can't do and it works.'[18] Wolfgang Wiens first worked with Wilson on *the CIVIL warS*, and they have now collaborated on a dozen projects. Wiens gave *Hamlet: a monologue* a textual coherence which provided a backbone of a different kind, running alongside Wilson's more drastic abstractions.

'First when he asked me to do it – well, actually he told me to do it – I said, "This is impossible, you can't do it,"' recounts Wiens. 'But he was going to do it. After a month I started, and then after I had the general idea it went rather quickly.'

The 'general idea' which Wiens conceived was the flashback frame, a crucial aspect of the production. *Hamlet: a monologue* begins with a major conceit: that the entire show depicts Hamlet in a moment of limbo before his death, casting back over the events of the play. Wilson plays – better, evokes – a number of characters, but the effect is that they are rolled into a single consciousness. 'I tried to tell the story in a realistic way, if it's possible to do that without knowing the play backwards,' says Wiens. It is hardly surprising that a reflective, first-person treatment is considered more 'realistic' in the late-twentieth-century than a straightforward telling of the story with its out-landish twists. The result is a Craigian Hamlet, a monologuist at the centre of a monodrama.

Knowing that Wilson wanted his pile of rocks to diminish, Wiens allocated scenes to upstage and downstage areas so that when Wilson was downstage the stagehands could prepare the next setting behind a curtain. The longer scenes were those upstage, with Wilson performing directly in relation to his set. Wiens describes the need, in making his adaptation,

> to find texts which [Wilson] could speak as Hamlet which are originally not his [the character Hamlet's] own texts. This was amazing. It's a mixture. Some lines are from Scene 5 of the 4th Act and edited in a scene of the second Act, *et cetera*. It's a complete mixture of texts.[19]

How were these initial ideas and structures developed in rehearsal? Wilson's co-director Ann-Christin Rommen was present throughout the devising, rehearsal and production period. Wiens, lighting designer Stephen Strawbridge and sound designer Hans Peter Kuhn were also largely in attendance. As with Lepage's process, design and technical members of the team are intrinsic to the work from very early on. Wilson's rehearsal room is a place of careful attentiveness and little frivolity. Abbie Katz describes the atmosphere as

> enormously concentrated. It always has to be completely organised, completely quiet. Every time I leave one of Bob's rehearsals or a process with Bob and work with somebody else I always feel as if I'm in the middle of a circus, because nobody else works in such a concentrated manner. And the people who have worked with him for a while understand that that's necessary. So you make sure that everything's in order, everything's been cleaned up, that it doesn't look messy, because that's distracting to him, that there's no talking. I've talked to assistants before we go into rehearsal about their posture, saying, 'No, if you stand like that it's going to disturb him.' . . . If he sees everyone standing properly, dressed neatly, it makes a difference.

This puts me in mind of Wilson's observation that 'Magritte painted in a suit and tie'.[20]

The set design is mocked up at the very beginning of rehearsals. Wilson then develops what he calls 'the book of gestures and movements'. 'We set up something in a small room that could represent the rocks,' says Rommen, 'and he started improvising movements. A lot of these movements from the very early stages are now in the production.' Wilson would perform without the use of the text. The second or third time through an improvisation, Wiens and sometimes Rommen would read in the text to accord with the movements, which Wilson might adapt in relation to the 'score' of the words. Rommen explains:

> He was being given this sound book from the outside, and he did something which was not necessarily illustrating what he was hearing, but was more an essence in his mind of what this scene would be. We would read the text, he did the improvisation and we taped that, and then worked from the video to recreate what was done in the moment. We went back to the rather tedious work of re-learning this kind of improvisation, which then became like a choreography, so you really measure your steps. You know, 'Do I have to stop on my right foot in order to swing around and throw the hat?' Then he had to learn the text with it.

The working method perhaps derives from Wilson's movement classes as a teenager with Byrd Hoffman, a dance teacher and therapist in his home town of Waco. Ms Hoffman would play the piano, Wilson would move his body to the music as he wished.[21] The initial improvisation is developed as performance in its own right – *presence* – rather than as a representation of any particular aspect of the text. As Rommen says, 'I don't think that in the first place the work is developed intellectually, no. It is very much in the body.' And as in Lepage's rehearsal-room, the video cassette supplants the written text as the authoritative resource. It allows Wilson to fix his 'instinct'.

Rommen reflects upon the intrinsic singularity of this procedure:

> In the Ophelia scene, when he is Ophelia – 'What a piece of work is man' – he comes forward, and then he would touch something. And he's very interior in this part of the text. 'And yet to me what is this quintessence of dust?' And I'm never quite sure what he is thinking, and I'm always curious about what he's thinking, and he won't tell me, I won't ask him, and I just hope the audience feels the same way. That there's this mystery, and there's a whole history of a person in the background, it's his history and his memories, and also the ones that he thinks Hamlet and Ophelia might have had.

What's interesting here? 'He won't tell me, I won't ask him.' The production promotes reserve, mystery, a 'freedom' to interpretation where common meanings – even amongst the production team – do not need to be agreed.

*

The production's sound design is developed alongside everything else rather than bolted on later. Wilson and Hans Peter Kuhn first worked together in 1979 on *Death, Destruction, and Detroit (An Opera with Music in 2 Acts. A Love Story in 16 Scenes)*, a show made for the Schaubühne theatre in Berlin, headed at the time by Peter Stein. The pair have since worked on over

30 productions together. Much of Kuhn's work takes place in the rehearsal room where he provides sound from almost the very beginning. He is accompanied by a sound operator, who is responsible for keeping the book of sound cues and playing the music and effects. Initially Kuhn plays live, but since he uses a sequencer – a computer programme that records exactly what he plays on the keyboard – he can store his improvisations and refashion them once rehearsals have finished. As we have seen, Wilson's improvisations are also recorded and learnt. The result is a production process which ascribes value to intuited spontaneity, whilst recording technologies allow authentic 'firstness' to be honed and reproduced.

'We always record,' says Kuhn. 'Very often the first thing is right.' The sound operator plays the recording of this initial version during rehearsals, so that the sound design is always a part of the ongoing development of the piece. Kuhn alters these recordings as he goes, or creates new arrangements if the piece demands it. He works extensively with samples (canned chunks of sound of all kinds which can be manipulated through the computer). The sequencer allows him to play back what he initially records by way of a variety of instrumental sounds and tonal treatments. He can adapt his material by overdubbing parts of the recording with the keyboard, or by altering the programme digitally by changing the readouts on the computer screen.

Kuhn describes his means of designing sound for Wilson's shows as a 'parallel process'.

It really gives the musician a lot of freedom. It creates two parallel worlds happening at the same time – you see something, and of course you hear the text, and then you have this other world which is aural. They run parallel, but not converging, and that gives a very

specific tension. It creates a very specific feel, like
Cunningham or Cage.

That is, the sound design is not necessarily literal or refer-
ential, illustrating what the spectator sees. The sound world
exists in its own terms. That said, Kuhn's sound design for
Hamlet: a monologue is closer to an accompanying score than
might have been expected. 'There's not much discussion [with
Wilson] about what the piece is about,' says Kuhn. 'I usually
set myself a theme, in a way. In this case I thought that having
made a lot of abstract work, I wanted to do something that is
a little bit like a traditional *Hamlet*, a Shakespearean direction
. . . music and not sound.' Kuhn's score combines Renaissance-
style music, period-based instrumental sounds (including
lutes, trumpets and hollow drums) and 'natural' sound effects
(waves, thunder, birdsong, raven-like cawing). In places the
music is closer to parody. It has a vaudevillian strain – Kuhn
acknowledges the influence of German cabaret music and
Kurt Weill – which conveys a cheeky humour alongside the
show's Wilsonian intensity. Wilson asked for sound effects in
scene 8 ('the dumb show': his back 'creaks', for instance, as he
takes a bow), to offset the 'straightness' of the mood, and
asked for the crashes which punctuate the final section of
scene 5 ('get thee to a nunnery'). Kuhn describes them as 'cuts
in the scene'. They are composed of 'all kinds of crashes,
sounds that are very impulsive, percussive, loud and harsh.'
They help to structure the action and provide a texture of
measured cataclysm, a precise evocation of disaster.

In this project, then, Wilson's collaborators found themselves edging closer to representational norms. Kuhn wrote a
different kind of music for the last scene – reflective, melancholic and grand, swelling as the scene progresses, then diminishing. It anchors the performance to a more conventional
sense of the play, as a place where meaningful actions get

resolved. Another paradox lies here in the teetering parallel between a cinematic sound design (cue story and emotion) and visual effects which strike at the heart of realism and meaning.

Wilson spends the last ten days or so dealing in particular with the lighting, a period which Kuhn uses 'to clean up. And I need that, too,' he observes. 'In this piece, if you were to do it on tape recorders, you would need four to five tape recorders and each of them running two to three reels of tape. There's an enormous amount of sound in there.'

Of course Kuhn has at his disposal not tape recorders but minidisks, CDs, computers and samplers, allowing the sound operator to access individual effects and play them at the touch of a button. The greater sophistication of sound tech-nology, especially since the 1990s, allows an increasingly sen-sitive relationship between sound design and staging. This means that the operator can 'play' the show live more easily than in the past, and this is the case here. 'He's doing a live mix every day,' says Kuhn. He has to, as well, accompanying Wilson's movements and observing a rhythm that differs from performance to performance. Such finesse is enhanced by Kuhn's control of the sound environment more generally. His design uses an 8-channel sound system around the audience in addition to the five channels onstage. This means that sound comes to the spectator from a variety of speakers all around the theatre. Every sound cue has its designated speaker, or is spread in due proportion around a combination of speakers. 'It's a complete composition of balances and timings,' explains Kuhn. 'It's like weaving and needs a lot of time to get it organised.' And time, as we have seen, is of the essence.

*

Wilson's proscenium arch productions play knowingly with flatness and depth. The picture is three-dimensional and it moves. And it usually looks sumptuous – thanks, in part, to Wilson's sophisticated command of theatre lighting. *Hamlet: a monologue* is lit by between 300 and 350 lighting units, depending on the size of the stage. A number of these are 'specials' used for specific single effects. According to A. J. Weissbard, the assistant lighting designer:

> It's normal in a Wilson show to have lots and lots of specials. A lot of other directors will work with designers who will make a light plot which is more all-purpose. This one is very specific for specific moments. It's minimal representation. Everything that we need to see we light, and anything that we don't need to see we don't light . . . It's like a painting: put light where you need it and take it away where you don't need it. Simple white light on top of the costumes helps to illuminate them, but we use a filter that matches closely the colour of the prop or the piece, so that it brings out the colour that's already in the material – the blue shoes, the gold doublet. We add more light to that and it punches in the colour. . . . The props on stage get light that hits their colour and their style.

The stage becomes a place of heightened phenomenal identity. Simple props are burnished by the gelled specials so that they glow with an intensity of colour. They are showpieces rather than everyday objects. Wilson observes, not without cause, 'If you know how to light, you can make shit look like gold. I paint, I build, I compose with light. Light is a magic wand.'[22] The luscious colour palette used for props and costumes contrasts with the colder colour temperature accorded to the central performer. Weissbard explains:

Most of the light that lights Bob in this show is a cold light, it's a white light with a slightly blue tint. He has a white make-up, it's certainly a little supernatural. His hands are white. Normally in a Wilson show any skin that's showing becomes white to pick up the light . . . It also helps to stand out against the backdrop. One of the things I've noticed with Bob's work is that he tends to push the identity of everything, so if something is white it becomes very white. . . . White skin, make it very white and push it to the limit. Find the quirks in somebody's behaviour and work with those. If you make a mistake, carry your mistake through, make it all go to the end, finish it. Nothing is an accident and nothing is halfway.

Tight visual focus – unusual in much theatre production – is also emphasised. 'I've worked on other shows with Bob where you have a follow-spot that's on a finger,' says Katz. The lighting design is characterised by a further stylistic trope more usual in dance productions. 'There's actually no front light in this show,' explains Weissbard, 'only for props – with the exception of follow-spots – which is very rare. . . . We felt that would make a mess and would wash things out. It's very simple angles – from above, from the back totally flat, from the side totally straight.'

The effect of this is to create a stage of striking contrasts, where the performer and his props are illuminated with crystalline distinctness. Side-lighting also gives luminescence to the *volume* of stage space. It lights the air. As Wilson moves across the stage he is caught in lit space – which is different from wandering around an illuminated stage. The fact that light is kept off the floor gives the space a buoyancy which holds up the bodies and objects within it. Side lighting further helps to separate the performer from the backdrop. He is a figure within three dimensions.

The lights for the cyclorama are composed of separate banks at the top and the bottom, with red, white, blue and green available, offering a vast range of washes according to the nature of the mix and the timing of gradations of change. There are also fluorescents top and bottom to provide a white-out effect, and a row of lights across the middle for the bar of colour that provides the dominant scenographic effect in scene 14. It is clear that Wilson conceives the visual dynamics of performance with their illumination in mind, although as Weissbard observes, 'the most effective and major part of the [lighting] work and design happens when you're in a theatre. . . . really it comes down to seeing it and having the tools at your fingertips and working in the theatre.'

Wilson took nearly 100 hours to light his production of *Madame Butterfly* at the Opéra Bastille in Paris.[23] That's two-and-a-half weeks' work, in old-fashioned currency. As we've seen, work on lighting during the get-in of *Hamlet: a monologue* takes six days. Such expansive attention means that Wilson's theatre always *looks* like theatre – illuminated, displayed, staged.

Framed

It's worth remarking that the entire text of *Hamlet: a monologue* is drawn from Shakespeare's play. There is no interpolated material from other sources, as was the case in celebrated Wilsonian works like *Death, Destruction and Detroit, the CIVIL warS* and *Einstein on the Beach*, where classic texts provide fragments amongst an undifferentiated mix of elements. 'One has the impression that [Wilson] assimilates and transforms what he reads without having to refer to it in a heavy-handed way,' wrote Julia Kristeva in 1994. 'But obviously he's increasingly interested in intense writing'.[24] In this instance Wilson appears to have found intensity by leaving Shakespeare's text undiluted.

The play is nonetheless given a good stir. According to Wiens, 'Trying to find a first line was the heaviest thing to do.'[25] The search eventually alighted on the phrase 'Had I but time . . . ' which Hamlet utters in his final moments. The production opens with lights gradually fading up on the pile of rocks, with the black-clad Wilson lying on top, his back to the audience, one leg slightly raised and one hand held behind his head, brightly-illuminated palm facing the audience (Image 11). An icy dawn-blue light washes down the cyclorama at the back of the stage. Wilson utters the opening line three times, then says:

> O, I could tell you – but let it be.
> Wretched queen. Adieu!
> I follow thee . . .
> Follow my mother! Drink of this potion!

The text then relays various lines from the duel towards the end of the play, ending with:

> 'Tis bitter cold, and I am sick at heart.
> O, woe is me!
> T'have seen what I have seen, see what I see.

Ophelia's famous couplet here doubles as the key to Hamlet's deathbed flashback. Wilson delivers all these lines slowly, leg raised, whilst displaying his outstretched hand – there is no attempt to present anything as vulgar as duelling actions or dying gestures. The performer then gradually sits up, stands and descends from his perch. There follows the memory (or re-vision) of the Ghost, with:

> Angels and ministers of grace defend us!
> My father, methinks I see my father!

and we are in the established chronology of the play, which Wiens and Wilson observe from here onwards, although the text continues to splice lines out of sequence.

Scene 2 opens with:

Be thou a spirit of health, or goblin damned

which Hamlet utters at his first sight of the Ghost. Wilson performs as if Hamlet sees the spirit before him. The movement from the top of the show, then, is from an abstract treatment in which the lone, tortured soul utters textual segments as if caught in some dreadful obligation, to the acting out of events within the play. The first mode is established as the priority. This is a highly idiosyncratic treatment of the text – whose main recourse, nonetheless, is to a form of intensely subjective reflection. Very 'Hamlet'.

The titular monologue is interior. Hamlet speaks to nobody but himself, obsessively working things out in a bubble of paused time at his point of death, play-acting, fantasising, replaying. The framing device situates Hamlet in an extended moment of memory. Apart from the very end of the show, everything shows him in this purgatorial present. Before he can die he must witness (and reenact) his own story. All the action is located in Hamlet's memory, desire and psyche – a paradox given Wilson's tendency to avoid anything which smacks of individual characterisation and psychological motivation. But this Hamlet is both more and less than an individual. He is a super-existential figure replaying an 'emotion text' of the play.

The flashback concept turns the production into an elongated death spasm. Such delight in morbidity is characteristic, notably in those few pieces in which Wilson performs. His short video work, *The Death of King Lear* (produced by Lois Bianchi for the Byrd Hoffman Foundation, USA, 1989), is

larded with overtones of doomed mortality. The piece includes footage from a black-and-white TV film, *Ages of Man*, in
which John Gielgud, dressed in a suit and tie, plummily
sounds Lear's desperate speech on the heath. This is intercut
with a sequence in which Wilson, also dressed in a suit and tie,
recites William Carlos Williams' poem 'The Last Words of my
English Grandmother'. The piece is less about King Lear and
his death, of course, than a presentation of formal contrasts
and comparisons – the black-and-white of the Gielgud film
and the blue-sky backdrop of the Wilsonian studio; the out-
door setting suggested in both; Gielgud's impeccably phrased,
rolling anglophone delivery and Wilson's slightly drawled
American vocalisation; and not least the tensions between
raging passions in the face of death and its calm report and
evocation. As so often in Wilson's work, what is staged is not
directly the content of the text (in this case revolving around
non-sense and death) but a set of formal constructs that may
have some oblique or even metaphorical bearing on it.

Wilson's 1994 film *La Mort de Molière* (produced by L'Institut
National de l'Audiovisuel and La Sept/ARTE) also has a
morgue-like cool. Wilson, in full period accoutrement, plays
the French playwright as a sickly roué on his deathbed. Where
you might expect echoes of seventeenth-century French comedy Wilson presents instead, with a blank-eyed scrutiny, details
of posture, costume and furniture, filmed by means of slow
and even camera movements within elegantly-lit studio settings. The film's texts, incidentally, were written and chosen
by Heiner Müller.

A repeated action links the staged deaths of these theatrical
figures. Wilson's Molière gives a long scream at one point,
revealing a bloody red interior to his mouth, before subsiding
into a wry smile. In *The Death of King Lear* the besuited Wilson
transmutes the word 'Cordelia' into a scream as he slowly tears
a sheet of newspaper. In *Hamlet: a monologue* the word 'Mother',

uttered four times at the point when Hamlet decides to visit the Queen in her bedchamber, builds to a strangled high-pitched scream. In each case Wilson is careful to stage the scream as something deliberate and controlled, surrounded by silence, 'quoted' by means of its contrast with other aspects of the scene. It becomes a sudden *interruptus* signalling primal horror and, simultaneously, the ironic *presentation* of that horror by the hyper-cool artist.

In each of these deathly scenarios time stands still, since the awareness of impending extinction is staged (albeit coolly) as an explosion of consciousness. The flashback device in *Hamlet: a monologue* further disturbs Shakespeare's organisation of time, but it also secures Wilson's place as the arch-joker of the event. Things have already happened (the story of *Hamlet* has already taken place), so everything is revisited and quoted. And here Wilson both panders to his audience's habits and catches you unawares. We are accustomed to experiencing 'depth' through repetition (rewinding our video, resetting our computer games, watching recycled news bulletins and slow-motion sports replays). Shakespeare's *Hamlet* has been replayed often enough, of course, and is ushered in as the most significant text in the western dramatic canon. *Hamlet: a monologue* uses the 'Replay' mode, but does so with a difference. It *stages* repetition and retrospection, and in the process *un*-stages the play itself. 'The nature of the project is that it's for people who already know the play,' says Wiens. The audience for Wilson's latest pieces – high-culture consumers and cognoscenti – are in the market for Shakespeare-made-strange. Pleasure lies in the teasing oscillation between the familiarity of the material and the novelty of its revision.

The framing concept additionally provides at least three of what Arthur Holmberg identifies as favourite Wilsonian 'images': the outcast (Hamlet, the inevitable loner – further exiled, we might say, from his own play), the journey (Hamlet witnesses his own progress through the events of the play) and the apocalypse (his journey ends inevitably in death).[26] There is another, more abstract, favourite image: the self-possessed iconoclast. One thinks of Sheryl Sutton in *A Letter to Queen Victoria*, Lucinda Childs performing her celebrated dance in *Einstein on the Beach*, or Honni Coles dancing in *When We Dead Awaken*. The black-suited Wilson also performs this type. Coutured, reflective, eccentric and unpredictable, the performer is always in control of his routine, always underscoring the *fact* of performance. His appearance as the Player, wielding a stick and sporting a sticking-tape black patch over one eye (Image 13), distils an effect which is present throughout. The solo nature of *Hamlet: a monologue* marks the production as part-celebration of the one-man show, a piece filled with routines of different kinds, impeccably performed by what the French would call *le comedien*.

On not being Hamlet

Wilson was 54 when *Hamlet: a monologue* opened in Houston, Texas. This might put us in mind of the likes of Kean and Garrick, who continued to play Hamlet when they could have been expected to put in a cameo as his father instead.[27] But the venerable thespians had triumphed in the role in their youth. Wilson was giving his version of the Prince for the first time. What's more, his star-turn came after a period in which he had performed only in short exchanges with longstanding collaborator Christopher Knowles; in the short films previously mentioned; and, in 1994, in his own adaptation of Dostoevsky's story *The Meek Girl*. Wilson appeared in the latter as one of three narrators, each wearing black formal dress. This arch trio 'visited' the story through a texture of quotations in French, German and English (the three actors spoke in their native tongues) whilst presenting a series of choreographed gestures and movements. Wilson's Hamlet, then, was the latest in a personal line of rarefied postmodern performances, and playing a character of any kind – youthful or addled – was hardly part of the director-performer's agenda.

'I wanted to get a less-ordinary Hamlet on stage,' he says. 'Most of the productions I have seen lately have been very conventional. Starting in the late-1940s with Laurence Olivier sitting on stage as if he were sitting in a bus, they have been so ordinary.'[28] In the same interview Wilson states his liking for John Gielgud's Hamlet, a feat of technical control and cerebral coolness. He is also a fan of Marlene Dietrich. 'She could be very cool in one sense – with her body and gestures formal and detached – yet at the same time vocally hot. There was something different going on between what I was seeing and what I was hearing.'[29]

Walking with the unlikely shades of Gielgud at one shoulder and Dietrich at the other, Wilson drew additionally on his own repertoire of techniques. His Hamlet distils over thirty years' worth of Wilsonian performance into the one iconic rendition. Some basic preferences were established at the outset of Wilson's theatrical career. In his mid-twenties he was using his own body as his means of artistic expression in ways which had more to do with contemporary dance than anything remotely like 'acting'. Towards the end of 1967, for instance, he presented his solo piece *Baby Blood* in his loft in Manhattan. According to Trevor Fairbrother, 'Wilson's first entry into the candle-lit space was accompanied by Bob Dylan's electrified blues song "Maggie's Farm"; wearing only a T-shirt he made a teetering walk across an elevated plank, using a giant lollipop as a balancing stick.'[30] Balance and imbalance; a bizarre activity seriously undertaken – the contours of the characteristic Wilsonian self-performance already show through.

The following year – 1968, the year of anti-Vietnam demonstrations in America and uprisings across Europe –

Wilson hosted weekly free-form dancing workshops in his studio. He and his acolytes in the Byrd Hoffman School of Byrds (named after Wilson's eccentric dance teacher in Texas) presented *BYRD woMAN*, an early outcome of the group's involvement with the deaf boy Raymond Andrews.[31] During this piece, 'Bob himself looking maybe like an itinerant hobo in drag [performed] some beautiful weird maneuvering . . . across the hay space and through the other relatively static performers . . . His progress was stop and go in a spastic rhythm.'[32]

In 1973 Wilson performed for the first time with Christopher Knowles, then aged 14, during the run of *The Life and Times of Joseph Stalin* at the Brooklyn Academy of Music. In a semi-spontaneous dialogue between the pair Wilson prompted Knowles to repeat his poem 'Emily Likes the TV'. The strangeness here was not provided by movement or costume but by Knowles's use of language. Diagnosed as autistic, he had struggled with his remedial schooling until he came into contact with Wilson, who relished the boy's highly structured but fractured and disjunctive treatment of words. He was particularly taken with the shapes they made on the page (perhaps, rather, on the 'screen' of Knowles's mind), and with the semi-random distortions they performed on overheard snippets from everyday communication (advertising lyrics and jingles and banal conversational exchanges). Knowles became a member of Wilson's performing troupe of Byrds, and the pair would perform dialogues together at different times subsequently.[33] According to Wilson, Knowles would treat words as entities ripe for manipulation, breaking them down into component parts and repeating or altering this raw material: '[he] was not afraid to destroy the word. The language was really alive, the words were really alive. They were always growing and changing . . . It was really three-dimensional, like in space or something.'[34]

The alternative consciousness of the afflicted boys expressed itself through distinctive structuring principles. Ed Knowles, Christopher's father, described his son's way of seeing as 'highly logical'[35] The shows which Wilson staged during this period remorselessly disturb those patterns, textures and relationships with which the audience might be familiar. This early work is the foundation for Wilson's own performance twenty years later. The strategy is always to present the strangely trammelled. The registers of the everyday – relaxed, easy body positions, gestures directly relating to utterance, 'normal' voicings – are renounced in favour of unorthodox vocal and physical articulations which emphasise their own production as performance. Paradoxically the authenticity of Andrews' and Knowles' special circumstances gave Wilson license to privilege fictionality and artificiality in his stagings – another flourish in his theatrical signature.

In the early part of his career Wilson was interested in movement qualities which emanated from, or expressed, the individual making those movements. According to Bill Simmer, one function of the workshops Wilson held for his group of Byrds in the 1960s 'was to help put people in touch with themselves – with their own bodies – and gradually to remove whatever blocks inhibited their achieving this.'[36]

During the 1970s Wilson's interest in improvised dance was overtaken by a fascination with the precision of routines and the careful calculation of choreographic minuteness. The overlap is illustrated by the movement qualities of Wilson's celebrated postmodern opera *Einstein on the Beach* (1976). The show featured thirty-six performers, whose routinised, automated movements were choreographed by Andrew de Groat. Lucinda Childs devised her own solo dance, a hypnotically repetitive series of steps and arm movements which lasted for half-an-hour. Wilson himself performed a 'torch dance' in which he swooped and swerved around the stage holding a pair of lighted battery torches. The production comes at a pivotal moment in Wilson's career as he moves from the surreal visions and unchecked improvisations of the preceding years to a cooler, more tightly choreographed style whose movement scores resist the rhythms of everyday activity. The liking of apparent randomness and of sudden switches of mood, rhythm or tone, however – so crucial to the effect of the earlier work – has never been supplanted.

In *Hamlet: a monologue* Wilson dovetails both approaches, constructing a disciplined movement score out of his own improvised, idiosyncratic self-expression, and placing it within a highly controlled *mise en scène*. Scene 5 ('get thee to a nunnery') gives a good indication of the results.

Wilson enters slowly, wearing a tall black hat, his hands held in front of him. After some measured and exaggerated turns right and left, he throws the hat offstage-right then, with a jerk, turns away and wafts to the pile of rocks. Elegantly but ridiculously he hitches up his trouser legs. He stands, slides his jacket off, gestures with it (Image 12), eventually throws it over his head and sits again. He moves stage-right, holds up his hand and then performs a low gesture as if throwing something or bidding someone be silent. He ends the section by exiting stage left.

This movement score provides the basis for four variations. A very simple pattern of repetition-and-difference is established. Each time Wilson removes his jacket, for instance, the lining is a different colour. Musical accompaniment plays throughout, although the music is different each time (with the exception of section three, which repeats the music from the first section). The text, taken from Ophelia's description to Polonius of Hamlet's strange behaviour, Hamlet's chastising of Ophelia, and Hamlet's first meeting with Rosencrantz and Guildenstern, is parcelled out across all four sections, so the sequence does have a through-line. *Something* is being developed – not necessarily the *Hamlet*-story.

The first time through, the instrumental palette suggests an oboe with a trombone oompah, a plunking banjo and drum and cymbal accompaniment. The effect is highly parodic. As Wilson sits holding his jacket, he utters Ophelia's lines:

> his doublet all unbrac'd,
> No [Wilson gives a flourish of his head]
>   hat upon his head, his stockings foul'd,
> Ungarter'd and down-gyved to his ankle,
> Pale [He holds his hand to his chin] as his shirt . . .

Wilson 'quotes' the lines, slowly and quite high-pitched. He exits on, 'He seem'd to find his way without his eyes', dragging the last word out in a stretched half-scream.

The second time through, Wilson performs the movement score more slowly as a mime. He is accompanied by a single melancholy oboe-sounding strain, and by his own voiceover in which he delivers Hamlet's lines, 'I have of late, but wherefore I know not, lost all my mirth . . . ' The section ends with the cawing of rooks.

Section three. Wilson is accompanied again by the trombone oompah soundtrack. With a screeching voice, he performs Hamlet's 'get thee to a nunnery' injunctions to Ophelia, with a good deal of vocal swooping, plucking out the word 'Why', twice, for special elongation. The colour-wash on the cyclorama changes throughout this section (blue, yellow, red, blue, white). Wilson's live utterance is intercut with his recorded voiceover of parts of the same speech.

The fourth time around, and the soundtrack is of twittering birds and a gentle musical line with an ambience of foreboding. Wilson/Hamlet shouts 'If thou dost marry I'll give thee this plague for thy dowry . . . ' There is a sound-effect crash, like a crate of glass dropping, as the cyclorama changes instantly from blue to acid-green. This introduces a series of crashes and colour changes which punctuate the text. Wilson runs stage-right to shout '*It – hath – made – me*', emphasising every word, before turning to the audience to say, in a muted voice, 'mad'. Wind effect. Wilson walks back towards centre-stage, now silhouetted against the white cyclorama. He ends the scene running off, shouting 'To a nunnery, go', extending the last word into a long cry. This is followed by the longest crash. The movement score is performed much faster during this and the previous sections.

What does this sequence present to an audience? Firstly, the act of performance. Through an array of devices (repetition, word-mangling, fixed posture juxtaposed with staccato movements) Wilson emphasises that he is delivering a routine. The four sections develop the scene between Hamlet and Ophelia and dwell on the performative ground of Hamlet's condition: play-acting, narcissism, melancholy, instability. The repeated movement score overrides the Shakespeare-material, however. Its different speeds and inflections add to the flavour of idiosyncrasy and, arguably, virtuosity. The different sorts of music, along with the effects taken from the 'natural' world (birdsong, wind, crashes), give the material an emotional colouration which is also deeply ironic. Visual and acoustic motifs – the coloured lining of the jacket, the repeated gestures, the sound-effect punctuations – are trailed like flags, making sure that you read the sequence's structuring principles. Wilson does little to contrive meaningful representation in terms of *Hamlet*'s narrative or themes. If anything, his treatment has traces of stereotype (Ophelia speaks in a fey, girlish voice, for instance), but the staging empties out even this sort of straightforward embodiment of character. If you didn't know the play you'd surely be unable to 'see' two different characters here. Not that that matters. Wilson samples *Hamlet* to produce corporeal, visual and acoustic effects which perform *alongside* latent aspects of the material (and it wouldn't matter what these were). We watch *structure* and *performance* first. The exchange between Hamlet and Ophelia comes a distant second.

The enemy is mimesis, and a long quote from Giancarlo Stampalia's unpublished interview with Wilson conveys the director's perspective.

> I hate naturalism. I think naturalism has killed theatre. I'm interested in what's artificial; I think that an actor who tries to act natural on stage is lying, because to be on the stage is something artificial; so if you accept it as something artificial, in a strange way you can be more natural about what it is that you are doing. I think the stage is different from the street, it's different from the restaurant, it's different from the earth, from a private house. To be on stage is something special; the stage space is like no other space. . . . the way you stand is different, the way you sit is different, the way you walk is different, because it's a stage. And it's something that you have to learn, the way you learn anything. . . . even if you want to sit in a naturalistic way, it's something you have to learn. So in that sense it's artificial. And not until we become really mechanical can we be free. And the more we repeat something, perhaps the freer we are. The first time you ride a bicycle it's awkward, but after a while you can do it and think about something else. . . . So I think that naturalism comes in a strange sense from being mechanical, through a formal approach to theatre.[37]

You can see the contours of a loosely Brechtian approach to acting: a respect for physical precision, for intellectual coolness and for a heightened register of presentation which calls attention to itself precisely as performance. It is no surprise to find Wilson lamenting elsewhere the lack of proper physical training for Western actors and expressing his admiration for the gestural modes of classical Japanese theatre.[38] There are shades here of Brecht's fondness for the stylised performance exemplified by the dinner-jacketed Chinese actor Mei Lan Fang on that celebrated evening in Moscow in 1935.[39]

Something of Wilson's own Brechtian performance style is explained by his use of a prompter during performances. Not trusting himself to learn all his lines for *Hamlet: a monologue*, Wilson employed Thomas Lehmann as his stand-in and prompter. The pair first worked together when Lehmann, then a student at the Ernst Busch Theatre School in East Berlin, performed in Wilson's production of Gertrude Stein's opera *Dr Faustus Lights the Lights* (1992), and he was a co-narrator in *The Meek Girl*. Lehmann acts as Wilson's doppelgänger during the get-in, standing in for him while the lights are focused. During the performance he reads the text to him through a discreet earpiece. He has a pronounced German accent, so Wilson must translate this Bardic prompting into his own vernacular before opening his mouth to speak. The entire arrangement is splendidly inimical to anything resembling a Method-based approach to playing Shakespeare.

The resulting 'quotation' of theatrical playing is precisely the thing that offended some critics. Clive Barnes, the prominent New York theatre critic, found Wilson's solo performance 'self-indulgently smug'.[40] Margo Jefferson provides a plaintive critique which Brecht himself might have relished. She suggests that Wilson

doesn't have great resources as a performer; his face, voice and body comment on emotion without containing or really expressing it. You felt that you were watching a workshop in which a fiercely intelligent director laid out his conception of the play. Of course you want to

> observe a theatrical intelligence at work, but you
> couldn't help thinking, why doesn't he stop now and
> turn it over to a real actor?[41]

A real actor might be expected to do some 'real' acting. He might find a through-line of motivations, a journey for the character and present the audience with a plausible individual – the paraphernalia of the psychological realism which Wilson's theatre so decidedly renounces. Instead, the manifestly artificial performance is part of a larger project: to underscore the theatricality of the event so that the audience is brought smack up against form and theatrical function. This is more than merely theatre. Wilson produces hyper-theatre – and a good deal of sweat and labour goes into its making.

Hyper-theatre and the theatre theatrical

Scene 10 ('now might I do it') begins with the traveller curtain open across a fifth of the stage. Hamlet, seeking out his mother, notices Claudius at prayer. In Wiens's version, Hamlet's reflections on this sudden discovery are spliced with Claudius's anxious mutterings.

> But soft, behold – who's there? – the King –
> 'O, my offence is rank, it smells to heaven –'
> Now might I do it, pat, now a 'is a-praying –
> 'The eldest curse – a brother's murder –'

Wilson's Hamlet notices Claudius as if the king is positioned behind the traveller curtain. He speaks Hamlet's line, then steps behind the curtain to speak Claudius's line, alternately stepping in and out of the audience's view. 'It is not that he is playing the King, but that he is quoting,' says Wiens. 'He is glimpsing what the King is doing and he is quoting the text of the King.'

Claudius's lines are delivered with studied anguish. What the audience can't see is that, far from performing such anguish as if in role, even though out of view, Wilson is having his face dabbed by the make-up artist, her assistant at hand holding her effects. It is a nice behind-the-scenes image. The backstage team springs into action to maintain the pristine appearance of the star, who remains in full performative mode whilst taking time out, metaphorically speaking, for a quick fix-up in front of the mirror.

The scene demonstrates the tension between the meticulous image presented to the audience and the scrabbling effort which goes into its manufacture. Throughout its course the curtain travels along a wire, so slowly as to be almost imperceptible, so that the stage is gradually opened and the site of Claudius's concealment reduced. The effect looks from the auditorium to be mechanised, as if the curtain is controlled by an engine which turns a pulley at a constant rate. In fact two stagehands at either side of the stage manually operate the pulley wires, whilst three of their colleagues crouch behind the curtain, straightening its folds as it slowly travels across the space, with the make-up artists retreating slowly so as to remain out of view. It hardly needs stating that this scene requires a fair amount of rehearsal to attain the smoothness that renders its timing precise and its operation invisible. It is a characteristically low-tech solution for a sophisticated-looking staging.

Towards the end of the scene Hamlet decides not to kill Claudius while he is at prayer. Wilson stands in front of the curtain, his back to the audience. He turns holding a sword, where before he had been empty-handed. Behind the curtain, one of the stagehands has slid the sword under the drape and into Wilson's hand – an obvious sleight, but neatly turned.

As Katz observes, 'It always feels like Bob takes these really old mechanics of theatre and finds ways to reinvent it and make it look really new and interesting.' Only the fly-rock (the slab on which Wilson is discovered, in mid-air, in Scene 12) is mechanically operated. Everything else – the contour drop which descends to frame the dumbshow scene, the rock-pallet (a small-scale model of the stage, flown in for the dumb-show), the traveller curtain, the tilting rock which slowly rises to stand perpendicular – is manually operated.

Each of these effects requires the spectator to recognise the 'hyper-theatrical'. They are not intrinsic to the meaning of a scene. Instead they *display* the theatricality of the show. Wilson's work is not, on the whole, metatheatrical. That is, aspects of the staging do not draw attention to themselves in order to point metaphorically to another field of meaning. Think of Shakespeare's treatment of the Players' arrival in *Hamlet*, which cues Hamlet's attempt at an impromptu perfor-mance and his eulogy of the First Player's talents. In slightly different vein, consider the appearance of the *deus ex machina* in Brecht's *The Threepenny Opera*, trotting in on his horse. In each case the play foregrounds the delightful operations of theatre (histrionic skills, staging panache) and the audience understands all the more swiftly the import of the things they are standing for (sincerity, simulation, royal pardon, [in]justice). Wilson's shows are not theatre *about* theatre, or theatre whose theatricality stands for larger issues of reality, illusion, pret-ence and performance. Theatrical effects are not there to pro-duce meaning. They are there to produce an *experience* of the theatrical.

In *Hamlet: a monologue* the flying slab and the rising rock are hyper-theatrical. The flying slab is suspended through the mechanics of stage wires and pulleys. The rising rock moves throughout the duration of a scene. Neither 'mean' anything in particular. Instead their function is to express their own theatreness. Wilson continually produces hyper-theatrical effects of this kind. In Scene 13 ('alas, poor Yorick'), for example, the lights fade up to reveal three skull-like objects on the floor and a shovel at an angle as though it is half stuck in the ground. Its handle, about six feet in height, is unusually long. At one point Wilson picks up the shovel, which is evidently on a stand, then places it on a different part of the stage. A little later he glides across the floor. So does the shovel, following his direction of movement. How did that happen!? We remember that Wilson moved the shovel in the first place, and there were no strings attached, so its independent movement is all the more surprising. In fact there *are* strings attached, although not to the shovel itself. Wilson places it on a small piece of carpeting with a smooth underside, indistinguishable from the rest of the stage covering. This is attached to a string which one of the stagehands holds. At the appropriate moment the device is pulled by the concentrating crewman and the shovel moves.

The trick works because of its illusionist nature. Wilson does not attempt, in Brechtian fashion, to unmask his secrets or to display the mechanics of the staging. Instead his control over the image and preservation of the mystery of its achievement is near-complete. The gliding shovel serves no immediate function in the graveyard scene. It does resonate with various themes in both play and production, to do with unorthodox behaviour and playful irresponsibility, but that might be stretching a point. It is an emblem of the hyper-theatricality of Wilson's work – a purely theatrical effect, only possible on the stage and through the devices of staging, full of its own staginess, empty of any other immediate signification. It celebrates the pure spectacle of the theatrical, with no other purpose than to display its own eye-catching presence as a theatrical device. It is a sign of gratuitous theatrical capability.

The wise-dreaming baby

Wilson has often talked about his dislike of 'interpretation' on the part of directors and performers, and his fondness for leaving things up to the audience. 'Theatre that imposes an interpretation is aesthetic fascism,' he says. 'By emptying out the meaning of a sentence, the text becomes full of meaning – or meanings. . . . in my theatre, the audience puts it all together, and each person puts it together differently. And each night the play is different. The audience makes the meaning.'[42] Utterances like this have led to the rather uncritical consensus that 'Wilson lets the public think'. What does the public think about? Surely thinking happens where there are provocations to thought? The effect of much of Wilson's theatre, by contrast, is to let the mind drift, to allow you to remain thoughtless.

Open-minded or empty-headed? For Wilson, the two are perhaps not so far removed. This, at least, is the premise of a favourite notion: the Socratic idea that one should aspire to a state of innocent wisdom, like the new-born baby who knows everything. The baby's pristine knowledge is lost in the process of acculturation. The task, then, is to 'unlearn' in order to approach wisdom. Wilson frequently couples this thought with another musing: 'A baby is born dreaming. I wonder what just-born babies have to dream about.'[43] This preoccupation with the uncorrupted, wise-dreaming baby is repeated often enough to indicate its central place in Wilson's thinking. It is one with his leaning towards dreamlike modes and interior mental landscapes, and disabling of clear meanings.

Invited to respond to an alphabetical list of words relating to his theatre, Wilson's entry under 'E' was 'Enfance = Genius recovered at will'.[44] According to the Socratic principle, genius involves the unlearning of that which we have learned, shedding the skin of our culture and education. Once experienced, genius can be recaptured again and again by the person who learns how to *un*think. According to Abbie Katz, if Wilson wants feedback in the rehearsal room, 'there's a tendency, certainly in the workshop sections, to invite contributions from whoever he thinks is the most naïve person there. So if there's a fairly alert child working on a production, I've noticed that he'll often say, "Well, what do you think of such-and-such?"' Wilson listens to the (inner) child. He produces himself as the dreaming baby every time a new task is at hand, but does so with the scrupulous rigour of a master craftsman. The naïf (Wilson) responds to various stimuli in primal and unpremeditated ways. The stage-magus (Wilson again) figures these responses in formal arrangements of colour, shape, architectural structure, gesture and utterance. Wilson's hyper-theatre doesn't need to be thought about or understood by a spectator, simply *experienced*. Form is visceral. The audience witnesses – and is sensually engaged by – the shaping of the instinctive and pre-rational. This is a kind of postmodern expressionism, revolving around the skilful naïvety of the artist. What it offers, however, is not a closed world of subjective individuality (for the 'I') but a repertoire of sensuous visual images (for the eye). And these images make you feel rather than think.

'Bob treats a text like a piece of furniture,' observed Heiner Müller appreciatively. 'He doesn't try to break it up or break it open or try to get information out of it or meaning or emotion. It's just a thing.'[45] It is a profoundly individualistic approach, although the results connect with other sorts of theatre. In Wilson's case, theatre-making depends upon the single vision of the infantly-dreaming artist, whose belligerent naïvety is its own defence against charges of mystification, indulgence and plain unreason. You cannot brook Wilson's vision, for it is self-authenticating. Only Robert Wilson (guru-initiate) can produce the theatre of Robert Wilson.

Müller suggests that 'Bob achieved what Brecht only dreamed of doing: the parting of the elements. Bob's theatre offers a more complicated pleasure than normal theatre.'[46] To its advocates this complicated pleasure comes down to a talent for formal patterning which provokes a kind of dumb joy. The first question is not, 'What is it about?' nor even, 'How is it structured?' but, 'What does it do with me?' The initial answer is that the hyper-theatrical offers an encounter with particular qualities of time, space, colour, light, movement, sound and utterance which *take* us. We are engaged without knowing anything. For his part, Wilson insists that theatre is not merely a seeing-place (to invoke *theatre*'s Greek etymology) but a *feeling* place.

> I think theatre is not something that has to be intellectual, something that you have to think about in [the] mind; this theatre is boring. It's a big bore. Theatre is something that you experience and experiencing something is a way of thinking. You don't experience something just with the mind but with the body: I'm moved; I'm touched; I feel something. My body feels it, it's not just with my head. So it's a kind of balance that exists but the experience is most important.[47]

Wilson means this formulation with regard to both performers and spectators. One issue for Wilson-watchers is whether *Hamlet: a monologue* makes you experience things in any significantly new way. I can't see that it does, particularly if you are already familiar with Wilson's output. It neatly distils a number of Wilsonian tropes. On the other hand it seems curiously familiar in its arch mannerisms, repetition of actions and tidy organisation of space. Familiar, and yet different – softer.

Wilson closes the show by pulling costumes relating to various characters from a costume box, upstage-left, and arranging them on the forestage (Image 15). Each item has its own lighting special, and the different objects almost float on the stage. Wilson then flings everything upstage and kneels. The lights are taken out except for a spotlight on the performer's whitened face. Underscored by a reflective instrumental, Wilson speaks a version of Hamlet's final lines (including lines interpolated from Horatio's tribute), ending with:

> Had I but time, as this fell sergeant, Death,
> Is strict in his arrest. O. I could tell you –
> But let it be – the rest is silence.

And Wilson turns and walks upstage into the blackness. It seems strangely obvious to end on this resonant line (Lepage made the same decision). Of course the rest will not be silence at all, as everyone knows. Applause fills the auditorium.

I find this last image touching, and wonder why. The single actor, only his face showing, speaks, stops, stands, turns away and enters the darkness. It all seems so simple – a stripped-down ritual of ending. The finale fits the play. The Hamlet-performer enters oblivion. And again, how paradoxical. In the age of Hollywood movies, television and Robert Wilson, the postmodern, high-art, Eurocentric, difficult, brilliant, anti-populist, late-surrealist Wilson concludes with a different signature. Closure is achieved. Meaning leaks out. Shakespeare's *Hamlet* leaks out. The showman's grace-note is a gesture of modesty. It is difficult to know whether this is another turn in Wilson's career, or the result of a sort of artistic menopause, or neither, just an obvious way to finish.

Hamlet • the director's cut

5

Hamlet • the director's cut

' . . . the theatre must not forever rely upon having a play to perform,
but must in time perform pieces of its own art.'

Edward Gordon Craig[1]

Reprise

As I write, there are productions of Hamlet in the repertoires
of the National Theatre in London and the Royal Shakespeare
Company in Stratford. Another two notches on the Shakespearean scoreboard. When Peter Brook, Robert Lepage and
Robert Wilson turned to Shakespeare's best-known work, they
did so in full knowledge of its gleaming theatrical currency.
Perhaps that's why in *Elsinore, Hamlet: a monologue* and *Qui Est
Là* they chose not to stage the play itself. They engage with it
but do more besides. They step outside the play's numinous
shadow to present new works. The titles of the three shows
make it clear that none offers a straightforward version of
Hamlet, but they also advertise their closeness to their source.
Of course each of the variations is, precisely, a variation. It still
needs a *Hamlet* to make the variation possible. The shows are
drenched in this spirit of revision. They are fascinated with

the very stuff of reassessment, of not taking the original for granted. After all, what is *Hamlet*? It is easy to forget that it is a five-act revenge tragedy written in blank verse in about 1600, which runs for over four hours. The play is hardly ever presented in its raw form. It is jumbled and sprawling. It absolutely demands alteration.

In the opening chapter to this book I visited some historical adaptations of *Hamlet*. The alterations made by Brook, Lepage and Wilson are different again. For a start, they are made at the end of the twentieth century. Their time is different. Inevitably, they are shaped by an evolving culture. There are another three twentieth-century staging posts which allow a shorter perspective on the trio of *Hamlet*-variations, before we take a final audit. None are actual productions of the play. One is a building: the new Globe Theatre on London's South Bank. The other two are critical texts about Shakespeare, which relate directly to trends in Shakespearean production: Harley Granville Barker's *Prefaces to Shakespeare* and Jan Kott's *Shakespeare our Contemporary*. We have been concerned, from start to finish, with theatre practice, and the three are milestones in this respect. They are situated at 1927, 1962 and 1996, although each is preceded by several years of development. They illustrate some of the shifts in what's thinkable and performable since the rise of modernity – the shifts which make possible the contemporary variations on *Hamlet*. Between them they help show up the theatrical innovations of the shows by Brook, Lepage and Wilson, and some of their continuities. We can then look more closely at common principles in the three renderings of *Hamlet*, and at the broader implications for contemporary theatre practice. A leitmotif throughout has been the pleasure of the audience, and this emerges as a dominant theme by the end of the chapter.

Shifting Shakespeare and the gathering postmodern

In 1927 Harley Granville Barker published the 'Introduction' to his *Prefaces to Shakespeare*, a critical project which preoccupied the author until his death in 1946. Uncelebrated now in many quarters, Barker was pre-eminent in his time as an actor, playwright and director. In his own Shakespearean productions, especially those shortly before the First World War, he put into practice some of the tenets of William Poel's Elizabethanism, overseeing clearly-spoken, ensemble-based productions on an apron stage, with Shakespeare's scenic fluidity unimpaired by cumbersome sets and scene-changes. At the same time he pursued the implications of the new realism in a way which spanned Stanislavsky's concern with characterisation and Brecht's awareness of the importance of stripped, meaningful action. As with Stanislavsky, Barker devoted his later years to extensive writing. The *Prefaces* come over as the work of a theatre professional for theatre practitioners, even where they draw upon scholarship and criticism. They codify a pragmatic response to Shakespeare which, whilst of its time, exemplifies the perspective of a good number of directors ever since.

Barker writes in glowing terms of Shakespeare's felicity with language, and champions verse-speaking where it conveys sensitivity to both the meaning of the words and the music which they express. But his Shakespeare is a playwright first, a poet second. For Barker, Shakespeare's plays are blueprints for performance, and were made as such. Shakespeare 'found himself . . . learning his playwright's trade amid the comradely give-and-take of the common theatre workshop . . . he was the genius of the workshop. What he learned there was to think directly in terms of the medium in which he worked'.[2] Barker is at pains to insist, nonetheless, that he isn't after an exact copy of the conventions of staging in force in

Shakespeare's time. In his view, a workshop-based Shakespeare created texts which demand workshop-like rehearsal,
in tune with prevailing conditions of theatre practice.

In spite of this, Barker might not have cared much for the
three shows which we're discussing. After all, he looked ask-
ance at 'production of Shakespeare according to this or that
even more irrelevant theory of presentationalism, symbolism,
constructivism or what not',[3] thereby dismissing a legacy
which includes Craig and Meyerhold. But the point is largely
about the perils of making Shakespeare according to theor-
etical fashion rather than theatrical verve, and in this respect
it is well made. For Barker's project is to save Shakespeare
from the scholars – more, from the bookshelves of a public
which was content to read Shakespeare – and celebrate him as
a playwright who 'must always be most alive – even if roughly
and rudely alive – in the theatre'.[4] How similar to the spirit
which informs the belligerent refashionings of Brook, Lepage
and Wilson at the other end of modernity's spectrum.

The strategies differ widely, however. Barker attempts to
imagine himself into Shakespeare's intentions, in order to
deduce the theatrical interpretations which Shakespeare had
planned. His project, then, is explicitly one of recuperation,
getting back to the unvarnished heart of the Shakespearean
drama. Barker analyses each of Shakespeare's plays to impute,
from the text, the intended Bardic staging. It is a sort of
criticism which is both pragmatic and idealistic, based on
close reading of the text in order to conjure theatrical solutions from the head of its maker. In the *Preface to Hamlet*
Barker argues that Shakespeare's art is to do chiefly with
characterisation, and the way in which characters are shaped
up for the spectator. The actor, identified with the character,
is kept in close relationship with the audience. The task for
theatre-makers is to be true to what Shakespeare intends for
his characters. Barker praises Shakespeare for discarding

'artifices' – perhaps the kind of 'pageantry' which Lepage and Wilson lean towards. His Shakespeare offers rich pickings for actors dealing with character, rather than directors dealing with *mise en scène*. And herein lies the shift in emphasis in cutting-edge theatre from one end of the century to the other.

Barker's modernist reading of Shakespeare is founded on principles of the new realism and psychological veracity. It is post-Freudian, confidently resting upon a notion of the deep subjectivity of individuals, which the actor taps into. And it is pre-Structuralist. Barker assumes that language means what language says. This is how he arrives through Shakespeare's words at Shakespeare's mind. A generation or so later structuralist critics were arguing that, far from being transparent, language operates through meaning-generating structures which conceal all sorts of fissures and glitches. Words slip, meanings slide, whether their authors know it or not. The notion of concerning yourself with Shakespeare's intention, let alone being able to deduce it in the first place, would eventually be deemed a basic schoolboy error. Brook, Lepage and Wilson, along with a host of their contemporaries, do not break stride to worry about what Shakespeare meant at any particular page. Barker cannot share this perspective. His approach to Shakespeare is founded on a more secure sense of Original Meaning. For Barker, Hamlet is fundamentally understandable, and so is Shakespeare, if we learn to unlock his art.

In *Shakespeare our Contemporary*, published in Polish and French in 1962, the Polish scholar Jan Kott implicitly realises that this is a fallacy. Shakespeare is so broad, so multifarious, that a completely comprehensive reading will escape even the most adroit disciple. Instead Kott celebrates the flexing of interpretative muscle on the part of latter-day directors of Shakespeare. 'What matters,' according to Kott, 'is that through Shakespeare's text we ought to get at our modern experience, anxiety and sensibility.'[5] Kott writes about a production of *Hamlet* that he saw in Cracow in 1956; the year that John Osborne's *Look Back in Anger* was premiered at London's Royal Court Theatre. This was also the year of Brecht's death, and of the visit of the Berliner Ensemble to London which so impressed Kenneth Tynan. Osborne's play, featuring its Hamlet-like complainer, Brecht's mature productions, the Cracow *Hamlet* – all were deeply committed to social commentary. Kott celebrates the Cracow production precisely for its limitation of focus. It was, he says, a political drama through and through, concerned with the rottenness in the state of Denmark and therefore concerned with questions of political organisation and resistance. Kott concedes that the production was necessarily simplified but notes that 'this interpretation was so suggestive that when I reached for the text after the performance, I saw in it only a drama of political crime . . . Hamlet is mad, because politics is itself madness, when it destroys all feeling and affection.'[6]

Kott's 'Hamlet of the Mid-Century' appeared in a book which helped define Shakespearean production in Europe and America in the 1960s. *Shakespeare our Contemporary* directly influenced the work of Giorgio Strehler in Milan, for instance, and that of Peter Brook and Peter Hall with the Royal Shakespeare Company in England. Brook's 1962 production of *King Lear*, a nihilistic Beckettian treatment of the play, drew directly upon Kott's essay '*King Lear*, or Endgame', and the company's tour to Eastern Europe in 1964 gave a fresh impetus to Soviet productions of Shakespeare. Kott eulogised Shakespeare as a technician, a writer whose organisational skills allowed a savagely even-handed world-view to take shape with compelling dramaturgical force. He offered an exciting vision of the modernity of Shakespeare, a playwright whose work was relevant to audiences if that relevance was looked for and shaped. At that particular historical moment,

Shakespeare's contemporaneity was largely to be found in a continuum of lacerating bleakness: 'Shakespeare – Cruel and True', as Kott titled his essay on Brook's 1957 production of *Timon of Athens*. In his 'Preface' to *Shakespeare our Contemporary*, Brook observes that, as a Pole living in a police state, Kott writes 'about Shakespeare's attitude to life from direct experience'.[7] Shakespeare's attitude seems a lot more benevolent to theatre-makers, Brook included, a generation later. Certainly the harsh pessimism which Brook's *King Lear* conveyed is largely absent from the *Hamlet*-variations, which play games with Shakespeare rather than have him represent such a remorselessly single vision of the world.

Kott is writing at a time when the principles of post-structuralism were beginning to take hold, but before the fuel-injection supplied by the various events of 1968. Shakespeare, at this point, has not yet been completely deconstructed, politically inverted, emptied of meaning altogether and hung out to dry. Kott's Shakespeare is still in one piece, his plays articulating a coherent world-view. Kott nonetheless finds that other currents run through the plays than those which might appear at first sight, and this is where his scholarship bears directly on staging practice. Coursing through Shakespeare, like an underground stream, is the throughline of our own modern experience. It is up to directors to divine such streams and have us drink from them. Such a vision asks for a direct – and very evidently directed – transcription of play-world into production, which partly explains why Kott has a claim as 'the Shakespearean critic with the greatest influence on the stage'.[8] His critical method embodies what he later described as a post-World-War-Two leaning towards 'an ideological and philosophical emphasis on contemporary interpretation in Shakespeare; an emphasis on thematic content, on what these plays mean and should mean to modern audiences'.[9] We have clearly passed another turning point, for the *Hamlet*-variations of the 1990s, Brook's included, have no taste for such a prescription. Kott's approach to Shakespeare depends on extrapolating social relevance and mapping it against the concerns of the present. His Hamlet is explicitly defined by latter-day history and politics.

Fast-forward another three decades. London's Globe Theatre, close to the Bankside site of its Renaissance predecessor, opened in 1996, a shade after *Elsinore, Hamlet: a monologue* and *Qui Est Là* had gone before their public. The project's architects attempted, as far as possible, to replicate the shape and substance of the original theatre which had accommodated the Lord Chamberlain's Men and, between 1599 and 1608, housed the premieres of many of Shakespeare's plays. So the new Globe is a polygon made of twenty sides, has a diameter of 100 feet and rests on foundations built with specially made bricks to match the dimensions of Tudor brickwork. The reconstruction is as scrupulous as you could wish in dealing with both knowable and disputed details, down to its painstakingly thatched roof and hand-turned balustrades.[10]

Of course the theatre is not quite as it was in Shakespeare's day. The roof houses a sprinkler system, for instance, and parts of the site are marked with plaques and logos celebrating the involvement of corporate sponsors. Facts like these, and the eery cleanliness of its forecourts and buildings, mean that the Globe quivers with the tensions between a yearned-for past and an inescapable present. As an experiment in the effects of a certain kind of theatre architecture (the circular auditorium, the thrust stage with its entrances, pillars and balcony) and playing conditions (the presence of groundlings, the fact of performance in daylight without theatrical lights) the project has value. In particular it furnishes actors with challenges which can be factored into their work in other environments.[11] Nonetheless, the warm hand of nostalgia rests upon the reconstructed theatre. The project is doomed always to be looking over its shoulder to a past which in many respects we can only guess at. Doomed, as well, to the associations that follow in its wake as 'a created heritage structure'[12] – a place inherently touristic in nature, and most intrinsically artifical where it attempts to be most authentic.

Contrast this with the drive towards innovation in *Elsinore*, *Hamlet: a monologue* and *Qui Est Là*. Part of the allure of the three revisions is their blatant renunciation of nostalgia and their independence from the heritage industry, even whilst they can't help but be part of it, Shakespeare being Shakespeare. These two zones of turn-of-the-century Shakespeare – recuperation and revamp – are not as far apart as they seem, however. The Globe is an artful sampling of ancient elements to create something which is inescapably of its moment. This well describes the three variations on *Hamlet*. They too are caught up in postmodernism's drive towards historical synthesis. There is a more functional connection between these two sorts of Shakespearean project, however, and it is to do with the pleasurable involvement of the spectator. The Globe offers an experience of Shakespeare which is supposed to be close to the experience of theatregoers in Shakespeare's day. You might think that, just as we cannot know what Shakespeare himself meant at every turn, we cannot hope to recapture what it was like to go to one of his plays at the beginning of the seventeenth century. That misses the point. The Globe's ersatz version of 'original' Shakespearean theatre allows the audience to play along with the fiction. We get a feeling of involvement in an event, even if we know all along that the feeling is fake. It might look as though the Globe transports us to the past, but (and this is its fatal contradiction) its purpose hinges on our presence in the here-and-now of the building itself. The new Globe's approach to Shakespeare is to make him available for participatory tourism. It offers its customers an experience.

These three twentieth-century staging posts – Psychological Hamlet (a subject in language), Political Hamlet (a subject in history) and Late-Postmodern Hamlet (the subject as consumer) – point the way to the contemporary remakings of Shakespeare by Brook, Lepage and Wilson. The shift lies partly in the audience's direction. Where previously we understood Hamlet as a person, then understood his connectedness with our own circumstances, we are now consumers of the event of which he is merely a part. We go to the theatre to be entertained, and this is where the three directors score. They offer audiences an exciting here-and-now experience of theatre itself. We cannot go back to the past, however much we pretend. If we could, we may well find ourselves bemused by Harley Granville Barker's production of *The Winter's Tale* in 1912, or by the Cracow *Hamlet* of 1956 – even by the Chamberlain's Men production of *Hamlet* in 1600/01. It's a nice game, to imagine the shows we wish we had seen. Culture shifts, however, and takes us and our entertainments with it. We respond to work which is stamped with the press of our own moment.

Elsinore, *Hamlet: a monlogue* and *Qui Est Là* cut their cloth accordingly. The three productions show little or no concern for Shakespeare's 'intention', regardless of whether or not it can be divulged. They do not attempt a return to 'authentic' Shakespearean performance conditions or staging conventions. Brook, Lepage and Wilson decisively relocate theatre as an activity for practitioners in modern workshops. They share Barker's concern with dramaturgical fluidity, although they necessarily move away from the psychological realism which is his mainstay. They place their characters within the evident frames of the production. The word gives way to the workshop, and realism gives way to theatrical gamesmanship. What would you see if you reached for the text after a performance of one of the three *Hamlet*-variations? Certainly not what Jan Kott saw when he did the same after watching the

Cracow *Hamlet*. More likely, you'd see a drama of subjective reflection, pretence and performance. For Kott, '*Hamlet* is a drama of imposed situations, and here lies the key to modern interpretations of the play.'[13] The protagonist is trapped not only by his personal history but by his historical moment. The variations by Brook, Lepage and Wilson are not marked with the same drive for interpretation, nor even with the same sense of social disablement. Quite the opposite. They are filled with signs of capability – whether it is performers running the show, feats of technical bravado or, simply, figures who think. The 'social energy' displayed by the three variations is not that which impelled the Cracow *Hamlet*.[14] Shifting again, Shakespeare has become a different sort of contemporary.

Or rather, different sorts. He cut two contrasting figures in 1996, wearing the fashion of the seventeenth century and that of the twenty-first. Unlike the Globe Theatre project, the *Hamlet*-variations are not designed solely to promote Shakespeare. They trade on the Bardic name, for sure, but they displace Shakespeare in favour of their own independent vision. They give off an identity as exclusive events which are not in any way copies of the past. There is an implicit resistance to standardisation. The Globe is similar in this respect – it is a one-off, although here too it is doomed, for the Globe is reproducible. There are Globe Theatres in Tokyo and Texas and another mooted for Berlin. The *Hamlet*-variations are distinctly singular. They might be influential, but they simply cannot be copied. This uniqueness, this utter newness, is part of their contract with the audience. And as touring productions by internationally renowned directors, they are also distinctly for international consumption.

Hamlet **made over**

What happens to *Hamlet* in this altered landscape? It goes without saying that the three productions are very different, one from another, and it's worth repeating that in *Qui Est Là* Brook wanted to stage theatrical issues which the play helps illustrate, rather than stage the play itself. Even so, these three approaches to the world's most celebrated playtext share some revealing tendencies. In reshaping the play for contemporary audiences, Brook, Lepage and Wilson make selections. Some parts of it appear a lot more interesting than others. The same or similar choices, made three times over, point to something larger than personal preference or the chance of the rehearsal room. They show those features of *Hamlet* which excite a contemporary pulse. These shared responses are what concern us here.

Common selections from the play include four cornerstones: the Ghost, Hamlet's dysfunctional family relationships (with Claudius, Gertrude and Ophelia), the graveyard and the question of 'acting' in order to create an effect. That is, the return of the dead father, the collapse of love, the place of death and the business of pretence. The pressing concerns of the three productions are with respect, trust, death and make-believe. In each, the Ghost is (to Hamlet) very believable. Hamlet is brutal in his abruptness with Ophelia (in the nunnery scene) and Gertrude (in the Queen's closet) in all three productions. Each show includes the image of Ophelia in her madness or her death. The texture created by these selections is one of instability and decentredness. What is being staged? A troubled relationship with fact, duty and sanity. Wasn't it ever thus, with *Hamlet*? Yes, except that in the three productions there is a distinctly modern sense of anxiety caused by an inability to find the solid centre of anything or anyone.

The text is fluid and unstable, so is its subject matter, and the same is true of the *mise en scène*. In *Elsinore* the set continually shifts its ground; *Qui Est Là* resists settling into one story, or one place; even *Hamlet: a monologue* features a grounded pile of rocks which erodes into nothingness. There is no fixed point. This isn't quite the 'empty space' which Brook wrote about in 1968. Lepage and Wilson fill their stages with visual stimuli. Brook's own work has moved out of the desert and back into the controlled environment of the theatre building. A trace of emptiness prevails, however, through a fondness for the blank canvas: the bareness of Brook's square playing areas, Lepage's screens and Wilson's massy structures. The space is abstract, rather than empty, ready for actions and images which can change in a flash. Perpetual renewal is the key principle.

How did the three productions renew Shakespeare's story? In each case, Fortinbras, Voltemand and Cornelius were removed, along with the entire sub-plot concerning the territorial dispute between Denmark and Norway, which is also about the frictions between adjacent feudal powers. The three variations do not deal with geopolitics. Nor did any of them reproduce Polonius's imprecations to Laertes on the latter's departure for Paris – a place, in his father's eyes, of dangerous modern decadence. They are interested in the story of Hamlet, and anything else falls by the wayside. They sharpen the play's focus on subjectivity.

None featured the two gravediggers of the text, nor any significant degree of banter between Hamlet and even a single gravedigger. But they all visited the grave. Their interest is not in the play's morbid comedy of mortality but in the grave as an image of resolution and finality, even where, in the case of *Qui Est Là*, the cemetery is a place of calm preparation. None of the productions ended with Fortinbras's promise of an efficient new political order. Instead, two closed with 'the rest is silence', Hamlet's self-fulfilling expiration, and the other on a buddhistic refrain. Their endings were not at all concerned with running countries properly or tidying up the metaphorical mess, but with achieving some sort of state of grace and dying as well as you can. They evoked a quasi-spiritual quietude, abstracted from the everyday world.

A striking blankness characterises the productions' treatment of power. Is Claudius to be despised for his crime, or admired for his grasp of realpolitik (one of the enduring questions for actors who play the character)? In these versions the question isn't really raised as an issue. They are not preoccupied with adjudicating the play's shifting balances of political efficacy and personal ethic. They do not present complex studies of power. Nor are they much interested in the tension between civic rules and individual autonomy. The material in the play is conveyed almost without comment, neutrally and even-handedly.

The way in which the three productions deal with gender reveals how little interest they have in socio-political questions. When *Hamlet* was performed by the Lord Chamberlain's Men in 1600/01 it featured boy-actors playing the parts of Gertrude and Ophelia. In *Elsinore* and *Hamlet: a monologue* these characters are played (or, in Wilson's case, evoked) by man-actors. The effect is extremely interesting, not really for what's done with the characters but for what's not done. You might think that cross-gender performance offers a prime opportunity to tackle the tricky sexual politics of *Hamlet* head-on. After all, the Prince vigorously – violently – insults his girl-friend and his mother, raising questions about the propriety of his behaviour which can hardly be ignored. But they are ignored. It is surprising how transparent the productions are in this respect – how little concerned they are with taking a position. It's not as if they blithely endorse Hamlet's vicious-ness. Wilson makes it a keystone of his rendition of the scenes in which Hamlet orders Ophelia to a nunnery and rebukes his mother for her 'o'er hasty marriage'. Lepage, likewise, expands upon Hamlet's difficulties with women by turning him into something closer to an obsessive stalker than a lovesick adolescent, in the scene in Ophelia's bedchamber, and by staging his meeting with his mother in her closet as a feast of vituperative accusation (certainly in Darling's rendition) like something out of *Who's Afraid of Virginia Woolf?*. Nothing here explicitly critiques Hamlet's behaviour. Nor, to be fair, is there any attempt to explain it away. Hamlet behaves in ugly ways with women. That's all there is to it.

Such a perspective might gain intriguing contours through the playing of the women, but here the exercise is one of technical achievement rather than interpretative muscle. Darling and Lepage play Ophelia, I think, not in order to develop a cogent image of a particular type of women at a particular historical moment, but to steer closer to archetype: reserved adolescent. This sort of woman, by the way, also emerges from Giovanna Mezzogiorno's playing of Ophelia in *Qui Est Là* and Shantala Shivalingappa's rendition of the character in Brook's full production of *Hamlet* a few years later. Wilson, meanwhile, keeps a distance between himself and Ophelia. He shows the girl/woman from Hamlet's perspective, rather than attempting an outright performance of character. The furthest he goes in impersonating the opposite gender is when he dons a sumptuous gold robe as the Player Queen in the play-within-the-play, to present a woman who is already a cipher rather than a feminine subject (Image 14). This proto-dominatrix wields a puppet King, a startling reversal of the assumed power dynamic in *Hamlet* where the King, whether Old Hamlet or Claudius, is unquestionably top-dog. The image hints at an object of anxiety which each production shares: the threat of the powerful woman. All three shows, just as *Hamlet* itself, predominantly give us men thinking and acting. And when the men play women in *Elsinore* and *Hamlet: a monologue*, we are connected more with the playing than the woman.

It's not that the three variations have nothing to say. But whether they say anything directly through the play is a very moot point. Brook says a good many things of note through the interpolations of the director-theorists whose ideas he brings to the fore. This is quite different from using *Hamlet* in order to reflect realities of modern life. The import of these shows lies somewhere other than in their overt meanings.

What of their treatment of the central character? The removal of Fortinbras is important here. The Norwegian prince operates in the play as an alternative conscience to his Danish counterpart, reminding the audience of the sort of person – man of action, leader of men, inheritor of a kingdom – that Hamlet might be. The three variations present Hamlet as a son first, a prince second (by a long way). This less regal Hamlet is recast as someone closer to the audience than to royalty. Hamlet's troubled relationship with fact and duty is also our troubled relationship with these things. Put upon, Hamlet suffers indignant anguish. He is a victim of his own expectations of autonomy. We know the feeling.

Each production features a self-absorbed, reflective Hamlet, with additional colourings. Wilson's is given to bursts of mocking tomfoolery; Lepage's to a cavalier sense of righteousness; Darling's to angry petulance and Sangaré's to dogged tranquility. In each case the central character's energy is alternately flamboyant and inward-looking. Again, the nature of the switches between these two extremes has a modern quality. Hamlet can never quite settle, never quite be defined as any one particular thing.

All three productions feature a Hamlet who is, so to speak, mature. This isn't some disaffected youth. At 54, Wilson was almost old enough to be Hamlet's grandfather. Lepage,

Darling and Sangaré approached the character from the vantage point of impending middle age. The consequences are a tone of voice which is more reasonable, an energy which is at least as much intellectual as physical, and a sense of reflection which has the savour of experience rather than the zest of teenage neurosis. Older than usual, Hamlet is more open. His age is no longer his excuse. He cannot be defined as a feeble adolescent, a narcissistic youth or an angry young man. He has already been round the block a few times, in the body of the performer playing him. It might appear that he speaks for more of us.

What does he speak about, this older guy? As we have seen, he is left little of the play's obviously political material to do anything with, and is denied the opportunity to reflect upon the manner of tackling things exhibited by Fortinbras. The productions all retain a good deal of Hamlet's soliloquising, and they privilege the things which the soliloquys traditionally allow. Put simply, the soliloquy is a form of speaking in the first person which gives the audience an undiluted shot of the protagonist's desires, anxieties and intentions. In the three *Hamlet*-variations the soliloquy is embraced not as a conventional part of the play's structure, needing to come in a particular place because of the run of the action, but as a mode of speaking which really fits with the tenor of the production. Each of the shows, as with the soliloquy in classical terms, makes much of speaking personally and directly to the audience. This approach is close to the confessionalism of other avant-garde performance. Even a rendition as mannered as Wilson's has something of this naked sharing of self about it. Lepage and Darling do this, as we have seen, through the camera as well as the more ordinary means of direct address from the stage. Brook's production features a Hamlet who reasons things out with the audience, and a host of supernumeraries drawn from the annals of theatre history who do the same. *Hamlet* is turned into a place of public-personal contemplation and confession. Having seen the productions, I don't remember a slant on the text which offered a striking new interpretation of Hamlet's thoughts, as a single, searing truth. But I am left with a strong sense of having been spoken to and performed to. All three shows are concerned less with shaping up a point of view than with the fact of communication *per se*. 'The medium is the message' has become axiomatic.

What Hamlet says matters less than how he says it. And that's hardly surprising, for although the three *Hamlet*-variations deal with a modern sense of self, none of them are really about Hamlet. None features a star actor in the role and, until Darling grappled with this problem in *Elsinore*, none was much preoccupied with Hamlet's 'inner' journey through the play. This is *Hamlet* without the principal, if not without the Prince. Hamlet the character melts into a strange unpicking of subjectivity, carried out in *Elsinore* and *Hamlet: a monologue* through doublings and redoublings and in *Qui Est Là* through the depiction of characterisation as something which is always 'put on'. Acting is shown to be fabrication and 'self' a question of role-playing or unwitting response. It becomes extremely difficult to find a centred, rooted Hamlet in the middle of all this, for the stuff of personhood is based upon multiple definitions.

In any case, the shows are less interested in Hamlet as a single character, and a lot more interested in how he is a device for metatheatre. None of the productions featured troupes of players (understandably so, in the cases of the one-man shows). But each highlighted the play's metatheatrical themes. All made a feature of the play-within-the-play. Lepage had fun with Hamlet's advice to the players. Wilson and Brook gave great emphasis to the Player's speech. All three were at pains, throughout, to underscore the play's motifs of performance.

The most striking connection in their work on *Hamlet* is their response to the play's themes of pretence and performance. In each case this is the centrepiece of their own renditions, not simply in terms of the thematics which they find most appealing, but as a key to their own well-worked theatricality. The latter seems to me their defining characteristic, and the basis of the pleasure they offer.

As Peter Brook observed, a turn to *Hamlet* by the likes of Brook and his team raises 'all sorts of immediate questions of theatre.' These are partly to do with finding theatrical solutions to aspects of the play, but they also spill out into questions about the particular qualities of the medium itself. There is a broader context, too, for they relate to what Brook describes as the 'why' of theatre – its efficacy or its function.[15] What sort of theatre practice we are addressing, then, and why do its outcomes seem so compelling to its audiences?

Immediate questions of theatre

The first thing to say is that distinctive theatre takes time. Not just time in the rehearsal room, but time outside it, between phases, to allow for a sifting of ideas. Each production was made by way of a number of stages of development, from research, devising, trialling and early showcases of work-in-progress, to refinement, rehearsal and production. In the case of *Elsinore* and *Qui Est Là*, the work was altered after the production had been in front of paying audiences. This is close to an industrial model of Research and Development, where products are developed through a cycle of testing and refinement. Theatre in Europe and North America is more usually geared to a single period of rehearsal and production, short-contract commitments of artists and fast turnarounds from one show to another. The long-term, slow-burn nature of the three *Hamlet* adaptations is entirely different.

Of course time means money – and there is money in these operations – but artistic strategy is paramount. The work is, literally, more refined. The staging posts of *Elsinore* provide a good example. Its first outputs were long and often literal, but the show became increasingly lean and cavalier. Phased workshops allow for greater integration of design and technical elements. There is time to get things built to unusual specifications. In fact all the technical departments benefit. More sophisticated sound, lighting and musical designs are possible, along with a more tightly controlled textuality.

More time also means a need for more space – and not just any rehearsal space. Each director has a customised place of work: Brook's theatre in Paris, Lepage's Caserne in Quebec City and Wilson's Long Island base. The working environment is more relaxed but also more dedicated. Bespoke theatre is made to specification in the workshop rather than a writer's garret or a hired rehearsal hall. The greater the access to specialist know-how, the more time available in carpentry and metalwork rooms, editing facilities and studio spaces, the richer the work is likely to be. Something like this state of affairs obtains in regional and national theatre organisations, but the exclusivity of focus is more pronounced in the sites in Long Island, Paris and Quebec. The shows are not made by different departments working independently and bringing their contributions together towards the end of the process. They depend upon a continuum of activities progressing in systemic interdependence. To lift a term from the corporate lexicon, these productions are all about synergy.

Each project involved extensive collaboration, although here contradictions abound. This is auteur-led collaboration. The three directors are figureheads in their own rehearsal studios and there's no question as to who's the boss. Nonetheless, these shows resulted not entirely from a genius waving his wand, but from a range of practitioners doing real work in the rehearsal room. Even Wilson, whose work seems the most authorial, relies to an unusual extent upon his sound designer and dramaturg. Brook's actors generate performance material. Lepage is the most extensively collaborative, forging close working relationships with and between designers, performers and other members of the team. Results are garnered through sophisticated team-working which maximises the inputs of key individuals.

There is also a loosening of role. We can talk of the actor as creator, the stage manager as deviser, the director as performer. In keeping with developments elsewhere in contemporary theatre, material for the shows is generated from initial improvisations – on the part of the performers, most obviously, but also in other spheres. The process is double-edged: it involves a mixture of intuition and organisation. Each director prizes instinct. The rehearsal floor is where free connections, hunches and spontaneous moves are given a go. The room is alive to the serendipities of the moment. And yet each director is also rigorously methodical, whether by way of Brook's painstaking research and dramaturgy, Lepage's lucid storytelling or Wilson's segmented storyboards. Systems of devising are planned in advance but the results only reveal themselves moment by moment in the rehearsal room. Improvisations are made through the space, through the set, through the body. They are staged in front of onlookers. How else can you know whether what you are working with is 'theatre'? This is the equivalent of a novelist jotting notes on the back of an envelope. There's nothing to stop a theatre-maker using the back of an envelope, but you can't go from that to the finished piece as you might with your novel. The envelope-sketch has to become a rehearsal-room-sketch, a three-dimensional activity in time and space. Only then do you have a draft for theatre which, to use a favourite Lepagean term, *incarnates* its material. And this incarnation is the stuff that is then honed.

If theatre-work can only be proved in front of an audience, it can only really be hardened once it has gone public. As Pierre Bernier observes, regarding Lepage's ongoing revisions, 'The way Robert works, he tries to do first what he wants, and then after when you go on tour, cut, cut, cut, polishing. It's not easy to polish in rehearsal because you don't have the public reaction. When you have the public reaction you know more about what's there.' In Renaissance playhouse practice, as we saw, a stable text emerged only after the trials by fire of rehearsal and performance. In the postmodern performance-workshop the same testing occurs.

The audience for postmodern Shakespeare is now nearly global. Shakespeare's footprint has expanded remorselessly over the last three or four decades.[16] Shakespeare himself has been decentred. He is no longer Will Shakespeare of London, or the Bard of Stratford. Even if I wanted to, I can no longer say as an Englishman that Shakespeare is 'one of us', to use Mrs Thatcher's resonant phrase. He has been recruited elsewhere – many elsewheres. You could argue that he is produced more interestingly elsewhere, too, and some critics point to Shakespeare's language by way of explanation. British Shakespearean production is bound to contend with the luminosity of Shakespeare's text. Working in translation and often in a culture which has a different relationship to the written word, 'foreign' productions can more readily explore scenographic and physical modes of performance.[17] There is an inevitable slippage from the primacy of the text. Shakespeare's language is now virtually foreign even to the English, although we do not usually translate Shakespeare into a more familiar idiom. Productions of the play in France, Japan or Peru must make such a translation. In the process the play is dislodged from its moorings even before the company sets to work in the rehearsal room. The text is more straightforwardly a blueprint for performance rather than verse-speaking.

Lepage and Brook both worked in French with translations of Shakespeare's play, and Wilson prepared visual and movement scores before working with the text. All three began at one remove from Shakespeare's language. This might help ease the play into the international market for which it is bound, but the three variations are international in more fundamental ways. Bruce Myers observes of Brook's CICT:

> an international group is the raison d'être. . . . The form has to be found which gives the greatest necessity for that group, where one sees – as well as the story that's being told or the play that's being played – the improvement made by the fact that everyone's from different races and different nationalities and languages. It's the opposite of any national theatre.

An out-and-out internationalism is also the lifeblood of Lepage's shows.[18] Characters in the devised productions of Ex Machina and, formerly, Théâtre Répère, for example, are international in their tastes (literature, leisure-pursuits, fashion) their work (they are photographers, actors, translators) and their schedules (they jet around between countries and continents). Lepage's Hamlet is a quasi-medieval version of the same sort of person – and he finds himself restaged by the machinery which characterises global communication: micro cameras, video screens and electronic imaging. A Renaissance text by Shakespeare meets New Age music by Robert Caux and video technology by the Japanese.

Robert Wilson, meanwhile, is the most itinerant of the three directors, as his work-schedule makes abundantly clear. In April 1999, for instance, Wilson performed *Hamlet: a monologue* in Shizuoka, Japan, as part of the Theatre Olympics. In the preceding three months he had staged an exhibition of artworks in Modena (*Bob Wilson: Relative Light*) and another in

Chicago (*Theater of Drawings: early artworks of Robert Wilson*), along with theatre productions of Strindberg's *A Dream Play* in Stockholm, *Saints and Singing* in Antwerp and Ljubljana, and Ibsen's *Lady from the Sea* in venues in Italy and France. During this period he also presented *Monsters of Grace*, his mixed-media collaboration with Philip Glass, in venues in the US, *The Magic Flute* at the Opéra Bastille in Paris, and preview-excerpts from *Scourge of Hyacinths* by Tania Léon, after Wole Soyinka (with Wilson reading excerpts of the text) in Geneva and Nancy. Whilst in Antwerp and Ljubljana he also gave his standard lecture, *1 HAVE YOU BEEN HERE BEFORE 2 NO THIS IS THE FIRST TIME*. Pause for breath. A number of these outputs were restagings of previous productions. Even so, it's a daunting schedule encompassing much of the post-industrial world. Wilson's lifestyle, let alone his work, is nothing if not intercontinental.[19]

We are in the realms of what Dennis Kennedy describes as the 'postmodern condition of nearly borderless theatre'.[20] Of course the three *Hamlet*-variations are not about the global market, but they work according to its operations. In common with an increasing number of theatre productions, they are made in their respective 'local' workshops by people accustomed to find many of their influences and materials elsewhere, and to sell their product around the world. As Brook says, 'Our financial basis is co-production. There's no play we have done for years without there being five or six big festivals or European theatres who have come together in advance as co-producers, which means that once they've paid, we have an obligation to go and show it in their towns. It's an obligation which is sometimes pleasant and sometimes a great burden.' Similar obligations bind Lepage and Wilson.

In a transnational environment, theatre productions travel across boundaries which used to be more constraining. In order to travel well, they must be welcomed in the places to which they journey. They might not share the same language, so the shows will depend upon other communicative systems: gestural, musical, image-based, rhythmic. The three *Hamlet*-variations are made for touring. Their very availability as international theatre is part of a wider performance-based imperative in work which enters the global marketplace.

Just as globalization produces a sense of decentredness, so the Shakespeare-variations present a decontextualised Hamlet, of no fixed abode. As we've seen, the extent to which the three productions reproduce the play is questionable. They reprise *Hamlet*, without actually being *Hamlet*. All the *Hamlet*-stuff in them therefore appears quoted – original but not the same as the original. This sort of intertextuality, pointing us back to the old play, puts something else in the foreground: the new show. We are made aware of the way the production wears its Bardic material. We respond not only to the material itself but to its gestalt – its overall pattern.[21]

This is more than mere adaptation. In his discussion of the status of 'the classic', Patrice Pavis suggests that

> The variable now is not the political teaching that the
> dramaturgy carries, nor the cultural and philological
> characteristics that all these foreign expressions
> discover in it, but rather the theatrical and aesthetic
> practices that can be manufactured out of it. In this
> sense, Shakespeare is now a machine to make theatre.[22]

We have arrived at the heartland of the three variations on *Hamlet*. What does it mean to suggest that Shakespeare is a machine to make theatre? Not, I think, that any turn to the Bard guarantees great performance, as though the plays are holy springs which revivify through mere contact. Instead contemporary practitioners find that Shakespeare provides fertile ground for all manner of performance explorations

and neo-formal developments. Theatrical and aesthetic practices are not there simply to deal with texts in new ways. They
shape up theatre for its audiences. As Bruce Wilshire says,
theatre is a place where 'things [are] made sensuously present
to us'.[23] That's also a nice way of considering the modern
theatre director – as someone who makes things sensuously
present.

The way to understand the three productions, and others
which share their theatre-world, is not to ask what they mean
but how they work on their spectators. What do they do with
their audiences? Brook involves the spectator in a play between thought and action. He ensures that we recognise the
fact of performance, through the careful presentation of acting as acting and the scrupulous use of items within the space.
He arranges Shakespeare's textual material in order to evoke
feeling through flow, rhythm and repetition. Lepage, too,
offers an experience of flux and transformation, through
dazzling shifts of images which themselves come layered with
metaphor. The visual and aural grammar belongs as readily
to cinema as to theatre, and it involves the audience in sen-
sorial enjoyment as much as thinking. Wilson's hyper-theatre
is no less sensory, presenting images in space and time which
are designed for consumption. This heightened, polished
theatre is made for the gut rather than the head.

Our meeting with the theatrical is sensual, libidinous,
visceral. It involves an experience of flow and of alteration.
We perceive the incarnation of meaning and the embodiment
of pattern. We watch. We feel wonder. We enjoy. We find
pleasure in this erotics of the theatrical. Theatreness is to do
with space, bodies, liveness and watching, and in the preceding chapters I have tried to consider the three projects in
this light. I've suggested that the variations on *Hamlet* by
Brook, Lepage and Wilson often cut more deeply because
they offer themselves skilfully for spectatorship. Space, move-

ment, sound and text are organised for sensual effect. And that is what characterises today's leading theatre directors. They trade in the sensuality of theatre.

At the top of this chapter I quoted Edward Gordon Craig asking for the theatre to 'perform pieces of its own art.' *Elsinore*, *Hamlet: a monologue* and *Qui Est Là* answer Craig's call. How piquant that they should demonstrate as much not by relying on a play, but by refashioning one. How apt that the play should be *Hamlet*. In the three variations, *Hamlet* is subjected to dramaturgy and to a neo-formalist approach. Dramaturgy is to do with thinking theatrically: the play is remade for a modern stage. Neo-formalism is to do with rhythm, space and image as primary sources of theatrical affect. Both locate the audience, rather than the text, as the first responsibility of the director; and the stage, rather than the text, as the place of excitement.

*

A team of practitioners produces theatre in a workshop. They operate a form of 'derivative creativity',[24] taking a well-known artefact and refashioning it according to their own preferences and predilections. They make their show in order to pleasure audiences – to make them think, feel and enjoy. Nothing gets in the way of this founding principle. The show is captured as a text, but the text is a phantom of performance and is therefore inert. It will be dynamised only by being staged. What's onstage is irreducibly present. The show itself is superbly volatile. It displays a taste for game-playing, metaphor and transformation. This is evidenced not just in what's said but in the staging, with its scenic fluidity and signalling of performance conventions. This is theatre which confidently plays upon its own theatricality. The audience is made complicit, aware of the point at which things in the theatre become other than themselves. The show at the very least remains ambiguous about questions of meaning and the nature of closure. Except, that is, for the point at which the spectators applaud and the contract between the company and the audience is fulfilled.

The above describes each of the *Hamlet* projects of Peter Brook, Robert Lepage and Robert Wilson. It also describes the practice of Shakespeare and his colleagues around four hundred years previously. In the 1980s 'Renaissance Man' became journalistic shorthand to denote someone who was supposedly multi-faceted, in comparison with the reduced expectations of modern culture – well-read, intelligent and able to get on with a variety of things. In this sense Brook, Lepage and Wilson are Renaissance men. These thoroughly postmodern figures connect rather more profoundly than this, however, with the Renaissance.

Why did all three directors choose *Hamlet*? Because *Hamlet* was most evidently there to be chosen – an icon of theatre, a playground for theatricality, a brand of theatrical credibility. Gliding through Shakespeare and around the world, the three variations on *Hamlet* share similar cutting edges. Their innovations are dramaturgical, technical, performative, the sorts of innovations which characterised Renaissance theatre-making. Have they been faithful to Shakespeare? *Hamlet* has certainly been taken seriously – and engineered into another kind of vehicle. The three shows play fast and loose with *Hamlet*. They have to. How else can they make the material fresh? How else, given the weight of the Shakespearean legend, can they stamp their own authority? The cultural myth of Shakespeare underwrites all three productions. By the same token, Shakespeare gives way to a postmodern dissipation of the text. Poetry defers to production, the Bard to the boards – just as in Shakespeare's day. Each show is about the authority of modern performance.

Point of Return

6

Point of Return

'What drives one is the sense that at any given moment there is only one way that is exactly appropriate.'

Peter Brook

I returned to Paris on 28 November 2000 to see Peter Brook's production of *Hamlet* at the Théâtre des Bouffes du Nord. It was a familiar journey – the Eurostar from Waterloo, the hotel near the Bastille, the walk from the Gare du Nord to Brook's theatre, past the shops selling saris and kebabs. Dinner at the Bouffes du Nord's cafe restaurant before the show, with its handful of tables, its bar across one end of the room, and its semi-private door off into the theatre, like a quiet promise. Adrian Lester, who was about to play Hamlet, was sitting with friends. Brook and Marie-Hélène Estienne, assistant director on this project, arrived at a reserved table.

As usual, a crowd of people gathers outside, thronging for tickets which they've already booked; the collection system still seems quaintly homespun. As usual, the small programme is handed out free of charge, and inside the theatre people busy to find their places and get comfortable – not always guaranteed. The audience is tightly packed along the benches, with a row of punters sitting on cushions around the perimeter of the playing area. This leaning, stretching line adds a touch of informality but also exclusivity to the proceedings. Brook's *Hamlet*. Tickets are rare. People are willing to sit on the floor to watch.

A square, coral-red carpet is on the stage. It is cotton, perhaps, and slightly faded, with signs of patching here and there – warm, used and artfully preserved, like the rest of the auditorium. As with the rectangular playing areas created for previous productions here, the carpet reaches back to the line of the proscenium arch. The floor-space behind is left empty, stretching to the ageing red wall at the back. Green, yellow and black cushions are placed around the sides of the carpet. Toshi Tsuchitori's musical instruments are gathered in a recess stage-left of the playing area. Two large, low, rectangular stools, each covered with a dusky-red cloth, are placed upstage. Shortly before the play begins, Adrian Lester sits on a pair of black cushions, his back against the proscenium arch stage-left. Another pair of cushions is arranged similarly the other side of the stage.

From the outset this is a characteristically Brookian evening. It is not just the environs and the front-of-house bustle which is familiar. The details of setting (carpet, cushions) suggest modesty, clear spatial definition and a near-neutral base for the work of the actors. The single musician plays live, shaping the piece's emotional environment through his accompaniment. The cast of eight is multi-ethnic and Hamlet is played by a black actor. The play is performed in English, but it is already being drawn into the Brookian system. This production is the apogee of Brook's work. 'Apogee' means not just 'culmination' but 'turning against the direction of gravity'.[1] Brook's *Hamlet* turns from the gravitational pull established by countless editors and directors of the play. It is the culmination of *Qui Est Là*, of Brook's encounter with

Shakespeare, and ultimately of the director's own system of theatre.

Nearly seventy years after his first production of *Hamlet*, aged seven, Brook returns to the Shakespeare's most emblematic play in his maturity. Anecdotal evidence suggests that the first foray lasted a good four hours or so. This latter version comes in at just over two-and-a-half hours without an interval. Wisdom brings economy. The play has been scrubbed down and in part Brook's achievement is one of dramaturgy. The evening is clear and spare. Simply, it tells Hamlet's story: here is a man, these things happened and as a consequence he died. Hamlet is a victim of circumstance (a modern theme). For this reason, perhaps, Brook gives the play part of its full title, *The Tragedy of Hamlet*, omitting *the Prince of Denmark*. Denmark doesn't really figure. There is no dispute with Norway, no Fortinbras. Much of the business dealing with Polonius's family is cut. Laertes is introduced only after the death of his father.

The excision of material is brilliantly, ruthlessly decisive. Where words are unnecessary or complicate the issue they are not used. Consider a moment during the duel between Hamlet and Laertes. In orthodox editions of the text, there is a break in the fighting during which Gertrude drinks from the poisoned cup. She then goes to wipe Hamlet's face and as she does so Laertes says, 'My Lord, I'll hit him now.' Claudius replies, 'I do not think't.' Laertes utters an aside, then Hamlet invites him to recommence the duel. It is a flabby little section. In Brook's adaptation Laertes says, 'My Lord, I'll hit him now,' and does so immediately, while Hamlet's back is turned. It is a killer cut, in both senses. The poisoned death blow is inflicted. The nature of the duel changes instantly. Hamlet spins round, the pair grapple, lock hands, their rapiers are thrown down one by one. Hamlet snatches up Laertes's sword and slashes, inflicting his own death-wound. A

passage which is often messy and ill-motivated in performance is cleaned up, tightly scored and given an effective
rhythm through judicious rejigging of the text. As soon as he
is hit, Laertes says,

> Hamlet, Hamlet, thou art slain.
> No medicine in the world can do thee good;
> In thee there is not half an hour's life.
> The treacherous instrument is in thy hand,
> Unbated and envenom'd. The foul practice
> Hath turn'd itself on me. Lo, here I lie,
> Never to rise again. Thy mother's poison'd.
> I can no more. The King – the King's to blame.

These are lines 319-326 in the Arden edition.[2] Brook follows
them with the business (the death of the Queen) which
immediately *precedes* them in conventional editions. Gertrude
says:

> The drink, the drink! O my dear Hamlet!
> The drink, the drink! I am poison'd.

And she dies. The duel begins as a formal joust, then turns
nasty. Both protagonists deliver fatal wounds which are immediately followed by Gertrude's death. The run of the action
is clean, brisk and cogent. *Hamlet* is remade from within.

Such deadly efficiency characterises this adaptation as a
whole. It is breathtakingly economical. The play begins with
Scott Handy as Horatio entering the playing area, cautious
and alert. He utters the opening words of the play: 'Who's
there?' No Barnardo, who usually has the first line, Francisco
or misty battlements loom into view. Instead, Horatio sees the
Ghost, played by Jeffrey Kissoon, who approaches slowly
along an aisle in the auditorium and walks magisterially
across the stage to sit on the cushions at the proscenium arch

facing Adrian Lester. Lester rises and delivers the play's first soliloquy, which begins, 'O that this too too sullied flesh would melt, / Thaw and resolve itself into a dew'. It usually comes after the first court scene. Its positioning here immediately places Hamlet in context: grieving son, critic of his mother and uncle. Handy, who had sat on the cushion vacated by Lester, re-enters and tells Hamlet that he saw his father. His manner is calm and measured. There is a soft, punctuating cymbal and drum accompaniment to this passage. Kissoon as the Ghost walks around the back of the playing area, and as he steps towards the centre of the carpet, the musician plays a shimmer on his cymbal, a rattling and a sound like an exhalation of dry breath.

The Ghost moves into Horatio's eyeline. 'Look, it comes,' he says. Hamlet waves Horatio away. He slowly approaches the Ghost. Both characters extend a hand, they touch, clasp hands and then embrace in a firm clinch. The spectre is flesh and blood, the meeting is between a father and his bereaved son. The Ghost reveals the details of his death, bids Hamlet take revenge, and leaves, but not before a second clinch. Lester plays the scene on an edge between incredulity, fear and desire. First and foremost, this exchange is person to person. The Ghost is not exactly domestic, but he is accessible. Kissoon underplays neatly. It is as if he grants his presence, allows himself to be touched. He moves extremely calmly and plays the lines for their directness of information.

After Horatio swears his silence, the lights brighten, the cast sets the stools, cushions and a small mat to create a court arrangement, and we are in Act 1, Scene 2 of the play as we know it, with the King and Queen quizzing Hamlet as to his melancholy. This scene usually comes before Hamlet has met the Ghost, so that he is maudlin and shifty at the outset. In Brook's version, the reasons for Hamlet's behaviour are more compelling. A man meets the ghost of his father and the ghost imparts awful information. His demeanour at court seems entirely understandable, indeed inevitable. And here we have the first glimpse of the consequences of Brook's stealthy smoothings. They make behaviour seem natural.

The run of action is like watching a series of 'french scenes', where every new entrance or exit signals the beginning of a new scene.[3] French scenes provide a helpful way of dealing with the rhythmic texture of Renaissance drama, which cuts swiftly from one scene to the next with no stage directions and only key words in the dialogue to indicate changes of place or context. They also help clarify the action and tone of each section of the drama. I haven't seen anything which renders the principle as clearly as this production. Usually when responding to a piece of theatre we talk about the ideas, the story, the acting or the images. The rhythmic texture of the event is no less significant, and here the pace and flow of the action are controlled with symphonic precision.

If the evening's narrative drive is both sensuous and austere, the work of the actors is also stamped with this Brookian double hallmark. Adrian Lester plays Hamlet as intelligent, decisive, extremely hurt. This isn't some distant royal but a modern everyman. Chloé Obolensky's costume – a long, slim collarless top outside tapered trouser-leggings, with slipper-like shoes, all black, of course – makes for a softened, fashionable but abstracted figure. Lester's Hamlet is still very obviously flesh and blood. In the 'What piece of work is a man' section, Hamlet's ironic eulogy to humanness, Lester tears off his shirt and uses his body, seizing Rosencrantz's hand to feel his flesh in illustration of the speech. Before delivering the 'To be, or not to be' soliloquy he feels his pulse, as he did a little earlier in Gertrude's bedchamber. Hamlet is hyper-present to himself, and Adrian Lester's body is a thing of substance to the audience. (The soliloquy, by the way, is shifted from its normal place before the nunnery scene to much later in the play. In Brook's version it comes after Hamlet has killed Polonius and been given his order to prepare to leave for England. This is Hamlet's nadir: he has mistakenly slain an innocent man and is about to sail into exile. Everything has gone wrong. The editorial move makes sense.) Another 'body' is given life when Yorick's skull is fixed on top of a staff, which Lester rotates to animate the grinning head. In themselves these are no more than touches, but they accumulate a biological and organic sense of bodiliness. The stage is always a place of embodiment. This stage, more intensely, is a place where flesh and bone are bodied.

Polonius is played by Bruce Myers as a good-humoured man who reasons things through honestly (the wheels turn a little slowly). Claudius is calm, reasonable, decisive. He outlines his plan to send Hamlet to England, then asks Polonius 'What think you on't?' It is an important retention, and the line is delivered in a way which makes the question appear genuine. The effect is to suggest two reasonable men responding to events. These are not caricatures, as is often the case. At prayer, Claudius is devastatingly self-knowing.

Finely-observed acting is accompanied by a curious shadow – finely-observed non-acting. Just as the production is marked by its verbal brevity, so too there is an absence of performance where performance is not required. The cast continually cede space to their colleagues by granting focus and not providing any distraction. This is more than merely a question of good manners. Scott Handy plays Horatio as though wearing a neutral mask. His very blankness makes you realise how rare it is to see an actor who avoids signalling with his face the thoughts or emotions of the character he is playing. He is studiously impassive when he might react and respond in all sorts of ways. Such restraint is stimulating for the audience. We are freer to assume what Horatio must be thinking or feeling. We must engage imaginatively.

It is common to overact Claudius's growing anxiety during the performance of the play-within-the-play. Kissoon merely stands, closes in on the Players' actions, then asks for lights. His face remains controlled, provoking the spectator to graft on to it an emotional disturbance which therefore seems much darker and more dangerous. When Hamlet cowers at the appearance of the Ghost in Gertrude's bedchamber, Natasha Parry as the Queen fixes him with her gaze, glancing only once or twice at where he appears to be looking. If the scene were 'real' her behaviour might seem strange. As it is, it fits with the ensemble's controlled minimalism of performance, constantly giving focus to the actor who is 'on'. When Rohan Siva as Laertes sees the mad Ophelia, he simply holds his ground and watches. No hands to head, no rushing over to her, no distracted (or distracting) glances at the King and Queen. After the tussle in the grave between Hamlet and Laertes, Siva remains still and silent, watching as the rest of the scene plays out. If your character has nothing to do, do nothing. Another actor is acting. Why complicate the picture? The show is filled with people who watch, listen and hold their place. Their reserve helps intensify the stuff that is actually performed.

And it is here that Brook's system is especially well-oiled. We watch the performance of performance. There is no doubt about Lester's Hamlet putting on his 'antic disposition'. At the beginning of his exchange with Polonius ('How does my good Lord Hamlet?' 'Well, God-a-mercy') he enters dribbling – more – frothing from the mouth. He drops to his hands and knees, coughing and choking over the book which he carries. On Polonius's exit, he wipes his mouth and says, very sanely, 'These tedious old fools.' Alone after the Players' first appearance, Hamlet goes into a mini-rehearsal of the piece which they will perform to the King. When he is with Ophelia ('Get thee to a nunnery'), he performs his confrontation with her in front of the hidden Claudius and Polonius, whom he has spotted. These are common enough interpretations. Played as deliberately as they are, they build a picture of a protagonist who is especially sensitive to strategies of presentation and pretence. This goes for the cast as a whole. Naseeruddin Shah and Rohan Siva exit as Rosencrantz and Guildenstern and return almost immediately as the Players, their outstretched arms virtually acknowledging their flagrant doubling. Meanwhile the audience is consistently reminded of the potency of *acting*. In true metatheatrical manner, Brook's production makes sure that we recognise its own steady trade in the currency of performance.

A number of staging solutions, retained from *Qui Est Là*, underscore this intent. When the First Player gives his *tour de force* speech, it is non-English and non-Shakespearean. Naseeruddin Shah performs in an *Orghast*-like set of onomatopoeic sounds, a pure display of rhetorical effect a little reminiscent of the sort of primal language which Brook and Ted Hughes developed in *Orghast* in 1971, and a direct descendent of Yoshi Oida's Japanese rendition in *Qui Est Là*. When Bruce Myers as Polonius hides behind the arras in Gertrude's bedchamber, he does so by kneeling on the floor and holding a sheet of material in front of him, as he had done in *Qui Est Là*, when he went on to compare Japanese and Chinese manners of dying. (Here, Polonius dies a mundane death, brutal in its swiftness, toppling beneath the sheet.) Shantala Shivalingappa sits on the floor as the mad Ophelia, with Toshi Tsuchitori seated directly in front of her accompanying her speech-song. Even this 'actual' insanity is evidently a piece of theatre. And think back to the pattern of action at the beginning of the play, which draws on the early workshops before *Qui Est Là* which explored the staging of the supernatural. Then, Brook preferred the version where the Ghost seemed as real possible to the son to whom he appears. The same is true in this full production of the play. The new beginning now partly depends upon the use of the cushions at either side of the proscenium arch. Adrian Lester sits here. Jeffrey Kissoon sits opposite. Scott Handy sits facing him once Lester is onstage. The movement has its dance, and non-acting actors are arranged within the *mise en scène*. They sit in a liminal onstage/offstage space to demonstrate the stuff of staging and their readiness for acting.

Ah yes, 'the readiness is all'. When Brook staged *Qui Est Là*, this was the final line spoken by Bakary Sangaré's Hamlet. Brook omitted virtually the entire last act of Shakespeare's play to end with Zeami's words on the eternal cycle of life, death and rebirth. This time round he nearly gets to the end of the play as we know it, but finishes in similar philosophical spirit. Hamlet dies kneeling, and is laid on the floor by Horatio. The rest of the cast are onstage. Those whose characters did not die in the carnage of the duelling room – Bruce Myers, Shantala Shivalingappa and Naseeruddin Shah – quietly lie down. Handy delivers Horatio's lines:

> Now cracks a noble heart. Goodnight, sweet prince,
> And flights of angels sing thee to thy rest.

The light brightens. Handy looks out beyond the audience, and speaks a couplet which Brook lifts from 1.1, where it comes after the Ghost's visit to the men of the watch:

> But look, the morn in russet mantle clad
> Walks o'er the dew of yon high eastward hill.

The bodies onstage softly rise, stand and look out to the light and to some imagined horizon. Handy has the final words, which close the circles of this particular performance and the Hamlet experiments which Brook set in motion with *Qui Est Là*:

> Who's there?

We are left with a group of bodies, quiet and alert, looking out beyond the audience. A refusal to end with death and closure. Another flamboyant edit. And a rhetorical question in the audience's direction.

What sort of *Hamlet* does this give us, four hundred years after Shakespeare first presented his version of the play? Answer: the play, concentrated, and not the play but a fluid and synthesised theatre event. Reworked in the CICT-laboratory, the text is stripped of its long-windedness, purged of its civic and political strands and turned into an organism for theatre. It emerges as a piece about personhood, personal experience, circumstances beyond your control, and the power of performance. Once again Brook's Shakespeare catches the currents of the age – except that this time, the show comes with an added sheen, a calm optimism in the face of the play's disaster. Is there really 'only one way that is exactly appropriate', as Brook suggests? I doubt it, but only a seasoned sort of theatre creates such an allure of inevitability. Then again, the 'exactly appropriate' way changes with circumstances. Only by remaking *Hamlet* does *Hamlet* remain appropriate.

I saw the show again, and headed home. My theatrical tourism was over for the moment. It seemed right, in the spirit of revisitings and change, that it should end where it had begun. I left Paris with the wind freshening, looking forward to coming back.

Appendix

Brook's
The Tragedy of Hamlet
a play in 48 French scenes

1. Horatio sees the Ghost.

2. Hamlet describes his circumstances.

3. Horatio tells Hamlet of the Ghost's appearance.

4. The Ghost appears to Hamlet.

5. Hamlet reflects upon the Ghost's words.

6. Horatio and Hamlet swear to observe the Ghost.

7. Claudius and Gertrude gently chide Hamlet for the extent of his mourning.

8. Ophelia describes Hamlet's visit to her closet.

9. Polonius tells Claudius and Gertrude that he has discovered the cause of Hamlet's 'lunacy'.

10. Hamlet enters and overhears Claudius plan with Polonius how they will spy on him.

11. Hamlet acts mad before Polonius.

12. Rosencrantz and Guildernstern enter. Hamlet divulges their mission and reveals something of his melancholy.

13. Polonius and Horatio bring news that the Players have arrived.

14 The Players enter. The actor gives his performance.

15. Hamlet, alone, reflects upon his own lack of passion.

16. Ophelia reads a book. Claudius and Polonius hide in wait. Hamlet enters, sees them, questions Ophelia and treats her roughly.

17. Hamlet exits, and Ophelia laments his demise.

18. Claudius, with Polonius and Ophelia, announces (with 'swift determination') that he will send Hamlet to England.

19. Hamlet and Horatio arrange the stage for performance. Hamlet explains his plan to stage the events of the murder in a play.

20. Claudius, Gertrude, Polonius and Ophelia take their places at the play.

21. The players enter and perform the play. Claudius (quietly) asks for lights as the poisoning is completed. Polonius quickly disbands the gathering.

22. Hamlet, with Horatio, is beside himself with excited vindication.

23. Rosencrantz and Guildernstern enter to tell Hamlet that Gertrude wishes to see him.

24. Hamlet, alone, announces his intention (''Tis now the very witching time of night'). As he exits, he takes up a black bamboo switch from under the downstage edge of the carpet.

25. The actors playing Rosencrantz and Guildernstern tidy the stage. Claudius enters, kneels, tells the audience of his guilty conscience and attempts to pray.

26. Hamlet steals up behind Claudius, who remains stationary in prayer. Hamlet has Claudius at his mercy. He decides not to kill him while he is praying, on the grounds that the King's soul will be saved if he is murdered at prayer.

27. Polonius and Gertrude discuss Hamlet's impending visit. Polonius hides behind the arras (the actor kneels and holds a drape in front of him).

28. Hamlet enters and remonstrates with his mother. Polonius calls for help as Hamlet appears to get rough. Hamlet stabs Polonius.

29. The Ghost enters to remind Hamlet to go gently with his mother.

30. Hamlet and Gertrude finish their bedroom encounter.

31. Claudius, accompanied by Rosencrantz and Guildernstern, quizzes Hamlet about the whereabouts of Polonius.

32. Ophelia walks across the back of the stage (her eyes meet with Hamlet's) and exits.

33. Hamlet feels his own pulse, kneels and takes stock ('To be, or not to be, that is the question.').

34. Rosencrantz and Guildernstern enter to take Hamlet to England.

35. Ophelia, accompanied by the musician (who moves on stage for this section), grieves by singing snatches of song.

36. Claudius and Gertrude enter and observe.

37. Ophelia exits. Laertes enters and demands to know what has happened to his father.

38. Ophelia enters wearing a red sash and carrying a bunch of flowers, which she distributes.

39. Ophelia leaves, with Gertrude following. Claudius briefs Laertes.

40. Laertes exits, Horatio enters with letters for the King, which tell of Hamlet's return.

41. Gertrude tells Laertes of the drowning of his sister.

42. Hamlet, Horatio and the Gravedigger set the graveyard, dancing a jig. Hamlet then questions the gravedigger.

43. The funeral procession arrives. Laertes and Hamlet struggle in Ophelia's grave.

44. Claudius and Laertes remain at the graveside as the other characters exit. Claudius outlines his plot to ensure Hamlet's death.

45. Hamlet explains to Horatio the circumstances of his escape from the ship.

46. Osric brings Hamlet details of the challenge to a duel with Laertes.

47. The denouement. Hamlet and Laertes duel, resulting in the deaths of both, along with the deaths of Gertrude and Claudius.

48. The actors not involved in the duel scene enter and lie down. Horatio delivers the last lines of the production, during which the company stands and looks out beyond the audience.

Notes

Chapter 1: The Play without the Play

1. For a discussion of the globalisation of Shakespeare in the twentieth century see Michael D. Bristol, *Big-time Shakespeare*, London and New York: Routledge, 1996, and Gary Taylor, *Reinventing Shakespeare: A Cultural History from the Restoration to the Present*, London: Vintage, 1991, 231-372. See Terence Hawkes, *Meaning By Shakespeare*, London and New York: Routledge, 1992, for an influential account of the ways in which Shakespeare's works do not yield 'final, authoritative or essential meanings' but are used 'as a powerful element in specific ideological strategies' (3).

2. W.B. Worthen, *Shakespeare and the Authority of Performance*, Cambridge University Press, 1997, 39.

3. For brief thumbnail sketches of each of the three directors in the same volume see the respective entries in Maria M. Delgado and Paul Heritage (eds.), *In Contact With the Gods? Directors Talk Theatre*, Manchester and New York, Manchester University Press, 1996, and Michael Huxley and Noel Witts (eds.), *The Twentieth-Century Performance Reader*, London and New York: Routledge, 1996. I give fuller bibliographic details regarding each individual director in the chapters which follow.

4. Huxley and Witts, *The Twentieth-Century Performance Reader,* 117.

5. Quoted in Arthur Holmberg, *The Theatre of Robert Wilson*, Cambridge University Press, 154.

6. Stephen Orgel, 'What is a Text?', David Scott Kastan and Peter Stallybrass (eds.), *Staging the Renaissance: Reinterpretations of Elizabethan and Jacobean Drama*, London and New York: Routledge, 1991, 83-4.

7. Peter Thomson, *Shakespeare's Theatre*, London and New York: Routledge, 1992 (second edition; first edition published in 1983), 61. In an endnote, Thomson quotes G.E. Bentley's conclusion that '"as

many as half of the plays by professional dramatists incorporated the writing at some date of more than one man," *The Profession of Dramatist*, p.199.' (182) . See also Andrew Gurr, *The Shakespearian Playing Companies*, Oxford University Press, 1996, 102.

8. See Andrew Gurr and Mariko Ichigawa, *Staging in Shakespeare's Theatres*, Oxford University Press, 2000, 23-5.

9. Taylor, *Reinventing Shakespeare*, 3.

10. Peter Davison, *Hamlet: Text and Performance*, London: Macmillan, 1983, 24.

11. Orgel, 'What is a Text?', 87.

12. For a discussion of the indeterminate first production date of *Hamlet*, see Harold Jenkins, 'Introduction', in Jenkins (ed.), William Shakespeare, *Hamlet*, London: Methuen, 1982, 1-13. For a conjectural reconstruction of the original staging of the play at the Globe in c. 1601, see Gurr and Ichigawa, *Staging in Shakespeare's Theatres*, 121-62.

13. Davison, *Hamlet: Text and Performance*, 13.

14. See Emrys Jones, *Scenic Form in Shakespeare*, Oxford University Press, 1971, 66-7. Shakespeare possibly follows a neo-classical division of plays into five sections (67-8).

15. Clement Scott, 'Henry Irving (1874)', *Some Notable Hamlets of the Present Time*, London: Greening and Co., 1900, 76.

16. The best way of doing this is by means of the parallel-text edition, which shows all three texts across two pages. See Paul Bertram and Bernice W. Kliman (eds.), *The Three-Text Hamlet: Parallel Texts of the First and Second Quartos and First Folio*, New York: AMS Press, 1991. Kathleen O. Irace (ed.), *The First Quarto of Hamlet*, Cambridge University Press, 1998, gives the text of Q1.

17. Thomson, *Shakespeare's Theatre*, 123.

18. Bert O. States, *Hamlet and the Concept of Character*, Baltimore and London: The Johns Hopkins University Press, 1992, xxiv-xxv.

19. For a book-length study of this issue, see States, *ibid*.

20. Ruby Cohn, *Modern Shakespeare Offshoots*, Princeton University Press, 1976, 138-9.

21. Taylor, *Reinventing Shakespeare*, 102. Taylor suggests that Coleridge's taste for the character – indeed his partial account of the character as reflective rather than active – mirrors and rationalises a certain 'political irresolution' on the part of Coleridge and 'his own generation'.

22. In *Characters of Shakespear's Plays*, 1817 (quoted in Davison, *Hamlet: Text and Performance*, 19).

23. Francis Barker, *The Tremulous Private Body: Essays on Subjection*, London and New York: Methuen, 1984, 38-40.

24. Hugh Grady, *Shakespeare's Universal Wolf: Studies in Early Modern Reification*, Oxford and New York: Oxford University Press, 1996, 222. This follows – and is written in the light of – Grady's account of the way in which twentieth-century critical approaches to Shakespeare are shaped by characteristically Modernist concerns. Grady's books indicate how Shakespeare is critiqued according to shaping intellectual forces of the age. 'There is no "authentic" Shakespeare there for the picking. After the Modernist Shakespeare comes – the Postmodernist Shakespeare. There is, simply, no other alternative – unless it is to revive an older Shakespeare.' (Hugh Grady, *The Modernist Shakespeare: Critical Texts in a Material World*, Oxford and New York: Oxford Univesity Press, 1991, 4.) Once again it seems that Shakespeare is as responsive as a weathercock, except that the weathercock twitches the more noticeably at times of cultural change. We should not look *into* Shakespeare for meaning, but look at what's *done to* Shakespeare.

25. Thomson, *Shakespeare's Theatre*, 116.

26. Bert O. States, *Great Reckonings in Little Rooms: On the Phenomenology of Theater*, Berkeley and Los Angeles: University of California Press, 1985, 15.

27. See Cohn, *Modern Shakespeare Offshoots*; John A. Mills, *Hamlet on Stage: The Great Tradition*, Westport, Connecticut and London: Greenwood Press, 1985; Anthony Davies and Stanley Wells (eds.), *Shakespeare and the Moving Image: the plays on film and television*, Cambridge University Press, 1994; and Bernice Kliman, *Hamlet: Film, Television and Audio Performance*, London and Toronto: Associated University Presses, 1988.

28. Bristol, *Big-time Shakespeare*, 65. For a discussion of Davenant and his production of *Hamlet* see Bristol, *Big-time Shakespeare*, 61-5. For a discussion of the embrace of the play in the Restoration period, see Taylor, *Reinventing Shakespeare*, 39-51.

29. See Mills, *Hamlet on Stage*, 27.

30. Peter Holland, 'The Age of Garrick', Jonathan Bate and Russell Jackson (eds.), *Shakespeare: An Illustrated Stage History*, Oxford and New York: Oxford University Press, 1996, 72.

31. *Ibid.*, 72. See Mills, *Hamlet on Stage*, 27-29 for a more detailed discussion of Garrick's handling of the denouement of the play.

32. Quoted in Mills, *Hamlet on Stage*, 27.

33. Scott, *Some Notable Hamlets of the Present Time*, 64.

34. Scott, 'Wilson Barrett', *Some Notable Hamlets of the Present Time*, 83, 84.

35. *Ibid.*, 89.

36. Taylor, *Reinventing Shakespeare*, 267.

37. Christopher Innes, *Edward Gordon Craig*, Cambridge University Press, 1983, 165-7.

38. The uncertainty over the date is explained by the difference between Russian and Western calendars. Craig and Stanislavsky's *Hamlet* opened on 23 December 1911 Old Style, 5 January 1912 New Style.

39. Richard Halpern, *Shakespeare Among the Moderns*, Ithaca and London: Cornell University Press, 1997, 235, 236, 254 and 277. Halpern's book addresses modernist critical readings of Shakespeare.

40. The production was directed by H.K. Ayliff, with Hamlet played by Colin Keith-Johnston.

41. See Cohn, *Modern Shakespeare Offshoots*, 201-5.

42. Bertolt Brecht in John Willett (ed. and tr.), *Brecht on Theatre: The Development of an Aesthetic*, London: Methuen, 1964, 202. I am indebted in this section to Ruby Cohn's account of Brecht's dealings with *Hamlet*, in Cohn, *Modern Shakespeare Offshoots*, 205-11.

43. Cohn, *Modern Shakespeare Offshoots*, 205-6.

44. *Ibid.*, 207n.

45. *Ibid.*, 221.

46. *Ibid.*, 225.

47. In *Time Out*, April 21-27, 1972 (quoted in Cohn, *ibid.*, 221).

48. Herbert Marshall, 'Introduction', Raymond Mander and Joe Mitchenson (compilers), Marshall (ed.), *Hamlet through the ages: A Pictorial Record from 1709*, London: Rockliff Publishing Corporation, 1952, xi.

49. *Ibid.*, xii. Margreta De Grazia argues at book-length that Malone's edition concretises a notion of 'authentic' Shakespeare ('the text closest to what Shakespeare put on paper' [4]) and of the relation between the Bardic texts and Shakespeare's biography. She suggests that the treatment of Shakespeare as a historical figure and as the producer of authoritative texts can be seen as an Enlightenment phenomenon. 'Authentic materials, the historicized and individuated subject, exclusive ownership, immanent or psychologized texts: all are part of a schema by which textual activity is regulated. This is the legacy of the 1790 apparatus and its enlarged successor

of 1821. It is a distinctly Enlightenment construct precisely because its terms appear so incontrovertible, as if, like truth itself, they could not be otherwise.' Margreta De Grazia, *Shakespeare Verbatim: The Reproduction of Authenticity and the 1790 Apparatus*, Oxford and New York: Oxford University Press, 1991, 225. The Variorum Shakespeare can be seen as pursuing an 'authenticating' recording project, although not in the terms which Marshall suggests.

50. Marshall, *Hamlet through the ages*, xiv.

51. Styan's mould-breaking *The Shakespeare Revolution: Criticism and Performance in the Twentieth Century*, Cambridge University Press, 1977, focuses on stage practice rather than textual criticism, and seeks to rediscover the original conditions of Renaissance production in order to get to the authenticating originality of Shakespearean stage practice. For a good discussion of Styan's book, noting its 'eccentric' (in twentieth-century terms) view of author-function, see Worthen, *Shakespeare and the Authority of Performance*, 156-160. Brown's *Shakespeare's Plays in Performance*, New York and London, Applause, 1993 (revised edition; first published 1966) attempts to read the plays and a number of (mostly British) productions in the light of theatre practice, staging implications and stage business. Granville Barker preempts this move in his *Prefaces to Shakespeare (1927-46)*, London: Batsford, 1972, reading the texts in order to understand the staging conventions which structure their dramatic strategies. In *Looking at Shakespeare: A Visual History of Twentieth-Century Performance*, Cambridge University Press, 1993, Dennis Kennedy explores Shakespearean production in scenographic terms, assessing how meaning is produced differently in particular productions through their construction of visual imagery and their use of the stage.

52. Worthen, *Shakespeare and the Authority of Performance*, 17.

53. States, *Great Reckonings in Little Rooms*, 20.

Chapter 2: *Qui Est Là* • Peter Brook

1. Richard Eyre, 'Shakespeare Alive!', foreword to Harley Granville Barker, *Preface to Hamlet*, London: Nick Hern Books, 1993, vii.

2. Quoted in David Williams, 'Peter Brook's "Great Poem of the World"', in Williams (comp.), *Peter Brook: A Theatrical Casebook*, London: Methuen, 1991, 354.

3. Whilst the publicity states that *Qui Est Là* is concerned with the work of these six director-theorists, the Russian directors Tairov and Leskov and the French director Jean Rouché each contribute a couple of lines. Rouché had shot a film in Nigeria which depicted 'a savage ritual played out in a state of extreme madness', which was shown to the company which presented Brook's production of *The Marat/Sade* in 1964. See Albert Hunt and Geoffrey Reeves, *Peter Brook*, Cambridge University Press, 1995, 86.

4. Peter Brook, *There Are No Secrets: Thoughts on Acting and Theatre*, London: Methuen, 1993, 102.

5. Peter Brook, *Evoking Shakespeare*, London: Nick Hern Books, 1998, 12, 14.

6. *Ibid.*, 21, 22-3, 31, 25.

7. *Ibid.*, 32.

8. Mary Blume, 'The How and the Why of Peter Brook', *International Herald Tribune*, 9 March 1996.

9. See Hunt and Reeves, *Peter Brook*, 136-41, for a chapter-length account of this production.

10. *Ibid.*, 141.

11. Barrault had invited Brook to work for him under the auspices of the Odéon Theatre in Paris. Brook was halfway through a two-month workshop exploring *The Tempest* when *les événements* of 1968 led to the sacking of Barrault as director of the Odéon, the termination of the workshop and the departure of its non-French nationals for London. See Hunt and Reeves, *Peter Brook*, 136-8.

12. Roland Barthes, trans. Richard Howard, *Camera Lucida: Reflections on Photography*, London: Vintage, 1993, 3.

13. Peter Brook, 'How Many Trees Make a Forest?', *The Shifting Point: Forty years of theatrical exploration, 1946-1987*, London: Methuen, 1989, 42. Brook suggests that Craig revolutionised the visual rhetoric of theatre by showing that scenographic information could be conveyed through bare and minimal means (one stick, for instance, can evoke an entire forest). Brecht's approach to acting, through simplification of physical disposition (something approaching Brecht's notion of 'gestus', although Brook doesn't use the term), is of the same representational register.

14. *Ibid.*, 43.

15. Quoted in Hunt and Reeves, *Peter Brook*, 204.

16. *Ibid.*, 215.

17. Peter Brook, 'Manifesto for the Sixties', in *The Shifting Point*, 54.

18. Brook's company was initially called the Centre International de Recherches Théâtrales. He explains the eventual substitution of 'Recherches' with 'Créations'. 'We felt that research in the theatre needs constantly to be put to the text in performance and performing, and needs all the time to be refreshed by research with the time and conditions it demands – and which a professional company can seldom afford.' Peter Brook, 'How Many Trees Make a Forest?', 105.

19. 'Peter Brook, du vrac au vrai', *Libération*, 8 December 1995.

20. Edward Gordon Craig, *On the Art of the Theatre*, London and New York: Heinemann Educational Books, 1980 (reprinted from the Theatre Arts Books edition, 1956), 264-80.

21. Kouyaté is from Burkino-Fasso, Sangaré from Senegal.

22. Odile Quirot, 'Peter Brook, Qui Est Là', *Le Nouvel Observateur*, 27 December 1995.

23. James Fenton, 'Peter Brook's Way', *The New York Review of Books*, v. 43 n. 5, March 21, 1996, 20.

24. See, for example, Rustom Bharucha, 'Peter Brook's Mahabharata:a View from India', *Theatre and the World: Performance and the Politics of Culture*, London and New York: Routledge, 1993, 68-87.

25. 'Peter Brook, du vrac au vrai', *Libération*, 8 December 1995.

26. Olivier Schmitt, 'Les bons esprits de la scène', *Le Monde*, 15 December 1995.

27. Peter Brook, *Threads of Time: a memoir*, London: Methuen, 1999, 212.

28. This took place on 23 November 1995.

29. This has been Brook's practice for many years, since *Songe d'un nuit d'été* at Stratford in 1970. See 'Peter Brook, du vrac au vrai', *Libération*, 8 December 1995, and Brook, *There Are No Secrets*, 114-16.

30. Michael Billington, 'Spinning Shakespeare', *The Guardian*, 10 January 1996.

31. John Peter, 'Any answers?', *The Sunday Times*, 4 February 1996.

32. Quirot, 'Peter Brook, Qui Est Là', 1995.

33. Frédéric Ferney, Les ressources de la joie, *Le Figaro*, 19 December 1995.

34. Quirot, 'Peter Brook, Qui Est Là', 1995.

35. Translations into English from the text of *Qui Est Là* are by the author.

36. See Bertolt Brecht, 'Alienation Effects in Chinese Acting', in John Willett (ed. and trans.), *Brecht on Theatre: the development of an aesthetic*, London: Methuen, 1964/1978, 91-9.

37. Artaud saw a Balinese theatre performance at a Colonial Exhibition in Paris in 1931.

38. Brook, *There Are No Secrets*, 119.

39. Michael Coveney, 'Can't make a Hamlet without breaking eggs', *The Observer* (*Review* section), 14 January 1996. For more theorised comments on the CICT's acting style, see Patrice Pavis, 'Wilson, Brook, Zadek: an intercultural encounter?', in Dennis Kennedy (ed.), *Foreign Shakespeare: Contemporary performance*, Cambridge University Press, 1993, 277, and David Williams, '"Remembering the Others that are Us": Transculturalism and myth in the theatre of Peter Brook', in Patrice Pavis (ed.), *The Intercultural Performance Reader*, London and New York: Routledge, 1996, 73-4.

40. Fabienne Pascaud, 'L'Insoutenable légèreté des spectres', *Télérama*, n. 2397, 20 December 1995, 57.

41. Peter Brook, 'Foreword', in Yoshi Oida (with Lorna Marhsall), *An Actor Adrift*, London: Methuen, 1992, x.

42. Michael Coveney, 'Can't make a Hamlet without breaking eggs', 1996.

43. See Oida, *An Actor Adrift*, 62-4, for a brief discussion of Brook's use of the principle of Jo-Ha-Kyû.

44. Albert Hunt, discussing *US*, acknowledges that Brook 'thought he was genuinely open to ideas, if the ideas were good enough. But I also think that he would never have found the ideas some of us were trying to put forward good enough, because they contradicted both his concept of what was "good" theatre, and his political sensitivities.' Hunt and Reeves, *Peter Brook*, 116.

45. Brook, 'How Many Trees Make a Forest?', 43.

46. See John Fuegi, *Bertolt Brecht: Chaos According to Plan*, Cambridge University Press, 1987.

47. Brook, 'Manifesto for the Sixties', 54.

48. Bertolt Brecht, *A Short Organum for the Theatre*, in Willett, *Brecht on Theatre*, 193. Hunt and Reeves discuss Brook's partial and selective appropriation of Brecht – and indeed his dismissal of the more radical formal and political aspects of Brecht's dramaturgy – in their chapter on Brook's productions of Dürrenmatt's *The Visit*

(1957-60) and *The Physicists* (1963) in *Peter Brook*, 26-43. Hunt sustains this critique in his comments on *US*, 117-18.

49. David Williams, 'Horizons of the Real: *The Tempest* at the Bouffes Du Nord', in Williams, *Peter Brook: A Theatrical Casebook*, 414, 416.

50. Patrice Pavis, Introductory note to Chapter 2.2, *The Intercultural Performance Reader*, 67.

51. David Williams, '"Remembering the Others that are Us": Transculturalism and myth in the theatre of Peter Brook', in Pavis, *The Intercultural Performance Reader*, 72.

52. Shomit Mitter, *Systems of Rehearsal: Stanislavsky, Brecht, Grotowski and Brook*, London and New York: Routledge, 1992, 4, 5.

53. Patrice Pavis, 'Wilson, Brook, Zadek: an intercultural encounter?', in Kennedy, *Foreign Shakespeare: Contemporary performance*, 277.

Chapter 3: *Elsinore* • Robert Lepage

1. Quoted in Pat Donnelly, 'Lepage's Hamlet', *The Gazette*, Montreal: 3 November 1995, D1.

2. In Rémy Charest, translated by Wanda Romer Taylor, *Robert Lepage: Connecting Flights*, London: Methuen, 1997, 173. First published as *Quelques zones de liberté*, Québec: Editions de L'instant même, 1995.

3. *Ibid.*, 173.

4. See Lepage's programme note to *Elsinore* (British tour, 20 November 1996-11 January 1997) and in Alison McAlpine, 'Robert Lepage', Maria M. Delgado and Paul Heritage (eds.), *In Contact With the Gods? Directors Talk Theatre*, Manchester and New York: Manchester University Press, 1996, 152.

5. See James Bunzli, 'The Geography of Creation: Déclage as Impulse, Process and Outcome in the Theatre of Robert Lepage', *The Drama Review*, v. 43, n.1 (T161), Spring 1999, 79-103, for a discussion of some of the processes and principles behind Lepage's work in the theatre.

6. For discussions of the details and cutural implications relating to the Caserne see Bunzli, 'The Geography of Creation', 82-3 and Jennifer Harvie and Erin Hurley, 'States of Play: Locating Québec

in the Performances of Robert Lepage, Ex Machina, and the Cirque du Soleil', *Theatre Journal*, 51, 1999, 305-6.

7. See Martin Hannan and Robert McNeil, 'Festival gloom as theatre showpiece cancelled', *The Scotsman*, 14 August 1996.

8. The Ex Machina archive includes video recordings of these productions.

9. Reviewing the first production of *Elsinore* in Montreal, Don Rieder made another Keaton connection, observing that 'The image of Keaton in "Sherlock Jr." comes to mind, the projectionist who enters the film he is showing only to find things are not quite what they seem.' Don Rieder, 'Robert Lepage's *Elseneur*', *Movement Theatre Quarterly*, Winter 1996, 2.

10. The British video artist Steve McQueen restaged his own version of Keaton's stunt in a piece entitled *Deadpan*, one among a number of exhibits which won McQueen the Turner Prize in 1999.

11. Moving sets point us towards theatre history. Machinery is a mainstay of Modernist artworks, as exemplified by the Constructivist productions of Meyerhold and the breathless eulogies of the Futurists. The early Modernists either celebrated the machine as a brutal, speedy harbinger of a new age or treated it with extreme caution (for precisely the same reasons). Lepage, by contrast, embraces technology as an unproblematic given of modern life – an ingredient, equal in value to actors and text, to be stirred in the theatre-maker's pot. This quick-handed approach to technology marks the post-modernity of Lepage's machines. But the machine in *Elsinore* also evokes the theatre of the nineteenth century, in particular the relationships between the 'active' set and the human bodies within it, and between the spectacle and the audience.

12. Spandex is a lycra-like fabric used in the fashion industry. It is cheap, tough and stretchy (useful for covering frames). It takes projection well but allows the audience to see silhouttes behind it if appropriately lit. It was also used in *The Seven Streams of the River Ota*, velcroed around the edges of a series of frames and easily ripped away in a moment to transform the stage image.

13. In Charest, *Robert Lepage*, 164.

14. Michael Marqusee, 'Introduction', *William Shakespeare, Hamlet, with sixteen lithographs by Eugene Delacroix*, London and New York: Paddington Press Ltd, 1976, 10.

15. Pat Donnelly, Lepage's *Hamlet*, *The Gazette*, 3 November 1995, D5.

16. The phrase means 'alone on the stage'; Luc Boulanger, 'Au coeur du sujet', *Voir Montrèal*, 2-8 November 1995.

17. Michael Coveney, 'First person singular', *The Observer*, 12 May 1996.

18. Interviewed by the author, 13 December 1995.

19. In Charest, *Robert Lepage*, 84.

20. I owe these observations to Richard Paul Knowles, 'From Dream to Machine: Peter Brook, Robert Lepage, and the Contemporary Shakespearean Director as (Post)Modernist', *Theatre Journal*, v. 50, n. 2, May 1998, 200.

21. I have not been able to find any conclusive proof of this myself. Lepage outlined the shaky textual evidence which might support this theory: 'One of the hints [that the soliloquy might have been presented as a prologue] is in "To be or not to be" where Hamlet says it's a place where no traveller returns, and the whole play is based on the fact that the ghost appears. It's somebody who says "There's this undiscovered country from whose bourne no traveller ever returns". So you establish that and you call for a ghost to come in.'

22. August Strindberg, 'Author's Note' to *A Dream Play*, in Strindberg, translated by Michael Meyer, *Plays: Two*, London: Methuen, 1991, 175. Lepage directed a production of *A Dream Play* at the Kungliga Dramatiska Teatern in Stockholm in 1994.

23. Raymond Williams, *Drama From Ibsen to Brecht*, London, The Hogarth Press, 1993 (first published 1952), 93. Williams refers to *The Road to Damascus*.

24. David Scott Kastan and Peter Stallybrass, 'Introduction: Staging the Renaissance', in Kastan and Stallybrass (eds.), *Staging the Renaissance: Reinterpretations of Elizabethan and Jacobean Drama*, London and New York: Routledge, 1991, 8.

25. See Andrew Lavender, 'Turns and Transformations', in Vera Gottlieb and Colin Chambers (eds.), *Theatre in a Cool Climate*, Oxford: Amber Lane Press, 1999, 180-82.

26. For a theorised account of this, see Shannon Steen and Margaret Werry, 'Bodies, Technologies, and Subjectivities: The Production of Authority in Robert Lepage's *Elsinore*', *Essays in Theatre*, v. 16, n. 2, May 1998, 139-51.

27. Until this point the Ghost's lines had been read in by Lepage (clearly enjoying this last shade of his own performance), from the vantage point of his high director's chair facing the stage. In sub-

sequent rehearsals Claude Cyr, the sound engineer, played the tape of Lepage's version until Darling's voice was recorded. Lepage's delivery, in comparison to Darling's, seemed strikingly calm and elocuted.

28. J. L. Styan, 'Sight and Space: The Perception of Shakespeare on Stage and Screen', David Bevington and Jay L. Halio (eds.), *Shakespeare: Pattern of Excelling Nature*, Newark and London: Associated University Presses, 1978, 202.

29. Barbara Hodgdon, 'Looking for Mr. Shakespeare after "The Revolution": Robert Lepage's intercultural *Dream* machine', in James C. Bulman (ed.), *Shakespeare, Theory, and Performance*, London and New York: Routledge, 1996, 87, n. 13.

30. Alvina Ruprecht, CBC Radio 1, 10 September 1997, transcript in Ex Machina archive.

31. Peter Marks, 'The Blips of Outrageous Fortune', *New York Times*, 9 October 1997.

32. Jocelyn Clarke, 'Theatre is dead, long live theatre', *Sunday Tribune*, 26 October 1997.

33. Quoted in Helen Meany, 'Projections in time and space', 'Dublin Theatre Festival Supplement', *Irish Times*, 24 September 1997.

34. Don Rieder, 'Robert Lepage's *Elseneur*', *Movement Theatre Quarterly*, Winter 1996, 2.

35. In Charest, *Robert Lepage*, 135.

36. Another Brechtian tint: Lepage attended a formative three-week workshop, as a young man, at the Institut de la Personnalité Créatrice in Paris, under Alain Knapp, who had worked with Brecht's contemporaries. In Lepage's account, 'I had always been told that I didn't commit myself enough, that I didn't know how to tell my own story, and there I was, suddenly being told the complete opposite. For Knapp, my reserve and control allowed me to act better, to tell my story better.' (In Charest, *Robert Lepage*, 156.) That 'reserve and control' seem quintessentially the stuff of the Brechtian performer.

37. For a balanced account of the postmodernity of Lepage's work, see Jennifer Harvie, 'Robert Lepage', in Joseph Natoli and Hans Bertens (eds.), *Postmodernism: Key Figures*, Oxford: Blackwell, forthcoming.

Chapter 4: *Hamlet: a Monologue* • Robert Wilson

1. Quoted in Jonathan Kalb, 'In Search of Heiner Müller', *American Theater*, February 1990, 51.

2. Sontag quoted in Arthur Holmberg, *The Theatre of Robert Wilson*, Cambridge University Press, 1996, 7; Rockwell quoted in Katherine Pew, 'The Wizard of Water Mill', *Quest*, July/August 1997, 73; Robert Enright, 'A Clean, Well-Lighted Grace: an interview with Robert Wilson', *BorderCrossings*, v. 13, n. 2, April 1994, 15.

3. Peter Sellars, 'Exits and Entrances', *Artforum* 28, December 1989, 23-4.

4. See, for instance, *Vanity Fair*, June 1995, 141.

5. For a more positive assessment of political aspects to Wilson's work, see Michael Vanden Heuvel, *Performing Drama / Dramatizing Performance: Alternative Theater and the Dramatic Text*, University of Michigan Press, 1991, and David Bradby and David Williams, *Directors' Theatre*, Basingstoke: Macmillan, 1988.

6. Vanden Heuvel, *Performing Drama / Dramatizing Performance*, 191. Heuvel discusses *The Forest* (1988), Wilson's collaboration with David Byrne, in this particular passage.

7. Holmberg, *The Theatre of Robert Wilson*, 23. In spite of extensive preparatory activity in Japan, Europe and America, Wilson's epic spectacular, comprising sections created in different parts of the world, was scuppered for lack of sufficient finance to bring its component parts together in Los Angeles. Wilson was denied a sweet revenge of sorts the following year when he presented a version of the German section at the American Repertory Theatre in Cambridge, Massachussetts. The jury adjudicating the Pulitzer Prize for Drama recommended the show for the award, but the Pulitzer Board vetoed the decision – one of the reasons being that there was no script available for members to consult. This risible verdict gives some indication of the unorthodox and uncomfortable nature of Wilson's work in this period, at least in the eyes of certain authorities (long after the experiments in contemporary dance, happenings and visual theatre of the 1960s).

8. The 30,000 square-foot laboratory was used by Western Union. Wilson converted it into studios and living and sleeping quarters. For a good account of Water Mill and its inception as Wilson's American workshop base see Pew, 'The Wizard of Water Mill', 70-80,

and Robert Stearns, 'Tangible Logic: Wilson's Visual Arts', in Franco Quadri, Franco Bertoni and Robert Stearns, *Robert Wilson*, New York: Rizzoli, 1998 (first published by Octavo [Florence], 1997), 230-32. According to one source, during the centre's earlier incarnation 'Hundreds of crucial patents were invented there, including the thermonuclear detection system and the fax machine' (Pew, 'The Wizard of Water Mill', 74).

9. Quoted in Pew, 'The Wizard of Water Mill', 76.

10. Schedule recounted by Ann-Christin Rommen and Abbie Katz.

11. See Trevor Fairbrother, *Robert Wilson's Vision*, Boston and New York: Museum of Fine Arts, Boston, and Harry N. Abrams, 1991, 120.

12. In the documentary video *The Making of a Monologue: Robert Wilson's 'Hamlet'*, directed and produced by Marion Kessel, USA, 1995.

13. Quoted in Enright, 'A Clean, Well-Lighted Grace', 16. Once Wilson had sketched the concept, the rocks were designed in detail by Christopher McCollum.

14. John Bell, 'The Language of Illusion: An Interview with Robert Wilson', *TheaterWeek* v. 7, n. 22, 3 January 1994, 18.

15. *Ibid.*, 17.

16. Fairbrother, *Robert Wilson's Vision*, 61.

17. Kalb, 'In Search of Heiner Müller', 51. Müller and Wilson first worked together in 1983, when Müller supplied the text for Act IV of *the CIVIL warS*. In the event he assembled bits and pieces of texts from literary and historical sources (including some self-plagiarism), writing only one original piece, a description of a dream. The collaboration was a happy one for both director and writer, who furthered their partnership over the next few years, with Müller contributing texts to Wilson for the director to use as he wished. Wilson's treatment of 'writing' as merely one of various contributing elements to the finished production suited Müller's poststructuralist view that texts should not subject their readers or audiences to any monolithic interpretation on the part of the author.

18. Fredi Böhm, Minu Shareghi, *Robert Wilson*, Hamburg: Verlag Ingrid Kämpfer, 1996. English version (unpublished) held in the Byrd Hoffman Foundation archive.

19. Kessel, *The Making of a Monologue*.

20. Mel Gussow, 'The Clark Kent of Modern Theatre', *New York Times*, 6 January 1994, C1.

21. See Stefan Brecht, *The Theatre of Visions: Robert Wilson*, Frankfurt, 1978, 14.

22. Holmberg, *The Theatre of Robert Wilson*, 121.

23. Bell, 'The Language of Illusion', 21. For a discussion of characteristic Wilsonian lighting, see Holmberg, *The Theatre of Robert Wilson*, 121-8.

24. Julia Kristeva, 'Robert Wilson', *Art Press* 191, May 1994, 64.

25. Kessel, *The Making of a Monologue*.

26. Holmberg, *The Theatre of Robert Wilson*, 108, 117.

27. As it happens Wilson appeared as the Ghost in *The Tragedy of Hamlet, Prince of Denmark*, a short film version of the play produced and directed by Richard Rutkowski. The film was shot at the Water Mill Centre in 1993 while Wilson was working on *Hamlet: a monologue*.

28. 'Das Hirn ist ein Muskel', *Der Spiegel*, 23.2.96, translation held in the Byrd Hoffman Foundation archive.

29. Quoted in Pew, 'The Wizard of Water Mill', 74. Interviewed by John Bell, Wilson acknowledges that 'Marlene Dietrich was a big influence. She has been an influence on a lot of my work: how she sings, how she walks, how she delivers a song, the way she can speak sing.' (Bell, 'The Language of Illusion', 21.)

30. Fairbrother, *Robert Wilson's Vision*, 110.

31. The group imitated Andrews' movement and sounds. See Bill Simmer, 'Robert Wilson and Therapy', *The Drama Review*, v. 20 n. 1, March 1996, 100-102. *Deafman Glance*, Wilson's mould-breaking show featuring Andrews as its central 'informant', was presented in 1970. It would claim a place in most canons of defining productions of twentieth-century theatre.

32. Jill Johnston, quoted in Fairbrother, *Robert Wilson's Vision*, 112.

33. The first of these, 'A MAD MAN A MAD GIANT A MAD DOG A MAD URGE A MAD FACE' was presented in 1974.

34. Simmer, 'Robert Wilson and Therapy', 109.

35. *Ibid.*, 107.

36. *Ibid.*, 103.

37. Robert Wilson interviewed by Giancarlo Stampalia, first draft copy (undated, unpublished) held in the Byrd Hoffman Foundation archive.

38. See Enright, 'A Clean, Well-Lighted Grace', 18, 20.

39. Brecht was in the audience, and the experience informed his emergent theorising of *verfremdungseffekt*. 'The Chinese artist's per-

formance often strikes the Western actor as cold,' wrote Brecht. 'That does not mean that the Chinese theatre rejects all representation of feelings. The performer portrays incidents of utmost passion, but without his delivery becoming heated.' Bertolt Brecht, 'Alienation Effects in Chinese Acting', in John Willett (ed. and trans.), *Brecht on Theatre: The Development of an Aesthetic*, London: Methuen, 1978, 93.

40. Clive Barnes, 'A no-holds Bard', *New York Post*, July 8 1995.

41. Margo Jefferson, '*Hamlet: a monologue*', *The New York Times*, July 16 1995, H5.

42. Holmberg, *The Theatre of Robert Wilson*, 62. Elsewhere Wilson suggests: 'The best actors are actors that perform for themselves, first, and let the audience come to them without having to go to the audience. There, in that way of thinking about theatre there's more space, there's more mental space, there's more virtual space, because the audience then can enter the stage at will, and participate in the exchange; if you insist too much on their attention there's less space.' (Robert Wilson interviewed by Giancarlo Stampalia, draft copy August 1996 [unpublished] held in the Byrd Hoffman Foundation archive.)

43. Jeffrey Hogrefe, 'Seeking Million for Arts Colony Robert Wilson does the Hamptons', *The New York Observer*, 14 August 1995, 16. See also Patrick Pacheco, 'Robert Wilson Tries To Go Home Again', *New York Newsday*, 5 July 1995; Robert Wilson, 'FOR AUTHOR ARTHUR MILLER', (fax to *Michigan Quarterly Review* in memory of the playwright), 18 November 1996, held in the Byrd Hoffman Foundation archive; and Enright, 'A Clean, Well-Lighted Grace', 16.

44. Robert Wilson, 'Le "A to Z" de Bob Wilson', *Technikart*, n. 2, Dec/Jan 1995/96, (Paris), 14-15. Fax of original held in the Byrd Hoffman Foundation archive. *Enfance* is French for 'childhood'.

45. Quoted in Laurence Shyer, *Robert Wilson and His Collaborators*, New York: Theatre Communications Group, 1989, 123. Müller's comment is made with reference to Wilson's production of Müller's *Hamletmachine*. Susan Letzler Cole describes the rehearsal work on this production. See Susan Letzler Cole, *Directors in Rehearsal: a hidden world*, New York and London: Routledge, 1992, 161-9.

46. Quoted in Holmberg, *The Theatre of Robert Wilson*, 52.

47. Böhm and Shareghi, *Robert Wilson*.

Chapter 5: *Hamlet* • the director's cut

1. Edward Gordon Craig, 'The Art of the Theatre: The First Dialogue' [1905], *On the Art of the Theatre*, London: Heinemann, 1968, 144.

2. Harley Granville Barker, *Preface to Hamlet*, London: Nick Hern Books, 1993, 31.

3. *Ibid.*, 3.

4. *Ibid.*, 4.

5. Jan Kott, trans. Bodeslaw Taborski, *Shakespeare our Contemporary*, London: Routledge, 1965, 48.

6. *Ibid.*, 50.

7. Peter Brook, 'Preface', in Kott, *Shakespeare our Contemporary*, ix.

8. Charles Marowitz, *Recycling Shakespeare*, London, Macmillan, 1991, 97.

9. Quoted in Marowitz, *Recycling Shakespeare*, 103.

10. For celebratory accounts of the inception and construction of the new Globe, see Barry Day, *This Wooden 'O': Shakespeare's Globe Reborn*, London: Oberon Books, 1996, Elizabeth Gurr, *Shakespeare's Globe: The guidebook*, Reading: Spinney Publications, 1998, and J.R. Mulryne and Margaret Shewring (eds.), *Shakespeare's Globe Rebuilt*, Cambridge University Press, 1997.

11. See 'New Voices from the Playhouse', a series of reflections by members of the company which presented the Globe's opening season in 1997, in Pauline Kiernan, *Staging Shakespeare at the New Globe*, Basingstoke: Macmillan, 1999, 129-57.

12. Dennis Kennedy, 'Shakespeare and Cultural Tourism', *Theatre Journal*, v. 50, n. 2, May 1998, 182.

13. *Ibid.*, 55.

14. The phrase 'social energy' is Stephen Greenblatt's. Greenblatt reminds us of the word 'energy''s Greek derivation, and its rhetorical origin evoking the exciting force of ideas given shape. Social energy, he suggests, involves 'the collective dynamic circulation of pleasures, anxieties and interests.' This seems especially appropriate with regard to theatre, which has always been a pleasure-industry, which depends upon collective agreement (in both makers and audiences) of the value of the event, and which might be expected to arrange things in response to 'interests' which resonate at the moment of production. See Stephen Greenblatt,

Shakespearean Negotiations: The Circulation of Social Energy in Renaissance England, Oxford: Clarendon Press, 1988, 5-6, 12.

15. Brook reflects upon what he calls the 'how' and the 'why' of theatre in his 'Foreword' to Gabriella Giannachi and Mary Luckhurst (eds.), *On Directing: Interviews with Directors*, London: Faber and Faber, 1999.

16. See Gary Taylor, *Reinventing Shakespeare: A Cultural History from the Restoration to the Present*, London: Vintage, 1991, 306-8.

17. See Dennis Kennedy, 'Shakespeare Without His Language', in James C. Bulman (ed.), *Shakespeare, Theory, and Performance*, London and New York: Routledge, 1996, 133-48.

18. Jennifer Harvie and Erin Hurley note that Lepage's productions are largely underwritten by city-based Western and Northern festivals, so their reach is inherently limited to the sorts of audience which these events attract. See Harvie and Hurley, 'States of play: locating Québec in the performances of Robert Lepage, Ex Machina, and the Cirque du Soleil', *Theatre Journal*, v. 51, n. 3, 1999, 307-9.

19. 1999 schedule from http://www.robertwilson.com/calendar, 16.2.99. See also http://www.robertwilson.com/works/workMaster.htm.

20. Kennedy, 'Shakespeare Without His Language', 145.

21. This point is informed by Judith Still and Michael Worton, 'Introduction', in Still and Worton (eds.), *Intertextuality: Theories and practices*, Manchester and New York: Manchester University Press, 1990. Still and Worton suggest that 'Quotation as fragmentation . . . [focuses] the reader's attention on textual functioning rather than on hermeneutics' (11).

22. Patrice Pavis, 'Wilson, Brook, Zadek: an intercultural encounter?', in Dennis Kennedy (ed.), *Foreign Shakespeare: Contemporary Performance*, Cambridge University Press, 1993, 287. Such a view arguably makes for some dumbing down, a 'fuzzy universalism', in the words of Richard Paul Knowles, that allows the work to reach its different audiences wherever they may be. See Knowles, 'From Dream to Machine: Peter Brook, Robert Lepage, and the Contemporary Shakespearean Director as (Post)Modernist', *Theatre Journal*, v. 50, n. 2, May 1998, 205.

23. Bruce Wilshire, *Role Playing and Identity: The Limits of Theatre as Metaphor*, Bloomington: Indiana University Press, 1982, 19.

24. The phrase is Michael D. Bristol's. See page 27, above.

Chapter 6: Point of Return

1. A. M. Macdonald (ed.), *Chambers Twentieth Century Dictionary*, Edinburgh: Chambers, 1972.

2. William Shakespeare, edited by Harold Jenkins, *Hamlet*, London: Methuen, 1982. Readers should be aware that here and elsewhere below I am quoting from Jenkins's edition of the play, and that Brook's edited text may not run exactly as shown.

3. See Mick Wallis and Simon Shepherd, *Studying Plays*, London: Arnold, 1998, 93-97, for a discussion of french scenes, which take their name from seventeenth-century French theatre.